PHILIP EULENBURG
THE KAISER'S FRIEND

PRINCE EULENBURG IN LATER LIFE

JOHANNES HALLER

PHILIP EULENBURG: THE KAISER'S FRIEND

VOLUME TWO

TRANSLATED FROM THE
GERMAN BY
ETHEL COLBURN MAYNE

 BOOKS FOR LIBRARIES PRESS
FREEPORT, NEW YORK

First Published 1930
Reprinted 1971

INTERNATIONAL STANDARD BOOK NUMBER:
0-8369-5651-6

LIBRARY OF CONGRESS CATALOG CARD NUMBER:
72-148883

PRINTED IN THE UNITED STATES OF AMERICA

CONTENTS OF SECOND VOLUME

BOOK THREE (*continued*):

AMBASSADOR TO THE ALLIED EMPIRE

	PAGE
V. BÜLOW	3
VI. THE EMPEROR	42
VII. THE END OF HIS CAREER	76

BOOK FOUR:

MARTYRDOM

I. YEARS OF SILENCE	145
II. HOLSTEIN'S REVENGE	169
III. PERSECUTION	188
IV. PUT TO THE TORTURE	225
V. THE EBBING TIDE	269
APPENDICES	287
INDEX	381

ILLUSTRATIONS

PRINCE EULENBURG IN LATER LIFE	*Frontispiece*
	FACING PAGE
COUNT HERBERT BISMARCK	60
THE ARCHDUKE FRANZ FERDINAND	94
BARON VON HOLSTEIN	172
MAXIMILIAN HARDEN	196
BERNARD VON BÜLOW	272

AMBASSADOR TO THE ALLIED EMPIRE

V
BÜLOW

WE know how the friendship between Eulenburg and Bülow began, and know who most profited by it. It was Eulenburg who obtained permission for Bülow to marry the Countess Donhoff, who had been divorced from her husband. Bülow once frankly acknowledged to whom he owed the happiness of his life (December 25, 1887) : " Perhaps I prize my present happiness so highly because it was so hard won, and gratefully do I think of those who so loyally stood by me—you above all, dear Philip." With every year their friendship grew more intimate. From the great number of written testimonies to this, we take a few examples. Bülow wrote on May 28, 1891 : " I have a great longing to see you again, dearest Philip. Life rushes by so fast—it will be over before we reflect that we must make use of what time we still have. . . . Year follows year ; a decade has been swallowed up since we were together in Paris." His letter of March 13, 1893, is a beautiful memorial to their friendship, and at the same time a valuable indication of both characters :

" MY DEAREST PHILIP,
" Heartfelt thanks for your letter received the day before yesterday. When you use the fraternal *Du*, you anticipate the wish as well as the sentiment of my heart. For God knows that for long and vicissitous years those sentiments have been

fraternal. It seems so natural to say *Du* to each other that I feel as if it could not be otherwise. Listen—outwardly unlike in so many ways, we are inwardly each other's true affinity. Not only because we have so many memories both sweet and sad in common, but because in the depths of our souls we think and feel alike, and in the daily round are each other's complements. Our spirits, like two sisters, crossed the mysterious bourne of being, only we were given differing raiment and variously-hued pinions. Since the Heavenly Powers conferred on you the magic gift of bewildering and brilliant talents, I cannot compare with you productively; but I *can* receptively rejoice in you, drink in your flow of soul, and admire you. Nevertheless I, by nature and training pointed to historical, legal, economical studies, can from the storehouse where I have gradually heaped up treasure furnish many a commodity that will assist you—drawn into the political arena as you have been, against your will but for the good of our Emperor and country —to enrich the temple which with lighter but surer hand than mine you are now building up. You are perhaps more Germano-Hellenic, like the Second Part of *Faust*, I more Prusso-Latin; you more knightly, I more soldierly; you more individual, I more the ζῶον πολιτικόν of Aristotle. But if your head touches the stars, your feet are firmly planted on this good round earth of ours; and if I am rooted in the soil, I can at least look upward to the star-sown empyrean. Our deeper unity, which consists in perfect mutual understanding, and leads to sympathy and harmony between two human beings, is the most precious gift that this poor life can offer. Ever since I have known you I have felt this kind of sympathy, and loved you from my heart; my wife has made me understand you still better; may you long, long be spared to me! While I live, my dear Philip, you will have a faithful friend in me."

Best of all is a letter of December 25, 1895: " When your songs were sung yesterday under the Christmas-tree, I looked at my wife, standing between her mother and her loyal friends, the whole household assembled around us, the various servants at their tables with their children—and I remembered past days, and tears of affection and thankfulness rose to my eyes; I thanked God, and thought of you. . . . Nothing and no one will ever be able to part us from each other."

A nature so genuinely modest as Eulenburg's could not fail to recognise gladly his friend's great abilities. " How often do I think of you," he wrote on January 29, 1890, " when serious problems and decisions present themselves to me, and how often have I wished you at my side, with all your experience! I don't conceal from that you I regard you —not as my own rock of defence only, but as that of many others, and I never let slip an opportunity of mentioning you." What self-knowledge and readiness to efface himself are revealed in a letter of February 28, 1893:

" I do not possess your erudition, but belong more to the intuitive diplomatists. Therefore I might in certain circumstances be dangerous, and only my self-knowledge protects me. You walk along the broad highway of erudition and experience; I on a tight-rope, and have to take care not to lose my instinctive balance. Because I judge you as I do (and I only wish I was as sure of everything!) I have only one thought—namely, to smoothe your way and remove any snags with which the envy and dislike of petty natures may have encumbered your path. I have had a good many successes of this kind, haven't I—and my friendship exults in the thought of them!"

The task was not always very easy. There were all sorts of unpleasantnesses for the husband of a divorced woman at the Court of Berlin. Eulenburg managed to overcome them; he contrived that Frau von Bülow should be presented to the Empress during the Imperial couple's stay in Venice in the spring of 1896. And he smoothed over a rebuff from Kiderlen (1893). But above all he used his influence with the Emperor. On March 12, 1892, he sent him extracts from a long letter in which Bülow had set forth his views on the political situation, and added: "Anyone who disparages Bülow's knowledge and capability in the political sphere is simply envious of him. There are, God help us, a great many mutton-heads of this kind among our diplomats, and I am glad that Your Majesty has an eye for talent and will know how to interpret the portentous countenance of such a green-eye in the moment of decision." We know that Bülow's promotion to the Roman Embassy, a deliverance from exile at Bucharest, was largely owing to Eulenburg's good offices. But he had something bigger in view even then. So long ago as 1890 he had written to Bülow: "You are the man to replace Herbert Bismarck"; he now saw in him the coming Imperial Chancellor, and was trying to instil that idea into the Emperor. On February 14, 1895, he wrote to him: "Bernard is the most valuable official Your Majesty possesses —the predestined Imperial Chancellor of the future." A little later: "With Bernard Bülow Your Majesty will be able to work smoothly, pleasantly, and safely." The Emperor was attracted by the idea. On December 3, 1895, he said of Bülow: "He and no other shall be the future Chancellor"—and on the 25th: "Bülow *is to be my Bismarck.*"

We have seen how the personal friendship became a political alliance; how the two Ambassadors exchanged ideas in the heated period of struggle for the Emperor's person; how Eulenburg sought his friend's advice in his own difficult and responsible position, and how he felt that their profound sympathy of mind brought out and supplemented the best in his own nature. On the other side, perhaps no people more appreciated and admired the character and rare qualities of Eulenburg than did the Bülow couple. In June, 1891, Bülow wrote: "It would have been too disappointing for us both, dearest friend, to have returned to the wilds of Wallachia without having seen you, clasped your hand, and told you how we bear you in our hearts. And besides I wanted to exchange opinions about grave practical questions—with you who combine such a forthright, honest point of view with such subtle insight and broad-mindedness." On December 12, 1893, discussing Eulenburg's position as Ambassador in Vienna, then in immediate prospect, Bülow said: "You with your infinite delicacy of feeling, a beautiful falcon in a forest filled with foxes, bristling swine, and cackling geese!" and went on:

"How glorious was that Saturday night of ours! Never while I live will it fade from memory. Past and present, visible and invisible —all combined to create such a mood as belongs only to rare moments of inspiration. Last night my wife said to me that you, sitting opposite with your dear face and gentle voice, seemed like some great philanthropist, some 'magic-working pilgrim' who passes through a country, succouring, saving, showering blessings, here doing good, there averting evil, now raising me, now supporting her, the messenger of some higher power. May the Everlasting Might which guides your steps uphold you always, my Philip."

Recalling a meeting, he wrote on January 7, 1894: "That day I spent with you in Munich seems like a refreshing pause and respite in these tormented days. You are surrounded by such an atmosphere of harmony and peace—that peace which comes from within, and which 'the world cannot give.' I was saying to my wife just now in Vienna that the motto of Novalis-Hardenburg fits you very well: 'Quiet and alert.'" On March 24, 1895: "That you, who have such a perfectly cool, steady head for politics, should have kept such depth and tenderness and delicacy of feeling, is the reason why I love you so dearly."

In the critical years up to 1897 the Eulenburg-Bülow alliance was the counterpoise to Holstein's intrigues. "If Holstein knew how we trust one another, he'd smash up the whole game," Eulenburg once wrote. For Eulenburg himself, Bülow was the man who was to put an end to the intolerable situation. It was merely a question of hitting on the right moment, when he might take the reins without their having to fear his falling victim to a fresh crisis. Holstein was the principal danger. When in March, 1890, there was discussion of Bülow's candidature for the post of Secretary of State in place of Herbert Bismarck, Holstein declared that in that event he would resign. And for long he was one of Bülow's opponents. It took Eulenburg some time to get him round. But that Bülow as his immediate superior was anything but welcome to Holstein there could still be little doubt. When he heard of the Emperor's expressions about the future Imperial Chancellor, he adopted the strangest methods of frightening Bülow off, telling him that he would wear himself out prematurely if he accepted the State Secretaryship, and spoil his chance of becoming Imperial Chancellor. He even tried to persuade him that the idea of his appointment as Secretary originated with the Military Plenipotentiary in Rome, Colonel von Engelbrecht, who was notoriously Bülow's enemy, and detested by him on account of his clumsy intrigues. Bülow himself showed little desire to come to Berlin. Was it a just appreciation of the fact that, despite all ambition, he was not suited to be leader of the Government? Was it the fear that in the tainted, enervating atmosphere of the capital he would quickly wear out or be knocked on the head by Holstein, and thus find his political career, which was life and death to him, brought to an untimely end? As ever, he was quite frank about it. On the very night before he was to have been appointed Secretary of State he telegraphed that in view of the state of affairs in the Foreign Office he could not possibly accept.

But he did in the end accept; and how that came about forms a tensely dramatic episode. Ever since the end of March, 1897, the suppressed Governmental crisis had been threatening to break out. The Emperor was under crossfire about it. First, the Big Fleet proposal had been rejected by the Reichstag on March 28. The Imperial Staff, with Admiral von Senden at its head, thenceforward urged dissolution, and if possible a new franchise, open battle, and a *coup d'état*—suggestions to which old Hohenlohe refused to listen. At the same time the Tausch case was impending, for which State-Secretary Marschall was held responsible. His days were really numbered now. The Emperor had already announced his speedy dismissal to the Austrian Ambassador, who himself declared it to be necessary in view of the very seriously strained relations between the allied Empires. On the other side Holstein was moving heaven and earth to keep Hohenlohe and Marschall. He pointed out—and in this he was right—that their retirement before the opening of the Tausch case would inevitably give the impression that the Government feared untoward revelations. At the same time he declared that Marschall was indispensable in view of the coming general election— it was not to take place until 1898. If it went against the Government, the Emperor would be blamed, and his position would be worse than before. Even Hohenlohe was convinced by Holstein's arguments, and made his son write in that sense to Eulenburg: "The situation has never yet been so serious."

Once more the Ambassador in Vienna had to take a hand. Under the impression of the news from Berlin, he wrote on April 8 to the Emperor, urgently warning him to abstain from hasty steps, reminding him of his (Eulenburg's) representations during the last Norwegian cruise, and telling him of something the King of Saxony had said—that the Federal Princes would not be able to follow the Emperor in case of a *coup d'état*. (He wisely suppressed the King's concluding words: " Because the Emperor himself is not to be relied on.") By some mischance his letter did not reach the

Emperor for twelve days. His Majesty then, in a state of extreme excitement, wired—not in cipher: "Much distressed about your gout! Hope it's not too excruciating! Your letter of the 8th from Venice reached me only this moment, through Foreign Office negligence! Contents very interesting, but I can tell you for your satisfaction that your so-called trustworthy source has planted a romantic fairy-tale upon you, of which not a syllable is true, but every one of them pure invention. I'm not surprised, for it's the fashion now to invent and spread the most fabulous lies about me, so as to cloak their own impotence and cowardice."

At that very moment, on April 21, the Emperor was expected in Vienna. Eulenburg, who shortly before had received a cipher telegram of 270 words from Holstein, went to Lundenburg to meet the Emperor, and thoroughly discussed things on the journey. Again the Emperor roundly declared that everything imputed to him was the outcome of lying and intrigue. He had never said a word about a breach with the Reichstag, never thought seriously of dissolution, open battle, *coup d'état*— might at the utmost have on one occasion discussed such possibilities, but in an academic spirit, as everyone else was doing. The originator of this mare's-nest was no one but Marschall. The sovereign expressed himself very bitterly indeed about the Foreign Office, whose officials he blamed for having lied about and persecuted him, in order to keep their positions. Of Holstein he remarked: "An old man for whom I have broken many a lance; full of intellect—and of hallucinations, who occasionally makes the Wilhelmstrasse even more lunatical than it is already." Eulenburg, during this talk, was most favourably impressed by the Emperor's personal attitude, of which he wrote to

Bülow: "The Emperor was quieter, clearer, cleverer than ever. What vile effrontery it is to represent him as neurotic, or actually crazy!" But he could not blind himself to the fact that the Emperor's story did not quite correspond with the truth. He relieved his mind by setting down the following reflections:

"The more I compare the letters and communications from Holstein, Hohenlohe, Alexander [Hohenlohe] with the Emperor's declarations, the more perplexed I grow. One thing is certain: All, without exception, are *exaggerating. Nobody is telling the absolute truth.* One might even ask: Which is telling the biggest lies? And the answer to that is: *He who has the greatest interest in injuring the others.* . . .

"The net result of all this was that I felt my every political relation to be *stinking*. There is not one breath of clean fresh air—I feel sick.

"How am I to go on living in this atmosphere? —to which at heart I do not belong, and to which I am forced to cling by the consciousness that I am bound to work for my country and the *poor* Emperor, because neither I nor anyone else knows any other means of steering this ship of fools from the destruction awaiting it every week of the year.

"'What is Truth?' asked Pilate. What is Truth, indeed? I believe that I myself could lie with a clear conscience *only* if, by my lie, I could get some poor creature out of mortal danger. Where is the mortal danger here? And yet everyone is lying.

"A lie, in political life, is no more than a move on the chessboard. A good move, *i.e.*, a good lie, means a *success*. Who is going to score a success in this lying-game ? *No one.* But all have perjured themselves. The air is positively alive with lies !

" I am really curious to know what I shall do. To-day I have no idea. ' It all stinks in my nostrils,' as my old uncle Louis Eulenburg used to say when he was cross."

In face of these intolerable conditions we now for the first time observe a certain lassitude in Eulenburg. For the moment he did nothing whatever, and left even Holstein unanswered. For several weeks his correspondence almost ceased to exist. In the early spring he had been seriously ill, and in May was obliged, on urgent medical advice, to go to Carlsbad. Even there he let a whole week go by ; then he pulled himself together for a fresh attempt at reconciliation. He wrote to Holstein :

" At the beginning of my stay here I was anything but well, and absolutely incapable of politics. Nor was it necessary to write to you in any detail, since in general the situation can be little changed. As I have always expressly told you, the Emperor is not thinking of a *coup d'état*, and as little of parting with the Chancellor, whose value for Germany he fully recognises. . . . "

(Here follows the Emperor's assertion that " only in an academic sense " had he spoken to the Chancellor of a *coup d'état.*)

" He said it would be *disgraceful* of the Chancellor if he had put any other construction on his words. He regarded the Chancellor as his friend, to whom he could talk frankly of anything and everything. If the Chancellor could not distinguish between words and deeds, there would be an end to all such confidences. . . . I begged the Emperor to tell me if he had had these academic discussions with anyone else. Perhaps with King Albert?

" ' No,' answered the Emperor ; ' I talked of it only with the Grand Duke of Baden, lately in Berlin. *He* can't have mistaken me either.'

" I have not a moment's doubt of the Emperor's sincerity, and his good faith with me. It is not his way to mislead me by a tittle—*absolutely* not. I am *perfectly certain* that remarks of his have been *maliciously* misrepresented.

" So things are not so bad with the Chancellor. Nevertheless I would urgently advise against letting it come to a trial of strength. . . . So I beg you to be *extremely careful*. Finally, I think it as well to mention that Lucanus has come very much into the foreground. He will play a big part in any sort of matters which may shortly be decided. But my experience teaches me that more or less open attacks (in the Press, etc.) upon the men who possess the Emperor's confidence are apt to turn out disadvantageous to those who do *not*. It is better to leave such men alone (and it was a great mistake not to have made Lucanus a Minister in his day !). What a concentrated attack on a man whom H.M. not only prizes for his capabilities, but believes himself to be indebted to, *may* lead to, we have seen in the case of the renowned Senden.

" I hear from Radolin, whom I see here daily and like better every time I see him, that poor Marschall looks terribly ill. How will it go with him? I am anxious about the Tausch case, which will be a great strain for him. I hope to goodness he won't take too prominent a part in it. I have been subpœnaed, but I have nothing more to say. I have just written to

Marschall, begging him to advise me what to do. I am to be at Prökelwitz when the case opens. I *might* make the excuse of Carlsbad, but scarcely of Prökelwitz! *Que faire?* In no circumstances do I want to find myself in that foul den again. I have said *everything* I have to say. There is nothing new for me to witness to."

Eulenburg's lassitude seems to have lasted all through May. He apparently took scarcely any further part in the development of the crisis, so far as we can judge from the scanty correspondence. Yet the final solution of the problem was entirely his personal work.

We shall let his reports speak for themselves, and merely remark for the reader's instruction that the case against Tausch was opened on May 24, and ended on the 31st in the acquittal of the accused. In the eyes of all those who had disapproved of the " recourse to publicity," this was a crushing defeat for Marschall. The position of another Minister became untenable about the same time. On May 18 had taken place the scene in the Reichstag when Eugen Richter made a most violent personal attack on the Emperor, wildly applauded in the House and the galleries—while the Secretary of State, Bötticher, representing the Government, uttered not a word in reply.

The Emperor arrived at Prökelwitz on the 25th, and there Eulenburg joined him. The sojourn was only of three days, and seems to have been marked by no important political incidents. Immediately afterwards occurred the dramatic events of which the following letters tell :

To Bülow.
"In the Imperial Train,
"Danzig, *May* 28, 1897.
"Yesterday I sent you a wire of no agreeable import. These lines are going to be still less agreeable. I have no time to go into particulars. I can only tell you that the fight we know of to keep going *à tout prix* the present system (and especially Marschall) is being carried on in the clumsiest way through the Press and so forth. Holstein's tactics are—and shrewd as he is, he is not far wrong in this—to *prevent Marschall's going on leave.* He cares very little, in this aim, that the unfortunate man is really on his last legs, and looks like his own ghost. Holstein feels that his going on leave might lead to a tolerably natural solution ; and so the poor man, who is as lean as a greyhound and getting leaner every day, has to await permission from the little rabid ruthless terrier. And now comes a sudden ring-down of the curtain in the shape of an *incomprehensibly* lengthy prorogation of the Reichstag.[1] Simultaneously, rumours about the reason. For instance, that the Centre is meditating surprises. So says the *Nationalzeitung* !

"*Of course* the Emperor sees through it, and has just said *very gravely*, very much annoyed : ' Well, I think you're shrewd enough to know as well as I do what all this buffoonery means. As it's no use sending the old Chancellor to plead Marschall's cause with me, I am to be terrorised in every sort of way by the Reichstag. You must see that I can't submit to that. There are limits to all things.'

"I was in a tight place, my dear Bernard.

[1] From May 28 to June 22, instead of finishing the debates and closing the session.

I said we should certainly have to investigate thoroughly, but one thing I *did implore* of His Majesty—not to make a breach immediately after Prökelwitz, for that would do neither him nor me any good. ' My dear Philip,' he answered, ' whether the decision takes place in three or twelve or any number of days after Prökelwitz, it will be the same thing—Prökelwitz will bear the blame ! But I will not suffer this any longer. The situation is unbearable, and *Prussia* is being injured by it.' "

" 6 a.m., *May* 29, 1897.
" I made up my mind in a hurry, and am now going on in the Imperial train (H.M. alighted at Berlin for the parade) to Lucanus at Potsdam. I foresee all sorts of heavy weather, and must try to fend it off. Lucanus is only waiting until the Emperor is in a thorough-going rage to take Marschall down a peg or two. So that that *easiest of all things*—namely, making friends with our peacock Lucanus, who is cunning enough to be very useful, Marschall has of course failed to accomplish !

" What I have to do is to gain time. A change during this accursed Tausch case would be lunacy, and would open the door to the most dangerous cabals. It will be no less disastrous to change over while the Reichstag is up. But the Emperor was right enough from his standpoint when he said : ' As they seem to suppose I should be more inclined to change over when the Reichstag is *not* sitting, Marschall has gone in for dragging on, with the help of the Centre. The prorogation is to last until July, when I shall be on the high seas ! So I simply cannot listen to any arguments from the Reichstag.'
c

"Another detail I must give you is that the Emperor's dislike for Marschall is now beyond *anyone's* power to mitigate. This has produced a state of instability which is scarcely endurable, and does great injury to public interests. If there has been a certain amount of unfairness, His Majesty is being well paid-out for it; and this is exactly what cannot be put up with much longer. Besides, H.M. seemed to me *quieter*, more lucid, and even more intelligent than hitherto. A talk I had with him about your candidature had exactly the effect I anticipated.

"'Can you seriously advise me to take a State-Secretary who is not *tanti?*' he asked me. 'The existence of Baron von Holstein, who is a rare fool, is not sufficient camouflage for a dummy official. How do you think he would get on with old Hohenlohe?' And on my hint about personal difficulties of every kind, which I vividly depicted, his answer was, regretfully: 'Well, after all it would only be a temporary measure—and not for long. Or do you think the old gentleman will stay more than a year?'

"His Majesty also observed: 'I am inclined to doubt if it would be well to make Bernard Chancellor at once.' And indeed, dear Bernard, so do I—*very much!* And if it *has* to be—if you, my poor dear, *should* come soon—your best course would be to lie low politically and assert yourself in foreign affairs only—gaining friends and a following *sub rosa* by your masterly handling of men.

"Thus, my dear good Bernard, do matters stand. You will grant that I have exhausted my resources.

"*Later:* I have just come from Lucanus, and have convinced him that we can't contemplate a change from Marschall and Bötticher before August or September. As the Emperor is going to discuss matters *with him alone,* and as I expect they will cool each other down, there is some prospect (though no certainty) of our staving things off.

"In any case go on leave *in good time,* so that you mayn't come to Berlin straight from your exhausting labours in Rome.

"Your old, faithful, solicitous,
"P. E."

Entry in Diary.
"*May* 31, 1897.
"(Apropos the Tausch case) :
"As certain 'friends' had cherished the silent hope that 'my relations with Tausch would put a halter round my neck,' I felt a certain satisfaction in disappointing them (by my evidence). Directly the proceedings were over, I was to go straight to the Emperor ; and I joined him at Potsdam station in his saloon carriage, where he was lunching with his suite on his way to Potsdam. I described the proceedings and the acquittal of poor Tausch, together with the savage disappointment of Marschall's enemies and all those who had cherished hopes of 'doing in'—say myself. By the faces of Plessen and Co. when I suddenly appeared, I could see that they had been talking of the case and my evidence. For there was an unmistakable pause of embarrassment when I came in and announced myself to the Emperor. Even he struck me as rather taken aback. So mine was the very congenial rôle of instantly reducing the mountain to a molehill by my extremely comical, but markedly sarcastic, description of the proceedings, in which our silly little grey terrier played the star part—

and *many* of those listening must have felt the pricks, though they would have died sooner than give themselves away by showing it."

To Bülow.
" In the train for Potsdam,
" *May* 31, 1897.
" Yesterday I had a wire from Lucanus, saying that Bötticher is to go at once—Marschall a little later. This morning I left at 6 a.m. for Berlin, to figure as a witness in the Tausch case. Thank goodness it went off without any serious mishap —but it was not pleasant ! Afterwards I spoke to Marschall. He is physically and morally *done in.* The picture of misery and woe. He told me he could stand no more of it ; wants to go on leave on Thursday and let it gradually come out that he is unable to fulfil his duties any longer. He is to be let go about September— any sooner would be injurious to H.M. As I saw that it was a physical impossibility for him to stay, I arranged as follows with him : He is not to say anything of his intentions to Hohenlohe and Holstein. He is positively terrified of them both—and in his wretched state of health ! I was to suggest to the Emperor that H.M. should dispose of Marschall's portfolio in the autumn— but keep absolute silence till then, so that Hohenlohe may not give us the go-by. After this came the news (through Alexander Hohenlohe to me) that H.M. has demanded Bötticher's resignation, and that Hohenlohe *père, after consulting Holstein,* has just written requesting an audience beforehand. He means to tell H.M. that he will go with Bötticher, if H.M. does not change his mind. . . . Well, the old Chancellor did go out to Potsdam, and he and the Emperor both

stuck to their guns. As soon as he got back to Berlin, the Chancellor sent in his written resignation. I instantly started for the New Palace, and will now see what can be done to save something from the wreck. Little, I fear—for I suppose Lucanus is in favour of the Chancellor's departure. It will be a great mistake if the Emperor lets it happen just now."

"Liebenberg, *June* 1, 1897.
"My despatches have told you where we stand. I shall give you just a few details here. Well, I went to Potsdam, and of course to Lucanus first, so as to find out what had *really* happened. You know how the Wilhelmstrasse exaggerates and distorts. Lucanus told me that on May 30 he was ordered to discuss Bötticher's resignation with Hohenlohe. The Chancellor had really made no particular objection to the removal of the extremely unsavoury Bötticher, and expressed his agreement with B.'s appointment to be *Ober-präsident*. The Emperor was satisfied —everything was all right. (His Majesty confirmed this later.) On the morning of the 31st, that is *next* morning, the Chancellor presented himself—' he had a report for H.M.,' and to the Emperor's utter amazement he announced his resignation, if H.M. did not cancel Bötticher's dismissal. The Emperor replied that he could not do that. Thereupon the Chancellor went back, and did not seem to be out of humour. Three hours later arrived his letter of resignation.
"I told Lucanus that we *must* discover some way of keeping Hohenlohe. He agreed with my arguments, and hoped we might find our solution in sending Bötticher on leave forthwith, and then letting his dismissal take effect.

"I saw no possibility of a solution in this, for Alexander Hohenlohe's slight acerbity (he feels that by his recent vote against the Bill introduced by his father he has incurred His Majesty's extreme displeasure, and lost his chance of a District Presidency) pointed to a rupture, and revenge on H.M. Besides, there was a storm blowing up in the Foreign Office.

"I went to the New Palace. Lawn-tennis—myriads of flies—heat. When the game was over and the Empress had made tea, came a walk with His Majesty on the terrace (how many other crises have I handled, *ambulando* with the dear sovereign !).

"The Emperor, wounded by the Prince's break with him, which he—*ex sese*—attributed to Alexander's influence, is prepared to concede so far as to agree to Bötticher's going on leave and postponing his resignation for a few weeks—*but no farther*. 'I enfeeble myself and the Monarchy if I demand no atonement for his unworthy silence after those monstrous attacks in Parliament,' he said. And he stuck to his guns in another long talk after supper on the terrace, during which *swarms* of flies were biting me on my legs, face, and hands.

"At 10.30 I drove back with August Eulenburg, whose inclination to see the 'absolutely worn-out' Hohenlohe replaced by Botho E. was plainly to be perceived. (Regarding this, a league between him and Lucanus might be serious.) On our arrival at 11.30 I went, as I had promised, to Holstein at the Office, to tell him whether there was any chance of an 'arrangement' or not. Alexander Hohenlohe was with him; and there arrived, smelling of wine and hiccoughing, Kiderlen from a drinking-bout.

I said that with the Prince's goodwill there was hope of a solution. His Majesty was conciliatory. It would turn on a little modification. Thereupon ensued a *positively malignant* concentrated attack by this venomous triumvirate on H.M. and myself. Holstein said that the whole crisis had assumed the character of a fight against the Emperor's 'cabinet politics.' His Majesty would have to submit blindly *and dismiss Lucanus.* ' His Majesty must be treated as the child or the fool he is.' Alexander backed him up ; and Kiderlen, the skunk, spat poison along with the saliva from his dribbling jaws—disgusting ! ' The Emperor would have to choose between submission and the *belle sortie* of the Chancellor, who had not acquiesced in H.M.'s cabinet politics, of which the nation was already talking and which the Press would soon take up in a tone which would bring H.M. to a sense of his mad folly.' (! !)

" I have seldom had a deeper sense of loyal love for my good, noble-hearted sovereign, who towered like another Siegfried before my inward vision ! It was only by tremendous self-control that I repressed such words as would have made an irreparable breach between me and the dragon-brood around me. All I said was : ' There is a profound difference between our views. I have done, and intend to do, everything possible to avert a crisis, which *at this moment* cannot but injure the Emperor. I hope too that the old Prince will behave more loyally than his three advisers, and refuse to make this *belle sortie.* For my part, I shall of course say nothing to His Majesty of what this horrible night has revealed to me.' Every one of them flinched ! Holstein tried to turn it off by fine phrases about this being His Majesty's best chance to learn statecraft, and the ' monarchical basis.' Alexander was ashamed. Kiderlen violently attacked Kuno Moltke—made venomous insolent insinuations against ' that friend of yours ' (!), so as to get out of his tight corner.

" It was then 1.30. I left, and Holstein came with me. Sounding his tragic note, like the Norn Uld—I felt sorry for him !

" I could not sleep. The Chancellor in the hands of these advisers—the rupture *must* come ; H.M. wounded, Lucanus not unwilling to cut the Gordian knot—and here, ' the driving to the wall.'

" Next morning I went to Marschall at 8.30. I told him that H.M. would see him to-day before he went on leave, and in case of his retirement in the autumn had in fact been considering an ambassadorship for him. I added that this intention would be frustrated if a smash came now, for that would sweep everything else away. But the smash was being prepared for (I then related the episode of the night before). He, Marschall, could do His Majesty *an immense service* if by his intervention he held up this smash. Marschall quickly caught on. He said that the Monarchy was to him a *principle*, and *that he had the last word with Hohenlohe* (*sic ! !*). He begged me to write H.M. a few lines, and recommend him for the appointment.

" I sat down that instant, and wrote :

" Foreign Office, *June* 1, 1897.

" With Your Imperial and Royal Majesty's most gracious permission, I beg to make the following communication :

" The situation is more critical than before.

The Chancellor declines to receive any further orders from anyone but Your Majesty *in person*, or to discuss matters with anyone but yourself. There are active influences behind this attitude of resistance. The clue is in Herr von Marschall's hands; and he, profoundly appreciative of Your Majesty's graciousness in granting him long leave and holding out the prospect of an ambassadorship, undertakes to smooth over the crisis. I beg Your Majesty to receive him as early as is feasible this morning, and to discuss the situation frankly. He has the last word with the Chancellor—so *he himself* confesses. It will be to Your Majesty's advantage.

"I took the letter to the Palace, while H.M. was holding the big Spring parade, and then started for Liebenberg."

"Liebenberg, *June* 2, 1897.

"To-day I received the enclosed letter from Marschall. The crisis is smoothed over—*vivat sequens!* I had little hope this time.

"But what now?

"I have asked Alfred [Bülow's younger brother] to come. He will tell you my views. I have too much to do—am worn-out with anxiety. Really wretched after that horrible impression of snakes in the grass. It can't go on like this much longer. *Most assuredly it can't!* "

It was of great moment to every new Secretary of State to know what Holstein's attitude to him would be—whether he would go, stay, fight him, or co-operate with him. What then did Holstein say to the turn events had taken?

At first he knew nothing of the wheels within

wheels. No one but Marschall himself, the Emperor, and Eulenburg had any suspicion that the leave was really the farewell to office. But some day it would have to come out. With good reason Bülow shrank from undertaking the post. Then something happened, which suddenly and entirely altered the aspect of things. An accident—indeed, a mere mistake—turned the tragedy into a satirical comedy.

Holstein discovered, or thought he had discovered, that Marschall, during his last audience with the Emperor, had asked for an unusual distinction to be conferred on an official of the Foreign Office who had fallen into disfavour and was on leave for an indefinite period—the same man who had been tacitly accepted as the author of the malicious pasquinades of 1894 in *Kladderadatsch*. Instantly Holstein's lively imagination put two and two together. What could have made Marschall take so singular and so utterly idle a step? He must be under very great obligations to the gentleman in question. An abyss opened before the suspicious eyes of the vengeful Privy Councillor: Marschall had all along known who was the author of those articles, had shielded him from discovery —nay, Marschall finally became the brain behind the whole series of attacks! From that moment Holstein hated no man so fiercely as Marschall, with whom he had long identified himself.

The reaction from this new enmity was a revival of old friendships. He positively overflowed with affection for Eulenburg. On June 6 he sent him this invitation:

" I am particularly anxious to have a talk with you about a personal matter which has arisen within the last few days. You will be astounded. I do not write it, because I want to see your face of amazement.

"Yesterday I ordered trout and a spring chicken with green peas. Likewise Steinberger. I am counting on your presence at lunch or dinner. Only we two. Who knows when we shall meet again?

"Your faithful H.

"Would you rather have a '75 Bordeaux?"

At this meal he confided in Eulenburg, who on his way back to Vienna on the 9th informed Bülow:

"Internal situation and personal relations have changed as if in a kaleidoscope!

"Yesterday I met Holstein and dined with him alone at Borckhardt's. Of course I had expected that he would challenge me about my manipulation of Marschall, which from its effect on Hohenlohe must have been evident to him (though of course he has no idea that Marschall has placed his portfolio at H.M.'s disposal)—but I *was* surprised at Holstein's paying me an enthusiastic compliment on that *coup*, which was to some extent directed against him!

"The explanation followed, and is in many ways of psychological interest." [Here follows the tale of Marschall's detection as a partner in the *Kladderadatsch* campaign, which was retailed by Holstein ' as a profound secret ' and ' in a tone of quivering excitement.']

"You can imagine the effect on Holstein! All the bitterness, all the rancour, which that trying period had left within his storm-tossed bosom, flamed high and were *suddenly and catastrophically* directed against Marschall. The perspective which opened before him, and which in his delirious fancy was decked with every suspicious circumstance of earlier years, has caused a complete *volte-face*. If Marschall were not a dead man—physically speaking—Holstein would now fight him as a mortal enemy. The first psychological effect was that of his being drawn back to those whom he regards as his *certain* friends—especially those to whom he attributes no evil. Simultaneously there emerged a tender, well-nigh impassioned affection for me and you. Yes; and as suddenly he was wholeheartedly on our side in his view of the situation—Emperor, public opinion here, Foreign Office, and all.

" The revulsion is so far a good thing that, if the cup is not to pass from you, if you *are* to be summoned to power, you will find Holstein in a totally different frame of mind and will be able to work with him.

" Among other things he said: 'Anyone coming to the Office now will have to bring a steel broom with him. Marschall has been conducting a pernicious secret campaign against all Prussians, aristocrats, and political functionaries.'

" Of course we talked about the coming man. He named no one but you, Kiderlen, and Monts as *possibilities*. . . . Of you he said it would be a pleasure to him to work with you at the end of his career. Under Monts he would not stay.

" This new departure of Holstein's will have an important influence on future developments. He will, I think (and without confessing it to you or me), move heaven and earth to have it represented to the Emperor that you and Monts are the only possible men. I *refused* to do it, because as your friend I could not, I said, help to put you in a position which would be extremely irksome to you. Holstein understood—but regretted it.

"His view is that we must stake all on keeping you on with Hohenlohe, and making you Chancellor when he retires. So *la force des choses* has brought him round to my opinion!

"You see from this—and *I* feel it distinctly—that, whatever happens now, Holstein won't move a finger against you and me. His rancour has turned towards others. So as to save his face with you, he wanted to saddle me with your candidature. How else could he make his revulsion plausible to you?

"I am very much impressed by this surprising turn of affairs. I am inclined to regard it as a Divine dispensation which will smoothe the way admirably for your appointment, inevitable in any event. Though of course I don't conceal from myself that Holstein's temperament must always make trouble for you.

"He had talked very frankly with Alfred, and expressed his objections to your candidature—that is now a thing of the past. Apropos he had declared (and did to me too) that he made his remaining conditional on *Hohenlohe's continuance* in office. I think he really means this. He tells himself, no doubt, that other Chancellors would not put up with him. But enough now! I repeat my urgent request—in your own interests —that you should *go on leave as soon as you possibly can*. I am yours, in anxious sympathy."

Faintly comical as is this sharp revulsion from love to hatred in a man of Holstein's age and standing, the episode becomes frankly farcical when it turns out that it was all founded on a mistake. Marschall seems either not to have asked at all for the decoration for the detested Councillor, or else to have merely pretended to have done so. At all events he was able, in a talk with Holstein in October, to convince him of his perfect innocence. They parted as good friends as they had ever been. And the Prussian Kingdom was to have been degraded for the sake of an hysterical fool's desire to domineer!

After Marschall's voluntary retirement there remained only the question of keeping Hohenlohe in office. He, though he did not know all, showed no slight desire to go. Eulenburg wrote of this to the Emperor on June 11:

> "The old Chancellor should decidedly *not go now*, and must, if possible, spend his closing years in Your Majesty's service. Your Majesty, I know, sometimes feels that 'it can't go on any longer'—and others feel the same (not in every case from purely patriotic motives); but the prestige which the old Prince still enjoys at home and abroad is too valuable to be lightly let go. . . . Hohenlohe's retirement, and his replacement by no matter whom, would set all South Germany by the ears—which is at least unnecessary, and could be of no advantage whatever to Your Majesty. On the contrary! I mean that the conversion to 'Prussianism' can be accomplished without convulsions.
>
> "On this ground I am convinced that it is to Your Majesty's advantage to keep the old Chancellor. To do this, as I have felt before now, some warming beams will be needed after the little storms we have had—otherwise he will freeze to death between one day and another,

like the secular beechen hedge at Liebenberg in the winter of 1894. In personal matters cordially considering his suggestions (he certainly will not now suggest Alexander !), not refusing him the wonted *Du,* and so on. Such a hoary gum-tree cannot have too much of the sun ! "

The Emperor answered by telegraph : " The old gum-tree is going on well, the sun is shining on it so that it bears the desired fruit, even to Bernard plums." His jest signified the end of the crisis.

On June 20 Bülow was ordered to present himself in the capacity of deputising Secretary of State. Hohenlohe had signified his assent. In October followed the final arrangements—Marschall got the Constantinople Embassy, Bülow was appointed Secretary of State, Hohenlohe remained for the present as Imperial Chancellor. Eulenburg's programme had been carried out. Simultaneously were attained the three aims which he had called, in a letter to Bülow, the most important ones— namely, to put off the change until there should be no public sensation, to keep Hohenlohe in office, and to restrain Holstein. Justice demands our pointing out that Marschall's admirable behaviour largely contributed to this success. At the last moment he had helpfully intervened by his urgent advice to Hohenlohe " not to make a Cabinet question out of my giving way to Bülow, but to acquiesce in it." He gave another proof of his unselfish attitude, when after his appointment to the Embassy he wrote to Eulenburg :

" I want very much to tell you how I regretted not seeing you in Berlin ; I heard too late that you were there for a day ; otherwise I should at least have made an attempt to look you up.

So now I must write to say how grateful I am for the friendly part you took with regard to me in the arrangements now decided on. I am perfectly content with my lot, have no regrets of any kind, and though it was painful to say goodbye to so many friends, my recent stay in Berlin impressed me with the sense that that was outweighed by having escaped from a state of affairs which was to me intolerable. When I think how worried I was in the Spring as to whether and in what way I could, without causing a serious crisis, lay down my office, I am sincerely thankful that it has happened as it has ; and I know how much I have to thank you for that."

Meanwhile the helping hand had been needed once more, to draw another brand from the burning.

In October Prince Hohenlohe had again contemplated retirement. The occasion was the reform of the courts-martial, which had been awaiting a decision for two years and more. . . . He wrote :

" My state of health is such that I really ought to spend the winter in the South. But I will try to stay on, if Your Majesty desires it, and if I can be of use. This, however, I can do *only* if I have to face a comparatively quiet Reichstag. My powers are no longer equal to contention and conflict. If I lay the courts-martial reform before the Reichstag, I shall have the prestige necessary to carry me through the session. But if I do not, my prestige will be so diminished that I can no longer be of any service, and should have to resign. Hence I prefer to make my exit *beforehand* as an estimable person, rather than afterwards as *un pleutre !* "

After weeks of negotiations the decision loomed

near, for the Reichstag was to assemble in December. On October 29, the Emperor was expected at a shooting-party at Liebenberg. There the die was to be cast. Days beforehand Miquel came to Eulenburg with the message " that the Chancellor would retire, if the reform was not brought before the Reichstag in the precise form desired by him."

Eulenburg thought the situation very ominous, and so he made a memorandum of his conversation with Miquel—a thing he did only at critical moments; and proposed to lay the document before the Emperor for His Majesty's guidance.

" Liebenberg, *October* 28, 1897.
" Prince Hohenlohe's retirement would at this moment have the following serious results:

" He would retire on account of the reform, and his successor would thereby be stamped as a reactionary Chancellor. The election slogan would inevitably be ' Fight against Reaction,' and the counter-slogan ' The German Fleet' would have no chance at all. Thus the skilful propaganda for the Fleet would as a whole be irreparably injured. In other countries Prince Hohenlohe's retirement would not be regarded as a break-up of the Foreign Office (for Bernard Bülow is known to be a powerful force), but rather as a symptom of a grave state of affairs within the Empire. Our neighbours to east and west would make their observations, and also would possibly draw deductions which might disturb the peace at short notice. The attitudes of Bavaria and Brunswick and the circumstances at the Court of Darmstadt would be made to appear worse than they actually are. The Chancellor's retirement would to a certain extent justify such speculations.

"This being so, the question of the courts-martial reform appears in a particularly serious light. It should not just now be allowed to cause the Chancellor's retirement.

"So once more it is indicated that we must persuade the venerable gentleman to a compromise. It is not unlikely that this could be done if the Chancellor were convinced beforehand that His Majesty really does wish him to stay in his service."

It *was* done. Emperor and Chancellor agreed on a compromise, and on October 30 Eulenburg was able to wire to Bülow that the crisis was over, and that the long contention had ended in the measure's being put upon the programme.

This was the last crisis that Eulenburg had to manipulate. When Bülow did finally enter the Government—he had still been in Rome in October, making ready for his move—Eulenburg's position and activities were altered. His task of keeping Emperor and Government in touch with each other then came to an end; the office of German Ambassador to the German Emperor had become supererogatory. For the Emperor at once found himself in full accord with the new Secretary of State. His letters are like honeymoon letters, as we who have seen the temper of the preceding period can easily understand. "Bernard—splendid chap! . . . He has done excellently, and I adore him! . . . What joy to have to do with a man who is body and soul devoted to one, who wants to and *can* understand one!" This mood lasted. As much as a year later the Emperor declared himself completely satisfied, and Eulenburg could give Bülow this quotation: "'From the moment that Bernard came, all went well; he did everything himself. Not only at home but abroad his position is very high. In the Ministry he plays first fiddle and shows all the old stagers their place; to him alone I owe it that peace reigns there too.' About the Foreign Office His Majesty said: 'The Privy Councillors are quite out of it. Who ever talks about Holstein nowadays? What *is* Herr von Holstein? He takes his proper place. When his enemies have remarked to me that the best thing he could now do would be to remove himself, I have answered quietly: ' Has he any sort of prominence now? Since Bülow took the reins, one positively doesn't even know the name of any one of his councillors, so we needn't worry our heads about them.' "

Bülow, on his side, was no less enraptured. After taking office, he collected his impressions (August 22, 1897):

" As a personality, His Majesty is charming, touching, irresistible, adorable; as a ruler, by reason of his temperament, lack of discrimination, and sometimes even of common judgment, his tendency to let his ' will ' (in Schopenhauer's sense) prevail over calm and sober reflection (in the Sophoclean sense), he will stand in the greatest danger unless he is surrounded by prudent and, more especially, *entirely loyal and trustworthy* servants. Upon this will depend whether his reign is a glorious or a melancholy page in our annals. With his individuality either is possible. . . . Now for the Foreign Office. There, in the winter, even worse things were plotted (and prepared for) than we suspected. Now the distinguishing marks of the principal group (Holstein, Kiderlen, Pourtalés) are an evil conscience and a devil of a fright. Holstein is elegiac ('For twenty years I have felt like a father to you'); Kiderlen makes me think of an earwig; Pourtalés is the tame attaché. . . . Of course the group has not yet abandoned all hope of their ideal future—Hatzfeldt Imperial Chancellor, Kiderlen Secretary of State; in the background the muzzled Emperor. . . . They cower at the very thought of Botho Eulenburg. They acquiesce in everything so long as H.M. is steady and reasonable, but are speculating on his possible blunders."

Bülow's relation to Eulenburg remained as of old. In December he wrote to him: "How constantly I am with you in thought! I say, write, and do nothing political without thinking of you—what *you* would think, what you would do in my place, and whether it is done according to your ideas! By your ideas, indeed, I measure everything that I do for the dear, dear Emperor, and he is always before me as the motive, the aim, the *raison d'être* of everything." In February, 1898, he wrote:

"I hang my heart more and more every day on the Emperor. He is so remarkable! Together with the great King and the great Elector he is far and away the most remarkable Hohenzollern that has ever existed. He combines in a manner that I have never before seen the soundest and most original intelligence with the shrewdest good sense. He possesses an imagination that can soar on eagle wings above all trivialities, and with it the soberest perception of what is possible and attainable; and—what energy into the bargain! What a memory! What swiftness and sureness of apprehension!"

Eulenburg on his side followed his friend's career in the new office with advice and encouragement. In a letter of August 23, 1897, he said:

" You *ought not* to write to me just now—wait until you are well in train and have thoroughly grasped the clues which will guide you through the labyrinth of 76 and 77 Wilhelmstrasse. Already, what has become of the hidden monster therein? The Emperor's remarks about you prove that you are *in personalibus* the plenipotentiary. Don't forget that! Build your nest as you wish and *intend* to have it, unhesitatingly, ruthlessly; show your teeth—if necessary. One doesn't get far in the Wilhelmstrasse with good humour. Even the monster is beginning to crawl whining round your feet. If you could but have been an eavesdropper at the last lunch at Borckhardt's!"

After a year and a half he wrote to Bülow on his birthday (May 2, 1899):

" You may look back on last year with pride and thankfulness. Few can estimate as I can the measure of your achievement, and with what unspeakable difficulties you have had to contend. It often makes me shudder to think that you are our dear good sovereign's last card. No other can—and still less will—do all for him that you are doing. That I can safely maintain. Another might have genius or erudition—but loyalty will always be lacking, the love of a faithful servant, which with you has taken the form of a father's love for a difficult child. How terribly *alone* the poor Emperor stands."

The same tone marks all their correspondence in this year, especially the letter in which Eulenburg on October 20, 1900, congratulated Bülow on his appointment as Imperial Chancellor:

"When I was young and in love with the then so beautiful Elizabeth Hatzfeldt, she wrote in my album: 'You must not dream away your life; you must do the things you dream of.' Well, in many respects I have done *more* than I dreamed of, but generally speaking *quite different* things—and horrible ones into the bargain. But you have done *exactly* what you dreamed of—and moreover always on a progressive scale, for which you must be very grateful to God. You have not been, like me, dragged and torn through terrifying cycles of experience, and have not, as a climax, been put off with a coronet —tilted all awry over the left ear—instead of the dreamed-of laurels round a harp.

"One of the *best things* God has given me to do was my intervention in your career—an intervention which I always felt to be my mission. I know very precisely what strange and subtle perceptions, sometimes overpoweringly insistent, I have had to cling to—they began with that extremely difficult task of gaining Holstein over so as to break the spell of Bucharest where you were languishing, fight to get you to Rome . . . until the moment when I could say to you: 'Now there's no escape; your destiny is fulfilling itself—to Berlin you must come.'

"Do you remember a long talk in a green field at Semmering, when we drew up our programme? You were to be Secretary of State for a long time, so as to learn the ropes in Berlin and thoroughly grasp internal policy. Then you were to be made Chancellor at a time when *no crisis* was in the air. It has all come *extraordinarily* true, though I frankly confess that the time as Secretary of State has seemed rather long to me. . . . How difficult you are going to find it, my dear Bernard, I can guess already from the newspapers, which quite barefacedly dilate upon the ' strong man ' who is to *bridle* the poor dear sovereign. Your motto must be : ' Pacify Germany, and never wound the Emperor.' God will help you to keep your balance on the tight-rope appointed for your feet ; that is my hope and my trust."

In a retrospect of that period Eulenburg, when arranging his letters some years afterwards, prefaced the year 1898 with the following reflections :

" The year 1898 was the great turning-point in my political life—that for which I longed as a sick man does for recovery.

" In a letter to Bernard Bülow of February 3, 1898, I find these words : ' My heart is full of thankfulness for the repose which has fallen upon me since your entry into office. No more explosive despatches, no frantic letters from Holstein, no lamentations from Marschall ! For me too it has been a new era. May you everywhere be as conscious of the blessing you have proved as I am, in myself. I am possessed by the sense that after terrible storms I have at last steered the ship we may call " The Emperor's Reign " into at least a tolerably safe harbourage. The steersman badly needed rest ; but will it be given him in as good measure as he hoped ? That is the question. Perhaps it is presumptuous to call myself the steersman in this instance. But if I honestly ask myself whether the vessel would have gained that haven without my help, I am bound to answer NO.

" For never in my difficult and responsible office of friendship have I deviated from the straight line of keeping the Emperor in touch with his instrument of government—by which I mean his legalised, established organs of administration ; never have I failed to fulfil what I regarded as a duty laid upon me by God himself. That again means to keep the *constitutional* King and Emperor—without wounding his dignity, his royal susceptibility—in a path which he owes it to the country to follow. Essentially it was a psychological work of art—one might even say a feat of manipulation—which was required of me. I could not prevent the envious, the malignant, from designating me as one of those who fostered and intensified the Emperor's absolutist ideas ; and it certainly did not make my arduous task any easier.

" In unimportant matters—whether they were political questions or purely superficial ones of the Imperial dignity and monarchical tradition —I have certainly held my peace (often filled with inward scorn) or else smilingly acquiesced ; for it was very essential that I should not be tedious in my capacity of pedagogue, but figure as the friend of that richly-gifted, if also undisciplined, Emperor, thus making my counsel effectual in *serious* matters and decisions—not rendering it *in*effectual by untimely opposition, or harsh and pedantic sermonising. Only by *consistently* rational and timely advice was it possible to keep the Emperor within the constitutional limits—temperamentally exuberant and imperfectly educated as he is, and, moreover, blinded by his military upbringing and narrow experience, or else influenced by the soldiers in his immediate environment ; and only so was it possible to restore the occasionally interrupted co-operation with the chief representatives of his Government.

"These tasks I have now consigned to the skilful hands of Bülow, in whom the Emperor saw 'his Bismarck.' I need scarcely say that to him, as to the Emperor—being the trusted friend of both—I shall, now as then, give my counsel in any thorny question or situation. For I have never failed in friendship, not even when it was inseparable from serious inconveniences or actual perils."

VI
THE EMPEROR

THE extraordinary sort of service alluded to in the concluding words of the last chapter was less often required of Eulenburg, and that only on very special occasions, after 1898. It was, moreover, very much less distracting and difficult now that it was performed in perfect harmony with the leading statesman. It is Bülow's incontestable merit to have in some degree restored harmony among the organs of Government —that harmony which, since Caprivi's retirement, had been lacking. Especially when the ever-intriguing Chancellor of the Exchequer, Miquel, had been got rid of,[1] could it be said with some truth that the Government was united. True, there was one important reservation : the Emperor himself continued to be an incalculable factor. His native tendencies would have made it difficult for any Chancellor to preserve harmony and stability of purpose and action. But he would not have become a permanent danger had it not been for the inordinate influence exercised upon him by his Staff. At this stage it is inevitable that some light should be thrown on an aspect of William II's reign which has been the subject of much discussion —namely, the political machinations of his military staff. That these existed was scarcely suspected by the public before the great war. And yet the fact is of the utmost importance, and must be

[1] On May 5, 1901, Miquel (to his own surprise) was requested by the Imperial Chancellor to send in his resignation.

The Emperor

elucidated here, if only because it represents a cardinal element in Eulenburg's life-work and was instrumental in deciding his fate.

The history of the most widely-differentiated ages and countries provides us with examples of highly-placed officers who, when they were able to influence their sovereign, have transcended their military functions. It may be the force of circumstances which leads them to do this—for instance, when they find that the military interests entrusted to them are suffering from an ill-advised or feeble policy ; or it may be, quite as often, ambition and lust of power. We need not cite the many examples, fresh in the memory of all, which prove the truth of this. The classic type of the ambitious, wire-pulling General is represented by Count Waldersee, whose two volumes of reminiscences have almost nothing to say of military actions, but treat incessantly of politics. A sound administration is called upon, and is able, to defend itself against that kind of interference. Bismarck had made short work of it, though sometimes at the cost of violent conflicts, until he was brought down by Waldersee. Since then there had been a permanent military camarilla—not, it is true (after Waldersee's removal from Berlin), conducted by the Army chiefs ; but by their *dii minorum gentium*, the Imperial Staff and the Military Attachés at the foreign Embassies. Eulenburg's painful memories of the conflicts that throughout his whole career he had to wage with these elements were set down by him in a document which casts a lurid light on his official activities, and likewise on the conditions prevailing in William II's Government and Court. They were as follows :

" The A.D.C.s are part of the ' Headquarters '

Staff, and are under the command of the 'General Commanding Headquarters.' They also come under the influence of the War Cabinet and the Adjutant-General. William II's predecessors in times of peace called this Imperial environment the *Maison Militaire*—which was more pacific and more logical. But even then there was a good deal of political wire-pulling, for 'aide-de-camp politics' are inseparably bound up with Prussian tradition, and only the rigid military discipline which prevails in Prussia can account for the curious fact that the nation does not believe in the existence of 'A.D.C. politics.' With touching naiveté the Prussian and the German subject connects the idea of intrigue with mufti and portfolio *alone*.

" But in the great era of William I an Albedyll, a Lehndorff, were too wary to venture on wire-pulling with Bismarck.

" Emperor William II (who, unlike his highly educated progenitors, 'finished' his education as an officer in the First Regiment of Guards) sucked in like an infant at the breast the tradition that every Prussian officer is not only the quintessence of honour, but of all good breeding, all culture, and all intellectual endowment. How a man so clear-sighted as William II could have attributed the last two qualities to *everyone* in Guards' uniform has always been a puzzle to me. We will call it a combination of military Hohenzollernism and self-hypnotism. From this essence of all excellence the Emperor further distils a concentrated extract—denominated the A.D.C.

" During my more than twenty years of intimate connection with the Prussian Court, I have seen as it were a long moving fresco of A.D.C.'s, with whom (as used to be said) I was on the best of terms. There were many honest, decent fellows among them, and of some it may even be affirmed that they did not intrigue at all, or only very slightly. The net result of my observations in the sphere of 'Headquarters' is that there were more donkeys than foxes among the Staff. But it is manifest that the donkeys would do even more harm than the foxes, because they were incapable of estimating the effect of their utterances on the temperamental, incalculable Emperor. So they frequently achieved more than they had at all intended, and I know of cases in which they vainly strove to moderate the storm they had raised.

"The Military Attachés at the Embassies and Ministries—whom one cannot call anything but 'official spies,' since their special function is to move heaven and earth to discover the military secrets of foreign powers—are usually A.D.C.s to the Emperor as well. And if the mere A.D.C.s form an extremely serious close corporation, by reason of the boundless over-estimation of their capabilities, what is to be said of those who are Military Attachés in addition, and feed at the very breast of diplomacy? These are so haloed in the Emperor's sight as to lose their glorified heads—if not entirely, at any rate to a great extent.

"They are permitted to send letters and reports direct to the Emperor, who takes for gospel every word such 'superior beings' may say. He thinks ever so much more of any communication from them than of reports from those ambassadors who do not happen to have been, as I was, at one time an officer on the active list.

Naturally such spoilt children come to think themselves incomparably more valuable than their chiefs. These gentry, cavalry-captains or majors, are solemnly preparing themselves to step into an ambassadorship one of these days. They intrigue, they write political letters, so as to demonstrate their brilliant qualifications, and often make their chief's life a hell.

" One asks one's self in vain why a Prussian diplomat should have to undergo an arduous examination in order to gain the promotion which falls like a ripe plum to some war-worn but entirely uncultivated military man—for instance, a Count Webel, who is now Stadtholder of the Reichsland, after having been Ambassador in Vienna.

" A similar figure (among many others) was Colonel von Engelbrecht, A.D.C. to the Emperor, Military Attaché to the Embassy in Rome, and the terror of his chief, Prince Bülow, afterwards Imperial Chancellor. How the Emperor could have been taken in by the humbug of that man, which was like a Jewish salesman's, ladled out by the spoonful, is incomprehensible to me. Like every official in the service (and even more so, because I knew more about them) I was infuriated by these A.D.C. politics, which all at Headquarters, whenever I permitted myself an allusion before any one of them, invariably repudiated 'on his word of honour.' What could I do against that word of honour, and the solemn incorruptible faces of those who assured me that no A.D.C. ever so much as dreamed of saying or doing anything but what the rigidly-disciplined Imperial service demanded of him? An A.D.C. had neither eyes nor ears for anything else!

" I have no desire whatever to prove my

point by examples. But over and over again I can trace the influence of the military group, which represents a *permanent camarilla*, but is not recognised as such by the militarised German State. For if anyone lets fall a remark about military intrigues, up gets some General or other, twists his moustache, and says : ' I, General So-and-so, herewith declare that any such expression as "Aide-de-Camp politics" is a foul slander.' And no one says a word. . . . And yet we have had plenty of experience of Adjutant-General von Plessen's interference in home-politics, and have gained a profound insight into the ways of political intrigue within this permanent Court camarilla.

" Unfortunately all my endeavours to convince the Emperor that it was inadvisable to permit political reports from military outsiders failed to take effect. That was a foregone conclusion. And, beyond a doubt, as the Emperor's distrust for Marschall and the Foreign Office increased and his respect for the venerable figure of Chancellor Hohenlohe diminished, the situation grew more and more uncomfortable. Especially as Holstein, who hitherto had been the real head of the Foreign Office and had worked in the Emperor's interest from the conviction that that course was the safest way to prevent Bismarck's return to the Wilhelmstrasse, now turned against His Majesty with the utmost effrontery. . . . He literally took it on himself to fight Emperor and Friedrichsruh. A lunatical proceeding !

" Stuck in Vienna, I could neither protect nor advise the Emperor. Nor could I suggest myself to him as Imperial Chancellor, or even force on a crisis whence I should emerge as Chancellor. My conscience forbade me to do that. But I longed for the moment when Bülow should be summoned to Berlin and make it his cardinal business to remedy the impossible conditions caused by the camarilla. . . .

" When Bülow undertook a responsible position in Berlin, my shoulders were to some extent relieved of the burden. Principally because of the quiet which ensued upon the Emperor's action, for in his characteristic delight over Bülow's stimulating and intellectual personality, he declared himself ready to let all military reports which touched on policy be sent in duplicate to the Imperial Chancellor (and therefore for the information of the Foreign Secretary). Nevertheless I cannot say I am convinced that this invariably happened. . . ."

Eulenburg's correspondence fully confirms the above description. We give an instance, which concerns the already-mentioned Colonel von Engelbrecht. He, under the incapable Ambassador Count Solms, had as Military Attaché in Rome become a political figure; and when he failed to obtain a desired ambassadorial appointment, he tried to continue his political activities under Bülow. He soon became the terror of Ambassador and Foreign Office. The Office made the mistake (Eulenburg describes it as "insane folly") of definitely warning a young attaché appointed to Rome in the beginning of 1894 to beware of Engelbrecht. Engelbrecht discovered this, there was a row, and the Emperor was in a state of white fury. Eulenburg, in a letter, tried to soothe him and enlighten him about Engelbrecht. In vain ! On January 11 he received the following answer : " As to Engelbrecht, you've been mistaken all along. I expressly desire you to warn the Foreign

Office against any further attacks on him. He has given me complete satisfaction, gained my confidence as well as that of King Humbert, and is *my brother officer and A.D.C.* If there is any more of this kind of thing in the Foreign Office, I shall have something to say about it. Once for all, I intend to have ' discipline on board ' ; else no useful work can possibly be done."

The following memorandum shows Eulenburg's agitation over this incident :

> " Such infamous episodes make my work of keeping Emperor and Government in touch during one of the most precarious periods ever known to the Prussian Kingdom and the new German Empire most horribly difficult. It is sometimes as though I despaired of my task of making these absolutely irreconcilable antagonisms appear to the world abroad and at home as a coherent organism—and they *must* be made to appear so. And now comes the spectre of that monstrous Prussian Hohenzollern atavism peculiar to the First Regiment of Guards, in the shape of the poor dear Emperor's letter ! After all, he can't jump over his shadow—and I really do think sometimes that in this lunatic asylum I myself shall go mad. The idea that an aide-de-camp is sacrosanct, the symbol of perfection in humanity, is one that I simply cannot get into my head. And especially when Engelbrecht is set up as a paragon ! Such men as he—and Senden, partly out of his mind, and Plessen, who when the Press was raving said to the Emperor : ' We must train the guns on them ; then they'll shut up '(! !). Whereupon the Emperor seriously declares that he will send his A.D.C.s to challenge the editors, if articles offensive to him,

the Emperor, are published. I fancy even Plessen himself wasn't quite prepared for that! It's really a blessing, after all, that in this witches' kitchen, not to say madhouse, there should be something to laugh at. But for a sovereign of the Emperor's impetuosity (called 'vigorous action') to be drawn once more into the atmosphere of Guardsmen's rant, when with infinite trouble and the sacrifice of my own time and energy he had been at last in some degree removed from it, is melancholy indeed. Nothing but good-nature and good-temper can save me from flinging the whole nuisance overboard, and betaking myself to the Elysian Fields of Liebenberg."

The man responsible for this minor calamity afforded, two years afterwards, a glaring proof of his dangerous ineptitude. In the beginning of March, 1896, Italy had suffered, in the Abyssinian war, the crushing defeat of Adua. This inspired the wire-pulling Military Attaché (who had meanwhile joined the Staff at Berlin as A.D.C.) with the brilliant idea that the Emperor should urge King Humbert, in a letter of condolence, to reduce the size of his army. Engelbrecht was to deliver the letter, as King's Messenger. He doubtless imagined that this would pave the way to his becoming Ambassador, in case Bülow left Rome. The Emperor was all on fire for the plan, though Hohenlohe said *he* should be obliged to resign. There ensued a very serious Chancellor-crisis, which Eulenburg had great trouble in smoothing over. On a telegraphic report from Marschall he commented: " So now A.D.C. politics really *are* getting dangerous! Engelbrecht taking the Emperor in tow! Where will it end? Thank goodness, the other A.D.C.s don't like Engelbrecht, so I hope they will disgust the disgusting creature with Berlin. The poor Emperor is sometimes like a new-born child." In a cleverly-worded letter he managed to calm down the Emperor (who had been beside himself over Hohenlohe's resistance) and make clear to him that *that* was not the moment to advise the Italians, smarting under defeat, to reduce their army. The Emperor perceived; and there was an end to the danger that the Italian defeat, which had already caused the fall of Crispi's Cabinet, would cause that of Hohenlohe's also, and lead to a public fiasco within the Triplice.

As time went on, other elements in the Emperor's environment became even more dangerous than the army officers. These were certain naval men. Long before it came to the ears of the public, Eulenburg had known of the extensive programme which was being drawn-up in those circles; had instantly perceived the danger when in 1891 Admiral von Senden, Chief of the Naval Cabinet, had revealed the Big Fleet-building scheme. Hence he was, in a sense, antagonistic to the plan—that is to say, he did agree that Germany must be stronger at sea, but most emphatically disapproved of any sort of naval rivalry with England, for his instinct told him that that first step must lead to the most fateful of all wars. He could not intervene against the scheme, because it was his well-considered principle never to mix himself up in warlike matters. Nevertheless the Emperor must have been well aware of his friend's opinion on this question, for he usually avoided any mention of it to him—probably so instructed by his suite, who recognised in Eulenburg an opponent of their plans. So he was reduced to being a helpless spectator of the approaching disaster. All he could do was to put up what defences he might against the threatening storm. Hence he became an advocate of the so-called " Continental System "—*i.e.*, the alliance of Germany with Russia, and if possible with France. It was no article of faith with him, and he would have preferred another policy ; but in that alliance he saw a possibility of carrying out the Big Fleet scheme (which he could not hinder) without endangering the existence of the German Empire.

Before Tirpitz took the stage in 1897, this scheme was incarnated in the person of Admiral von Senden-Bibran, whom the Emperor had placed at the head of his Naval Cabinet. Eulenburg had known the man—narrow, a prey to suspicions, " stubborn as a goat "—from his youth, when they had attended the same college at Dresden. He thought him a disastrous influence ; hence for once he had—entirely against his wont—resolved to bring down this opponent, who had laid himself open to attack by a monstrous political blunder. This was on November 12, 1896, when there were chronic Ministerial and Chancellor crises. Eulenburg had written the Emperor the following letter, which—unfortunately—was fruitless, but gives us a good idea of the writer's character :

> " Your Majesty, on reading these lines, will understand that I have not enjoyed writing them. But I am perhaps the only man who can tell Your Majesty the truth without wounding Your Majesty. My subject, then, is the ineptitude of our friend Senden.
>
> " I am very far from forgetting how loyally devoted he is to Your Majesty (and it is that which, personally speaking, inclines me to overlook the very many respects in which he can

afflict me—and Your Majesty is in a like position !). But there is a limit to everything. If he is like the bear in the fable, who for love of his master tried to slay the flies on his forehead and thereby slew his master too . . . well, something must be done to save the situation.

"Your Majesty will remember my telling you at Wilhelmshohe how Senden informed me on the 'Hohenzollern,' carefully avoiding any encounter with my eyes and delicately lisping, that the *Berliner Neuester Nachrichten exactly represented his views*, and that he regarded it as his duty to express those views in public to all and sundry—even when he was not asked to do so. When I said that criticism of Your Majesty's Government, from him who was known to enjoy Your Majesty's confidence, could not fail to have a disturbing and perplexing effect, he answered with his usual superior smile that he did not share that opinion, and would, now as before, give expression to his convictions with manly determination.

"I then besought Your Majesty to put a stopper on this dangerous folly. It is indeed perfectly evident that it has given much, and serious, support to the legend of an 'aide-de-camp camarilla.'

"Perhaps nothing was done to stop it—or perhaps with his wonted obstinacy the good Admiral has taken no notice. But now my story is getting very serious indeed.

"For some considerable time—and again and again—Senden has been saying in the casino (where he goes daily and always finds a submissive audience) to everyone who will lend an ear that in his view the Reichstag will have to vote the 300 millions to make the Fleet what we need it to be—and that the Reichstag, when it has been dissolved *ten times*, will see that it must grant what is wanted. As he is known to be Your Majesty's closest confidant—especially in naval matters—this view is regarded as Your Majesty's throughout the City, the Parliament, the Press ; and Your Majesty's ' unlimited Fleet-building ' is more and more believed in, and more and more the cause of public uneasiness.

"But that is not all. Some days ago Senden, dining at the Casino, made a longer speech . . . about the *extraordinary flabbiness of Prince Hohenlohe and the Government*. Hohenlohe was said to have made his statement about the courts-martial measure in the Reichstag *without Your Majesty's* authorisation : ' We must get fresh blood,' and so on.

"Bitzthem [the Saxon Military Plenipotentiary] vigorously contradicted these assertions, and repelled the attack on Hohenlohe. (A Saxon, to Your Majesty's A.D.C. !) When Senden left, the conversation of all present turned on the question of foreign Secretaries of Legation, parliamentarians, etc.

"Again I must remind Your Majesty of the fable about the bear. What will be the result of this ? I can no longer wonder that ' A.D.C. politics ' are perpetually talked of. But I am sorry for the other A.D.C.s, who sedulously avoid talking politics lest Your Majesty should be injured by some heedless remark. I expressly repeat that I highly value Senden's loyalty and attachment to Your Majesty, and that therefore these lines are *horrible* to me to write—but really, this *will not do !* Such a stupid fellow ought not to be in such close proximity to Your Majesty— the bear will destroy Your Majesty !

"Your Majesty is always in a position to bestow favour and distinction on anyone who deserves them, and Senden does deserve them for his loyalty; but there are other fine feathers than those he is now sporting.

"I assure Your Majesty on my honour and conscience that such incidents do immeasurable damage, because Senden figures as Your Majesty's most trusted of all beings. And with the excellent Senden himself it is perfectly useless to reason. Your Majesty knows that even better than I do! I also assure Your Majesty that *not a soul* knows or shall know anything about these lines—but I cannot help writing them, extremely disagreeable though it is to me. If I had the smallest hope that the good Admiral *was capable* of altering his ways, I should not now be writing.

"I beg Your Majesty to burn this letter at once—for I value Senden for his good qualities, and I hate writing as I have done. But, as I have said, who else is there to do it?"

The battle with the military elements in the Emperor's immediate environment was no more to come to an end than was that with his own inborn characteristics. The task of protecting the sovereign against himself was indeed lightened for Eulenburg by Bülow's entry into the Government, but he was not relieved of it. With every year it grew more harassing and more hopeless, and his endeavours more unsuccessful. Seldom did it happen that a warning took such good effect as in August, 1897, when Eulenburg had written, urgently and eloquently advising the Emperor not to take a prominent part in the agitation for the Fleet, "lest the people should come to look upon the naval proposals as more the gratification of His Majesty's sporting instinct than a German necessity." On the 20th the Emperor answered amicably : " Dear Phili, sincerest thanks for your valuable and interesting letter . . . I am glad to have your voluntary expression of opinion about the handling of the naval business, and am particularly grateful to you ; for if *you* don't speak out, who on earth will ? " The Emperor went on to say that he was delighted with Tirpitz's successful handling of the question, and promised in future to " hold my jaw ; and use it exclusively for eating, drinking, and smoking."

The sovereign's feeling for his friend did not alter as time went on. Ten years after his accession, on June 15, 1898, it found expression in the following telegram : " For your faithful, active friendship I thank you from the deepest depths of my heart. May I always have your idealistic presence to fortify my efforts ! That is my daily prayer. I have appointed you acting Privy Councillor, with the title of Excellency."

But the friend's counsel did gradually lose some of its effect. It was during the annual Norwegian cruise that Eulenburg was especially called upon to exercise his influence over the Emperor. Since 1896 he had been the only representative of the Government on these occasions, for through some intrigue of the Staff, in which Bülow was not wholly unconcerned, Kiderlen had fallen into lasting disfavour and was no longer invited. For Eulenburg these cruises had always been the most detested of his official ' extras,' and participation in them was perhaps the greatest sacrifice he made to the Emperor. But now it was evident to all that the long duration of these trips was not beneficial to the Emperor himself. In August, 1899, even

Surgeon-General Leuthold, who was of the party, declared that it was folly to let the trip last longer than three weeks; it did His Majesty more harm than good. Eulenburg commented on this: " He is quite right, for everyone! " As a rule the Emperor's restlessness was accentuated, he was seldom really well, and the prevailing mood made it harder than ever to keep the sovereign within normal bounds. The journal-like reports sent by Eulenburg to Bülow give a striking picture of the difficulties of his task. We shall give but a few examples.

In the summer of 1899 " everything seems bewitched." The Emperor had started in a state of high excitement about the Reichstag, wherein the Bill for protection of the non-strikers—the so-called House of Correction Bill—had no chance whatever of finding support. He had been trying to help on the cause by vigorous speeches, but—as was to be expected—they had had precisely the contrary effect. The extremely unfavourable impression created by them was strengthened when on July 12 a telegram appeared in the newspapers, sent by him to Hinzpeter from Norway. He there announced the presentation of a statue of the great Elector to the town of Bielefeld, calling it " a symbol that in that ancestor as in myself there resides an inflexible will which will proceed, in face of all resistance, to the goal felt to be right." This could refer to nothing but the House of Correction Bill ; and it was sought to read into it the intention of dissolving the Reichstag and letting it come to a fight. Excitement increased when it became known that the Emperor had cancelled a visit to Dortmund, which had been announced, in case the Bill did not become law.

The effect on German public opinion is displayed

in a letter from the Master of the Household, Count August Eulenburg, to his cousin (June 16, 1899):

"Here at home the unfortunate publication of the telegram to Hinzpeter has raised a storm like that of last autumn about the telegram to Detmold, and the '*Suprema lex*' affair of some years ago. Were it not for these perpetual upheavals of public feeling—which are not only futile but directly injurious to the Most High's authority—we could (despite Canal and Penitentiary Bills) live in such bléssed peace and harmony, let the political parties tear one another to pieces, and rejoice in the fine successes of our foreign policy. But it is not to be, and it never will be any different!"

Philip Eulenburg's diary-letter to Bülow shows us what *he* thought:

"In the newspapers I read the Emperor's telegram to Hinzpeter! I must hope that this telegram did not go off on the very day that I talked about 'rash words and telegrams.' However that may be, the fact depressed me. It is really a mystery why the Emperor should choose the occasion of a memorial to the great Elector for a resounding manifesto, and why Hinzpeter should publish it! These are truly most melancholy moments, with which you too, alas! are sufficiently familiar."

But he did not content himself with lamenting in secret; he made use of the opportunity to tell the Emperor the truth, in the way we know of old. Of this he wrote to Bülow:

"On a quiet walk which I had with the Emperor in the beautiful avenue running along the banks of the Molde to the beach and gardens, His Majesty once more led the conversation to Prince Bismarck. . . . I managed to bring in the remark that the prudence and self-restraint shown by the Emperor during the last years of the Prince's life were no less desirable to-day, for ' Bismarckism ' was a force whose roots were still very deeply and firmly implanted in the German heart. His Majesty did not like this. He expressed the opinion that ' the Emperor ' was more deeply implanted than any other root. . . . The Emperor said that though he never had at any moment thought of restoring Herbert to office, the publications which with Herbert's acquiescence appeared after his father's death, and which were one mass of lies and shameful slanders about the Emperor's grandparents and parents—these publications had *à tout jamais* severed any slender link which might still have subsisted between him and Herbert. ' If ever you hear any remarks about a restoration to office,' he concluded, ' I earnestly beg you, and empower you, to declare that *never* can any such thing be contemplated ! ' I answered that I thought it wiser to hold my tongue and let the facts speak for themselves, since I did not wish to rouse the ire of those who set their hopes upon the Bismarck name. Prudence and the Emperor's interests dictated that attitude. His Majesty broke out rather vehemently against such elements—' they deserved no consideration, nor need we be afraid of them.' I then said that despite His Majesty's opinion that the ' Emperor ' was too deeply implanted in the German heart for anyone else to find a place there, I could not depart from my attitude of *bearing with Bismarckism*. I said that

H.M. underestimated certain dangers which might at any moment affect the State. If H.M. offended public opinion in any way, he might in certain circumstances find himself in a dilemma. There were plenty of people to exploit any uneasiness, any 'self-assertion.' So, as usual, I could only earnestly advise him to be *cautious* in words and deeds, both at home and abroad.

"The Emperor was much perturbed by this, and asked me what sort of dilemma I meant—and who were the people I feared in that respect?

"I answered that, for example, the Government might be forced to resign in case of a dangerous political situation arising and becoming uncontrollable; and this, as well might happen, by reason of some incautious proceeding on His Majesty's part. Circumstances might then create a national movement in the direction of abdication or a Royal Commission. A mechanism like the German Empire was (I said) a subtle, intricate bit of work—a masterpiece of the kind we put under glass. If the glass-case were broken, the masterpiece was endangered. Careless handling of so precious an object might incense the nation.

"The Emperor looked very grave, and asked with *whom* such ideas could originate. How would such people proceed?

"I answered very firmly that I did not wish to give any names, for I possessed no proofs and had no desire to turn an academical discussion into a question of fact. But I *could* tell His Majesty of something said to me by Cardinal Hohenlohe, whom His Majesty had greatly revered. Shortly before the Cardinal's death he had said to me *very earnestly:* 'I know that you are absolutely devoted to the Emperor, and

COUNT HERBERT BISMARCK

moreover in a position to give him really outspoken advice. Tell him to be *very* much on his guard, *very* careful! I know for a positive fact that the idea of declaring him to be irresponsible for his actions has been widely discussed, and that very many persons, among them highly-placed ones, would be willing to support such a proceeding. You must warn the Emperor.' I added that accident had led our conversation in this direction to-day, and I *was* ' warning the Emperor '—but (I said) I was not anxious now, since *you* were beside him and in his confidence. You were watching faithfully and devotedly over him. There was no danger for him, while you were at his side—and while he himself was careful.

" Very much against his wont, the Emperor did not break off with a joke or some strong language *à la* Royal Regiment of Guards. No—he was very thoughtful for some time."

" *July* 21.

" In his eleven years of sovereignty the Emperor has outwardly grown much quieter. We, on our eleventh Norwegian cruise, have been very much struck by the alteration. But psychologically speaking, there is not the slightest change. He is the same explosive being, if not even more violent and unaccountable, from his sense of being more experienced—which in fact he is not in the smallest degree. His individuality prevails over the effects of experience. That might well be a roundabout way of saying something else—but it is not ; it is just as I have stated it.

" He does not belong to our times—and in all times there have been natures which broke the frame of their epoch. *Real* genius shapes the age to its own pattern ; weaker spirits are ground in the mill. When so markedly eccentric a nature dominates a realm there cannot but be convulsions, and we are heading straight for a period which will decide whether the age or the Emperor is the stronger. I am afraid that it will not be he, for at the moment his strength consists chiefly in the skill of his advisers, especially you. If he perceives that through you he *may* become great, the laurel may be his in spite of himself.

"I close this long letter, feeling wretched and sick at heart. The last few days have been too gloomy—have opened too uncertain a vista. I am so sorry to cast these dark spells upon you—during your holidays. But I think it necessary that you should be acquainted with our sovereign's present train of ideas."

"*July* 26.

"Home politics have been in abeyance for some days—though the suite eagerly discusses the situation as gathered from the newspapers received, and puts its own constructions on the Bielefeld telegram. Not always in a friendly spirit. Hitherto I have had to contend with two or at most three faultfinders ; now they all without exception find fault in a languid, hopeless sort of way, which gives everyone of them a tinge of Oriental fatalism and—peevish terror of the Sultan ! This experience makes me very melancholy. The poor dear sovereign is more alone than ever. There is so much I should like to say to him, but I am struck dumb by the 'Caliph' in him who a moment before seemed like a good Haroun-al-Raschid mixing with his people."

"*July* 27.

"I said yesterday that home politics were in abeyance. To-day they're very much to the fore again. I walked to Lomvard with the Emperor, in pouring rain. He was very much under the impression of the sensation caused by the Bielefeld telegram and the cancelled visit to Dortmund, and said : 'When one sees the way people are behaving at home, one really loses all desire to go on reigning ! The only thing to do is to take no notice *whatever.* The frightful loss of prestige, the collapse of parliamentary government, is making public opinion *sick*—just as Russia is sick internally. But there they can take refuge in foreign policy ; with us the sickness finds an outlet in delirious discontents, which impede the aims of government, and put every possible spoke in everyone's wheel ! "

"I summoned all my courage, and spoke almost word for word as follows : 'I have long observed this dissatisfaction, and it is beginning to alarm me because the parties, usually so divided, are united in embitterment against Your Majesty.' The Emperor said : ' That's nothing new. If I could fight Bismarck for eight years, no one else is going to frighten me. You might use that argument the next time people come bothering you ! '

"I answered : ' The two battlefields are very different. The head and front of the offending is now the serious conflict between Your Majesty's personality and the views of the nation. Your Majesty is undoubtedly modern-minded ; you might even be called progressive—but that side of you is invalidated by an excessive public display of energy. By your speeches and telegrams Your Majesty gives the impression of desiring to revive the idea of the absolute monarch. But there is not a single party in the Empire which will ever again accept that idea. Parliamentarianism is in the German marrow, and what you call the collapse of Parliamentary Government is merely dissatisfaction with some of its forms.'

"The Emperor replied, somewhat tartly: 'I claim the right of free speech, like any other German! I must say what it is I want, so that reasonable people may know whom they are to follow, and how. If I said nothing, how could the perfectly "willing" members of the middle-class know what they were supposed to do?'

"'Deeds are better than words in a ruler,' said I.

"'And they shall have those too,' exclaimed the Emperor. '*You're* only afraid that I may show the Reichstag who is master,' he added, laughing.

"'No,' I replied. 'I am not afraid of that, for Your Majesty has often told me that you would not contemplate a change in the Constitution unless people and Parliament manifested a desire for some such thing. You know very well that you are far too modern-minded and far too intelligent not to recognise that Germany will never again do without a Parliament.'

"'Then it will have to be a *modified* form of Parliament—not what we have now,' interrupted the Emperor.

"'There may be something to be said for that,' I answered; 'but even so it would have to keep the established course. And that course becomes *impracticable* when the majority of the nation is in conflict with its Emperor.'

"'If that were true, it would mean Revolution

—and one way or another we'll have to face it. Everything points that way, and we may as well accept the challenge.'

"'Which the coalition of the European Powers,' said I, 'is waiting for, in order to attack us. The Russians pay the newspapers, the English finance the strikes in Hamburg, the French are setting the Slavs at our throat—and we are playing their game for them.'

"'Oh,' cried the Emperor, 'if they'd only see what I mean by my exhortations! But the Germans are too limited and short-sighted for that; they are absorbed in petty squabbles.'

"'And thus we are back at the beginning of our argument,' I cried in my turn. 'The movement is against the "absolute" Emperor, and anything which awakens that impression must be avoided, unless we want to rush into the most dangerous and sinister of controversies.'

"'*I*, an absolute monarch!' exclaimed the Emperor almost sneeringly—but at this moment Görz came up, and interrupted the conversation, which as I have told you I give almost word for word. The 'will-to-power' shows plainly through all the limitations that H.M. imposes on himself. I was forced to recognise a fatal misconception of the situation, which cannot but fill us with anxiety and apprehension. Will *you* succeed in restraining him from incalculable proceedings—*in removing the elements which urge him to do things of which he does not know the import?*

"Afterwards the Emperor recurred to our talk and said: 'When I get back to Germany I shall make Bernard set the Press on the lunatics who see in me the "absolutist" Emperor. Have I ever taken a single step which could be said to infringe the Constitution? Never! How on earth do people get hold of such ideas?'"

The summer cruise of 1900 started under very unfavourable auspices. The incidents in China, where the Boxer rising had just broken out, and the opposition from the Conservatives and Agrarians, had made the Emperor extraordinarily excitable; so that from the first Eulenburg had a difficult game to play. Even before they left Kiel there was a tussle, and when he insistently urged a pacific attitude, a definite quarrel ensued. But again the Emperor bore no malice; he was soon as good friends as ever, full of trust and consideration. During the cruise they at first thought he had calmed down; but this did not last long. When in casual conversation something was said about the Conservatives, he flew into such a rage that Eulenburg felt as though he were looking into an abyss of hatred and embitterment, and for the first time feared that the Emperor might " throw himself into the arms of the Liberals, so as to ' do in ' the Conservatives."

" I regard the situation as very perilous," he wrote to Bülow, " and don't know what to do. What we discussed on our walk at Kiel might be useful. Whether it would *help* us, only time can tell . . . Leuthold, too, is uncertain. He regards this state as a sort of nervous breakdown, but *decidedly* rejects any fear of mental disturbance. I feel as if I were sitting on a powder-magazine, and scarcely dare to breathe. Please let political reports be as few as possible, and ask him for none but *unavoidable* decisions."

" *July* 15, *late at night.*
" At dinner and after dinner there was so much excitement about mere nothings that one

can't tell what the outcome of this state of mind will be. Leuthold has just told me that he is at his wits' end. Every suggestion of a different régime is angrily rejected. Life on board ship is no relaxation but the reverse, he says; yet he doesn't know what to advise. Neither do I; we can only wait and pray God that no sort of complication in affairs may now arise. For many such scenes as I went through at Kiel would lead to a nervous crisis of some sort—no one can tell what. Good-night. It is one o'clock, and I am very tired. These things affect me deeply. I have trusted so much to the Emperor's talents—and to time. Now both are failing me; and one has to look on at the suffering of a man one loves without being able to help him.

" P.S. Please—the utmost caution about this letter and its contents."

The mounting excitement which characterised this cruise broke out on July 27 at Bremerhaven on the return journey. Then was delivered the address to the troops embarking for China—the notorious " Hun speech." Eulenburg, who on that sultry day had to stand beside the Emperor as representative of the Government, thought at first that he had succeeded in putting the journalists off the scent. In this belief he made some notes on the day's proceedings:

" The speech which the Emperor intended to make on the departure of the troops was known to me only in part, and that by word of mouth. He took the murder of Ketteler [1] and some German nationals as a *personal* insult, and wanted

[1] The German *chargé d'affaire* at Pekin, Baron von Ketteler, had been assassinated on June 20, 1900.

the troops to avenge it! As I knew that reporters from Berlin must have arrived to see the troops depart, I sent a request through some police officials that they would come to me on the 'Hohenzollern,' and arranged it so that they should miss the Emperor's speech. I was most polite to them, and told them that H.M. was very much upset by the insult put upon the German nation; he had told me (I added) pretty much what he intended to say. I then read them the speech, which they took down in shorthand. They were very grateful, and instantly left for Berlin. But one of them slipped through the officials' fingers, and *had* heard the Emperor's speech—though he had not been able to get very near. So in *one* paper there did appear a phrase of the Emperor's, and a very bloodthirsty phrase. But not the whole speech, thank God! Among other things there was this order: 'Give no quarter'—'blood for blood,' and so on.

"It was like a weight off my chest to have got the better of that horrid little gang of reporters. The publication of the speech would have done the Emperor *great harm*."

Unfortunately he had deceived himself. Enough of the speech filtered out to do the Emperor considerable injury.

During the customary sojourn at Cadinen and Rominten at the end of September Eulenburg found the Emperor decidedly calmer than in the summer, and seized the opportunity to have " a long serious talk with him about giving his nerves a rest, leading a quieter life"; and the Emperor's amiability showed that he took these remarks in good part as of old. But now as before, it made

Eulenburg extremely anxious to find him frequently wiring, as he had done in Norway too, to foreign lands—now to the Tsar, now to England, and to Waldersee besides, whose answers, moreover, he sent straight to the General Staff without informing the Foreign Office. At the same time perfidious articles were appearing in the *Hamburger Nachrichten*, designed to influence the Emperor against Bülow. Eulenburg, to get some sort of help, arranged—and was supported by Mackensen as A.D.C. in attendance—that the despatches should be forwarded " through the Foreign Office," so that the Secretary of State might at least see them. In a long talk he tried to enlighten the Emperor on the gravity of the situation : " The Chinese question was immensely complicated, the risk of an understanding between Russia and England, in order to expose him, was great. . . . A mistake made by him, which his officials would not now be able to gloss over, would unite *all* the hostile elements in Germany against him, and give rise to a coalition within the Empire which would be more difficult to overcome than one outside it." The trouble was, as Eulenburg reported to Bülow, that the Emperor regarded the Chinese expedition as a purely military affair, which did not concern the Foreign Office and was to be directed by him " from the saddle, as it were." This view, remarked Eulenburg, was impossible, from both the political and the military standpoint, and would inevitably lead to a catastrophe. " You must, at Hubertusstock (where the Emperor is shortly to betake himself), establish the position with Schlieffen and Tirpitz ; otherwise there'll be some disastrous arrangement made there with Scholl. *There is no time to lose* . . . I ask myself where are we all coming to ? Anyhow, this can't go on."

Those who can remember that period will not have forgotten the extraordinary upheaval of public opinion that now ensued. For it was a fact that the expedition had been undertaken without asking the Reichstag for the wherewithal. When it assembled in the winter, people were prepared for anything. It was in such a situation that Bülow became Imperial Chancellor. His first task was to ask for an indemnity; and such was his tact, and the attractive power of his personality, that he actually succeeded in laying the storm. But he naturally wished to show the Emperor from what perils he had momentarily rescued him, and that they were not yet completely over. It is significant that he did not do this in his own person, but—put forward the Ambassador at Vienna! On November 22 he wired to Eulenburg:

"J'ai réussi dans deux discours à sauver la situation devant le Reichstag et le Bundesrat, qui semblait presque désespérée. Le danger depuis longtemps prévu par toi d'une coalition entre les princes allemands et le Parlement allemand contre Sa Majesté Impériale est imminent. A présent tout dépendra d'une conduite sage de Sa Majesté. Trouve un prétexte pour lui écrire, ou télégraphie-lui le plus vite possible en lui recommandant d'être prudent, dans ses discours, jusqu'à l'arrangement de la question chinoise et des questions dépendantes du Reichstag."

On the same day Eulenburg sent the following long cipher-telegram to the Emperor, on the draft of which he noted: "This shows exactly what my relation was to the Emperor and Bülow."

The Emperor

"I must remind Your Majesty of a certain political talk we had in Norway. By a concatenation of circumstances I have learnt that a very clever move was in preparation. This was based upon well-intentioned speeches and actions of Your Majesty's, which laid themselves open to attack and might have had a very serious, and probably a *dangerous*, effect, if they had been fully carried out. Certain speeches in the Reichstag will give an idea of what I mean. Bernard, by his answer and his attitude, has evidently parried the blow. A *waiting game* seems now to be the word of order. I implore Your Majesty to put your trust in my sure knowledge of the situation; and I can only very, very earnestly beg Your Majesty to abstain *for the immediate present* from any kind of public manifestation— be it civil or military—if it is in the least likely to cause a sensation of any sort in any place. *Especially with reference to China*, but also to internal questions, whatever their designation may be— water or land, administration or parliament (Diets, etc.). Your Majesty may rest assured that this wire is not scaremongering or pessimism. The *actual position obliges me to send it.* For I must keep the promise I gave Your Majesty in Norway —of warning you *in good time*. That is why I telegraph. I shall inform Bernard of the situation. May God protect Your Majesty! A friend has but a limited power to do so."

The Emperor's answer was not very reassuring :

"Kiel, *November* 23, 1900.

"Just got your telegram. . . . Am very grateful for your hint, to which the attitude I had prescribed to myself fully corresponds. I have, moreover, strictly adhered to it. . . . Of course the duty and the right of speaking to my soldiers is an exception, and I shall never allow that to be interfered with, or censored."

The conclusion shows that the Emperor had taken the warning to refer to the intrigues of the Herbert Bismarck party !

The poor Emperor was simply not to be reasoned out of his illusion about himself and the world at large. He really was not aware of what he was doing and causing. Even in July, 1901, he could say to Eulenburg : " I allow Bernard to rule in peace. Since I have had him, *I* can sleep in peace. I leave everything to him, and know it's all right." Eulenburg, passing this on to Bülow, merely remarked : " All very fine, if the dear thing only did ! But anyhow the saying is significant as a mark of character."

The mordant King Edward VII took a malicious pleasure in saying of his nephew : " He is the most brilliant failure in history." It is difficult for a mere looker-on to realise what a personal friend must have felt in view of that failure. " The Emperor is the greatest disappointment of my life," Eulenburg once said to a trusted woman-friend. " I hoped everything of him, and he has not fulfilled one of my hopes." We have been able to follow the course of that disappointment—how it first appeared in the form of slight anxieties, like little spots of mildew on a fine picture ; how it grew more and more substantial, spread, and left no part of the picture untouched, until finally the whole was covered as with a melancholy grey film. His sentiments of love and friendship for this unusual man, who possessed so much personal charm, had not diminished, but they were mingled with sadness and compassion. For Eulenburg William II was now only " the poor dear Emperor."

A year and a half before his death he summed up his verdict on this one-time friend in his mild, fair-minded way :

" His intentions, which were always noble, were frustrated by his incapacity for seeing things as they were, and his complete lack of any insight into character was the vulnerable spot in his undeniable equipment of genius. For he was more or less the victim of those immediately surrounding him, and these ruled him craftily, and never contradicted him ; they also managed to remove those who *had* the courage openly to oppose the sovereign, when duty dictated that course."

Who can wonder that after so many painful experiences Eulenburg should have wearied of his political exertions, and lost his interest in politics as well ? Especially as he told himself that he could safely take the second place and leave the Emperor to the guidance of the Imperial Chancellor, who was his friend, with whom he believed himself to be in perfect agreement on all important matters, and whose expert knowledge he trusted to. That this Imperial Chancellor was to be another " brilliant failure," and this friend to prove another bitter disappointment, he did not then dream—perhaps could not have dreamt. With a clear conscience he thought he could go back to the ordinary duties of his more restricted sphere. What he believed to be still his personal duty to the Emperor, we shall see a little later. He wrote of it in a description of a meeting brought about by him in October, 1901, at Liebenberg between the Emperor and Houston Stewart Chamberlain, whom His Majesty very much admired.

"The Emperor's intellectual interests had at one time brought us together and made us friends. His personal authority, when he came to the throne, had bound me to the wheels of his chariot, and he made use of any talents I possessed in the service of Emperor and Empire. . . . My artistic temperament was, nevertheless, constrained to what was from the purely human point of view a sort of slavery, a spiritual martyrdom, which often became unendurable under the stress of increasing physical exhaustion. But it was unchangingly my duty to be " something to " the Emperor, mentally and artistically speaking. If it had once been my music and my literary ability (whenever political toil did not fall like a blight on that flowering garden), it was afterwards my constant endeavour to keep spiritual ideals before that explosive nature, so prone to be impassioned by questions of personal authority. But in the end all I could really do was to keep him in a good temper, and relax his mind by my amusing talk. And that to me, who so deeply felt my vocation as a friend, was mighty little. However, I did not fail in vigilance and never missed an opportunity of being faithful to my more spiritual duty."

These words, written in later years, may lay greater stress on his dislike for the political sphere than was actually felt at the time of which we are writing. It had always been there, as we know ; and if it usually slumbered on the threshold of consciousness, there were moments in which, under disappointment or over-exertion, it made itself strongly felt.

At the turn of the century, however, it had become irrepressible and prevailed over all else ; fostered as it was by many and many a trying experience in the narrow sphere of the Viennese Embassy, and accentuated by increasing physical suffering—until one day the resolve was taken to turn his back once for all upon the diplomatic service, and as a consequence, on politics in general.

VII
THE END OF HIS CAREER

THE position of German Ambassador in Vienna did not become any easier as years went by. The allied Dual Monarchy was creaking and cracking all over, its foundations were quivering, the whole structure threatening to fall asunder. The first sign of approaching dissolution, the fall of the Badeni Ministry—which fell a victim to street-rioting—at the end of November, 1897, had not directly affected the German Empire. But when after an unsuccessful experiment with a preponderantly German Ministry in the beginning of November, 1898, a representative of the Czech clerical nobility, Count Thun, became Prime Minister, the situation showed symptoms of strain. For this orientation looked towards Russia and France and secretly hated the German alliance; and as at the same time relations with Hungary grew more and more complicated, no one could fail to see that the Triplice was seriously menaced. It was no accident when immediately after Count Thun assumed office, the leader of the Czechs, Kramarz, wrote an article for a French paper, in which he called the Triplice a worn-out piano on which no one could play, and pointed out that Austria need no longer regard the German Embassy as the principal arbiter of her destiny. Eulenburg had cognisance of the article before its publication; he also learnt that it had been written, if not at the instigation, at any rate with the knowledge of the

Minister Kaizl. This made the Foreign Minister's position no less difficult than Eulenburg's.

Count Goluchowski, personally a convinced supporter of the German alliance, was nevertheless not powerful enough to be able to steer successfully against the feudalist-clerical-Slav tide, if this should submerge the Austrian Emperor. Moreover, the heir to the throne, Archduke Francis Ferdinand, was against Goluchowski; it was said of him that he was " more Russian than the Tsar."

In these circumstances the German Ambassador had to be doubly circumspect. Any self-assertion might easily assist the anti-German side to victory, and what might then happen no one could foresee. However, Eulenburg stood so high that he could face coming events with a certain amount of confidence, provided no tricks were played on him from Berlin. But this was precisely what was soon to happen.[1]

On November 29, 1898, Count Thun, in the Austrian Council, answered a public interpellation on the expulsion of Austrian subjects from Prussia (it concerned some Galician Poles who had been agitating in Poland) by an aggressive speech which concluded with the declaration that in certain circumstances he " would not hesitate to protect to the fullest extent the rights of Austrian subjects, that is to say, to make use of measures in accordance with the principles of reciprocity." Whether this was a considered challenge or merely a display of truculence, its effect was the same—the German side had to display the greatest possible circum-

[1] The official documents are to be found in the Foreign Office publication: *Die grosse Politik der europäischen Kabinette*, Vol. 13, pp. 121, *et seq*. They give, as will easily be understood, a very imperfect picture, which is filled in by private correspondence, making part of them for the first time comprehensible. This must for a while be withheld from complete publicity.

spection if they wished to avoid a serious clash, which after all could not well be contemplated. Bülow parried the thrust by a subtly evasive reply in the Reichstag. But Emperor William, on whom at that time the influence of his suite was again all too powerful, could not refrain from writing the Emperor of Austria a reproachful letter, at which the latter took great offence.[1] It required an interview of three-quarters of an hour with Eulenburg, and all the reliance the old Emperor placed on him, to mitigate the impression in any degree. But he could not prevent Francis Joseph from soon afterwards appearing on the Tsar's name-day (December 18), demonstratively clad in Russian uniform, at the Russian Embassy. From Berlin it was then demanded that Count Thun should explain and apologise. That was not to be obtained.[2] Austria's self-respect was wounded by the Emperor's missive, and took pleasure in emphasising a great Power's independence of its ally.

This incident, unpleasant enough in itself, was made still more so by Holstein's (as before) seizing the opportunity to take Goluchowski down a peg. Eulenburg learnt that an attempt had been made from Berlin to insert an article in the *Pester Lloyd* in which the Minister's position was represented as badly shaken. At the same time German newspapers fastened on the pretext of the article by Kramarz to attack Goluchowski as the friend of this most dangerous of all Czech agitators. As Bülow denied all participation in the manœuvre,

---

[1] According to the documents, State Secretary von Bülow composed the draft of this letter. Whether he was induced to do this by his knowledge of the Emperor's mood, or was urged thereto by Holstein, only the initiated could say.

[2] A semi-official explanation, which after some time appeared in the *Fremdenblatt*, could not be considered satisfactory.

it could only have originated with Holstein, whose methods it precisely embodied.

This affair put Eulenburg between two fires. Convinced that at this moment any sort of clash would play the opponents' game for them—the French Ambassador was only waiting for his German colleague to show his teeth, and was visibly disappointed when he did no such thing—Eulenburg had done his best to protect Goluchowski. By this attitude he incurred the displeasure of the Foreign Office. On February 13 he commented on the above-mentioned articles in the German Press :

" This badgering has its *spiritus rector* in Friend Holstein. He has been gradually withdrawing from me ever since I have held by Goluchowski, who now represents the *only* guarantee that Austria will not throw herself into the arms of Russia. If H.M. and Bülow did not listen to my counsels, we should be confronted by a Franco-Russian-Austrian alliance. On Goluchowski, Frau Schratt,[1] and myself the whole Triplice depends at this moment, for Hungary is internally so riven that it can offer me no satisfactory guarantee as a counterpoise. For peace, everything depends on keeping Holstein in check and replacing Banffy " [then Prime Minister of Hungary] " who no longer has a following. It is *devastating* when Holstein carries a personal hate into policy !

" My nerves are suffering badly, but I know where my duty lies, none the less."

[1] Frau Kathi Schratt, a popular actress and the intimate friend of the Austrian Imperial couple, did not actually concern herself with policy, but through her daily intercourse with the Emperor she exercised no little influence on his mind. Eulenburg was on very friendly and confidential terms with her.

The troubled waters gradually subsided, and Eulenburg's wise and circumspect attitude was conspicuously justified by events. The clerical-feudalist-Slav Ministry was not able to carry on beyond October, 1899; the danger to the Triplice was averted, and Eulenburg even had the somewhat questionable gratification of being held responsible by the entire Czech-clerical Party for the fall of Count Thun. But the crisis had left an unwelcome legacy—Holstein had broken with him once for all. Ever since the conflicts in the summer of 1897 their relations had been definitely cooler. That unexpected flaring-up of Holstein's former friendly sentiments, at the end of the crisis, had been of brief duration. True, he still now and then despatched those lectures ostensibly saturated with unselfish loyalty and friendship, which argued that Eulenburg ought not to assert himself when the Emperor ran amuck in home politics, but should make himself felt as a moderating influence (as if that advice were needed!) for in this way he might " possibly " survive the coming catastrophe. Or he would abound in reproaches for Eulenburg's having let himself be seduced by family influences. This letter (May 15, 1898), which has not the shadow of a foundation in fact, is a classic example of the lengths to which the man's diseased imagination could drive him. " Your high-strung nature needs to be objectively influenced; instead of that it is like a swimmer among weeds, perpetually and increasingly entangled in subjective ones. . . . Last summer you did the Emperor the great service of painlessly ridding him of two troublesome Ministers " [an allusion to the retirements of Marschall and Bötticher]. " What effect has that had upon your own position? None—or at any rate none for the better, that anyone can perceive.

To-day you are not so much ' Phili ' as ' Eulenburg '; and that means the end of many things which at one time would have been in your favour. ... In my view, you must be harder (or shall we say, more egotistic) even towards counsels coming from the side which has your sympathy—or else you will go aground."

It is no wonder that Eulenburg left such demented " badgering " unanswered. To him Holstein's behaviour—nay, Holstein himself—seemed more and more a subject for the pathologist. When in the autumn of 1898, during his holiday at Liebenberg, he paid a promised visit to the Foreign Office, he found Holstein—" who is getting more and more like one of Böcklin's phantom forms "—not at home. He had vanished, no one knew where. The mysterious absence lasted nearly two months. Not until December 4 did he reappear in his place. His letters had long been few and far between. For the whole of 1898 only five are to be found, and since August he had been mute. Eulenburg wrote to him about this on January 2, 1899 :

" I cannot enter on the New Year without sending you my greetings and sincere good wishes, with all my heart. May it bring you all good things, and protect and strengthen your poor eyes! Our correspondence has been very limited since Bülow took office. This I regret *personally*, because I now hear less of you as an individual. Politically I don't mind, for I know that all is safe with Bernard and yourself. . . . Keep your old friendship for me. We have put through so many stiff jobs together that it cannot well die out; we have been, so to speak, roasted and stewed in company. But we will always keep those times in memory. The older one grows, the more one clings to familiar conditions; new ones leave us cold.

"Your P. E."

Holstein's answer shows as a masterpiece of refined malice when we remember that since the beginning of December the friction about Count Thun's manifesto had been going on, and that the Ambassador had had to strain every nerve to save the situation and the alliance. Certainly he had not pandered to Holstein by attacking Goluchowski; and this probably accounts for the letter written to him by Holstein on January 5:

"Many thanks for your New Year wishes. That I could not personally exchange with you here what modern Americanism calls 'the compliments of the season' was a source of regret to me. But as you were obliged for once to stay in Vienna, I cannot understand why you didn't go out to Semmering and amuse yourself there with sleighing and so on. That indeed seems to display a dutifulness which I, it is true, still retain, but which is not the general rule. As to the interior affairs of Austria, they cause me the less anxiety because I do not see what we can achieve by interference either for ourselves or her. So we bide our time, and drink to each other in goodness knows what—tea, for choice! I hope that the month of frost prophesied by Falb and Co. will assist you and yours to a more cheerful view of life—in so far as that is not yours at present.

"With heartfelt greetings,
"HOLSTEIN."

This was, on Holstein's side, the closing of a correspondence which had extended over twelve years and a half. Eulenburg had written to him once more in April, 1899, a chatty letter about various interesting events in Vienna—probably supposing that Holstein's ill-temper had, as so often before, evaporated in the interval. He received no answer, and when he tried to see him in September at Berlin, Holstein was " not at home." That was the end of the end. Holstein's enmity had, in the January and February of that year, manifested itself in the way we have seen. There can be no doubt that the campaign against Goluchowski was ultimately designed to make the German Ambassador's position in Vienna an impossible one. That aim had not been attained, but Holstein did not lose sight of it. For three years he had been secretly opposing Eulenburg— we shall have clear proof of that in future pages. Henceforth he worked, with all the tenacity of his morbid powers of hatred, for the downfall of his one-time friend.

It was against Eulenburg's nature to retaliate in kind for such sentiments. When in November he received the first proof of Holstein's enmity, in the shape of a sudden newspaper attack upon him as the prospective Imperial Chancellor (there was not the slightest foundation for this), he merely sketched out for his own information a history of the rupture, and added the following reflections :

" To be ' not at home ' is, after all, no deadly insult. If it were, how many hundreds of gentlemen should I have had to call out ! But it did wound me very keenly ; for even if Holstein *was* rather (or very) crazy, he was a lonely, unhappy being, and my pity for him was *very great.*

" The cause of his rebuff was not, however, only the fact that Bülow and I are friends, and powerful enough to put him in the background ; but also my political 'apostacy' about Goluchowski—as Holstein, possessed by his old burning hatred, calls my attitude towards the man with whom, in my position as German Ambassador in Vienna, I discussed affairs, regarding him as the only person with whom I can properly do so. From the moment I refused to 'down' Goluchowski, Holstein had done with me. And I placed the country's interests higher than the Holstein caprices. What will be the outcome of it all, I cannot tell. I imagine that my none too easy life will be made as difficult as he possibly can make it. He used to call that 'breaking people in.'"

Two years later, on September 11, 1901, when the enmity of his former friend was already painfully perceptible, Eulenburg again alluded to it in a letter to Bülow :

"How strange a thing is life ! When I think that I never did Holstein anything but good, interceded for him, helped him whenever I could, suffered a *great deal* on his behalf—and now this enmity, this hatred ! It really is perfectly inexplicable. I shall never let myself be led into showing him any active hostility, because I am sorry for him, and in spite of all cannot forget what we once were to each other."

He was true to that principle ; he never did anything against Holstein. Even when the terrible persecution of himself broke out, behind which from the first we know that Holstein, and no other, stood as instigator and moving spirit (and that Eulenburg was not deceived has now been made clear by a witness from the other side), he spared his foe, he never uttered his name, though he could have greatly improved his own position by forcing Holstein to appear in person before the court. Only the thought of his posterity and his family-name could have finally induced him to lift the veil for those who came after, and thus ensure that, when he was dead, the truth should not for ever be suppressed.

It is for history to deliver the verdict. Which of the two was the better man is a question which does not admit of a moment's doubt. But even when we weigh their political achievement, Holstein's scale kicks the beam. Without any exaggeration we may say that whenever he disagreed with Holstein, Eulenburg was in the right. Every time that he, as Ambassador, opposed Holstein's views about Austria, he was conspicuously proved the better statesman. But even where he did not succeed, we cannot say that he was wrong. Of Holstein's grand scheme for depriving the Emperor of governing power in one way or another, we have had occasion to judge, and could not fail to condemn it. It was an impossibility; and Eulenburg's opposing policy represented a sense of what *was* possible. True, his also failed in its modest aim of preventing the sovereign's blunders, and when they could not be prevented, of smoothing them over as best he might, so as to pass through that difficult constitutional period (which could not last for ever) with as little damage as might be. In Eulenburg it was the symbol of a profound disappointment; we have seen how often he expressed that disappointment and how often, too, his anxiety about the future made itself heard. But for a convinced adherent of the Monarchy there was no other course; and it is not a proof of error, but the profoundest of historical tragedies, that this course too led finally to disaster. If anyone should reply that a course which so ends must be wrong in any circumstances, we can only answer, in our turn, that that end was not to be foreseen, nor was it inevitably appointed ; and that the great mistakes which caused the downfall of the Emperor were made in the period when Eulenburg was but a looker-on at events. When he made his exit, nothing was irretrievably lost, and even afterwards things might have turned out otherwise. Nay—even when the Emperor, through gross blunders which were not of his making, was obliged to stake the destiny of Germany on the precarious wager of battle, all was not yet lost. How high he still stood on that Fourth of August, 1914! Perhaps it depended only on the issue of a single battle—and the statues of conquerors might have stood in all the German cities, and the renown of William II have fallen in no way beneath that of his grandfather. Such a thought seems like an idle dream to-day. But—German hands on German hearts—are there many of us who did not once dream that dream? And which of us, could the picture of Germany as she is to-day have been presented to him, would not have declared it to be the phantasy of a lunatic? There are indeed moments in the history of the world when reality is the phantom and the wildest of phantasies the reality, and when the most widely-differing conceptions are brought into close touch with one another.

But let us admit this—that there was no intrinsic probability that William II's photograph would come to represent the glorious victor in a mortal combat. Having come to know the Emperor as he was, we cannot so conceive him. Such sovereigns are ill-starred. Initiates knew this before we did, and Philip Eulenburg knew it best of all.

That was precisely why his policy was above all designed to prevent the larger kind of crisis, and why he moved heaven and earth to do so. Every page, so far, has given us the proof of that. Whatever the occasion might be—whether at home or abroad, whether a practical or a personal matter—Eulenburg's advice was always based upon prudential considerations. This was not merely an outcome of his nature, which disliked the appeal to force ; for when it was necessary he could, as we have seen, take a resolute attitude. If in all big questions he preached prudence, and again prudence, this was on the one hand because he quite rightly considered that only by tranquil and pacific evolution along her appointed path would Germany prosper, and on the other because he knew his sovereign and realised that his nature was not fit to cope with great vicissitudes.

From this standpoint, indeed, one might reproach him for not accepting Holstein's challenge, once he had realised how dangerous the man was. Then one might say that he ought to have caused Holstein's downfall, in order to protect himself, the Emperor, and Germany from that evil genius. But this would be to demand of him what was contrary to his nature, for nothing was further from Eulenburg than the very thing with which his enemies, those who envied him, and mistaken public opinion have so often reproached him—namely, intrigue against his nearest colleagues. Philip Eulenburg was not a belligerent person, and more than anything else he disliked attacking others ; even in self-defence he found it difficult to use the weapons at his disposal. So it is very doubtful if he ever could have brought himself to get Holstein out of the way. " Bringing people down " was not to his taste ; and it is significant that he, who so often succeeded in reconciling and smoothing over the most troublous incidents, should have failed in his one exceptional attempt to remove a dangerous influence. He did try very hard to bring down the egregious Master of the Household, von Liebenau. In that he failed, and the credit must be given to another. Similarly, he came to signal grief in his attack on Admiral von Senden. But in Holstein's case he could, besides, assure himself that it was not his business to purge the Foreign Office, of which his friend Bülow was chief. Of Bülow he *had* confidently expected that he would in time get rid of Holstein. The reader will remember the advice given in a letter of August, 1897: " Show your teeth— build your nest as you want it to be ! " But Bülow —nay, we must not anticipate ; let us return to the Viennese Embassy.

The new century brought Count Eulenburg his elevation to the rank of Prince. For a long time the Emperor had cherished the intention of enlarging the group of princely Prussian Houses, which were mostly Catholic, by the addition of some Evangelical members ; and naturally he thought first of his friend. To him he mentioned it first on October 30, 1899, during a visit at Liebenberg, and was somewhat vexed to meet with an alarmed refusal. When next day, on the way to the railway-station, Eulenburg tried to reiterate his refusal in milder terms, he saw at once that it would be fruitless. " I felt very distinctly," he writes, " that the Emperor was quite determined. From years of intercourse I have learnt not to mistake that ' sovereign accent ' which only gets more sovereign with opposition ! And how could I wound him in the moment of his greatest favour, and his pleasure in thus exalting me ? Looked at in a practical light, I was faced with the alternatives of becoming a Prince in opposition to the Emperor, or in agreement with him. I could no longer doubt that the latter was the part of a friend. 'Your Majesty will decide my fate, as you have done ere now,' I said. 'I have received nothing but kindnesses from Your Majesty, and so I shall be grateful for anything that your favour bestows upon me.' 'Come, this *is* a pleasure to me!' said the Emperor, so warmly and gladly that I instantly felt I had done right. It was as if some kindness had been done to *him*. His gladness really touched me!

" Meanwhile we had reached the station. A few minutes later the train disappeared, the dear kind Emperor waving to me so cordially—nay, almost tenderly!

" I never drink brandy except when I have influenza. But now, to the astonishment of the station-master, I went up to the buffet in the waiting-room and ordered a small glass. The 'Prince' was all of a shiver at first, but the brandy wasn't a bad cure for that. I sat down, wrapped in my big cloak, in the coupé, and thought over the conversation that the blue cushions had heard ten minutes earlier. A sort of melancholy came over me, shot through by various reflections on names and coats-of-arms, which played distractingly against the gloomy background. Then I sank into a heavy-hearted anxious reverie upon the effect of this worldly glitter on the souls of my dearly-loved children . . . God will guide them. What can *I* do to keep their youth untouched by the hideous sin of arrogance!"

New Year's Day arrived, and with it the anticipated tidings. Congratulations poured in. The Emperor wired: " Congratulate Your Highness from depths of heart." King Oscar of Sweden likewise telegraphed : " Cordial thanks for your wire ; I send my most heartfelt wishes for the new century and my pleasure at the princely rank conferred. Please greet the Princess, too, most warmly. She will be glad, I am sure, to be able to keep the old name of Sandels for herself and the princely head of the family." [1]

" OSCAR."

In all there were 390 letters and telegrams, and 340 calls and visiting-cards. It took the aspect of a tribute to the German Empire, in which all the peerage, even the Czech peerage, all the princes, the diplomatic service, Ministers of State, Court functionaries, famous artists, numbers of financiers, parliamentarians, etc., participated. Even the town of Elbogen, near Carlsbad, which had belonged to the Eulenburgs in the 14th and 15th centuries, was represented. But the recipient of all these honours wrote in his diary for January 1 :

" Naturally the effect on the personnel of the Embassy and all the officials and servants was very great, and they all felt honoured in my person. The visits of congratulation went on and on and on—and *nobody* could see into my heart. My official and social position was girdled round with envy, and I felt the full pressure of that girdle. I knew perfectly well that this ' elevation ' could not fail to stir all the venomous elements into one deadly potion. And so that which to a worldly-minded man would no doubt have been a great delight, was mingled

---

[1] With the King of Sweden's sanction, the Emperor had decided that the new Prince zu Eulenburg should likewise bear the name of Count von Sandels, which was the Princess Augusta's family name, famous in Swedish history, and then extinct in Sweden itself.

with so much of bitterness that I could not help feeling a sort of terror.

"Undeniably it had given the Emperor the greatest pleasure of all. And therefore I had to be careful not to say a word of my uneasiness to anyone. The pleasure it gave *him* must not be spoilt, for after all it was only a *heartfelt* affection for me which had urged him to this token of his highest recognition and friendship."

Three days later he went on with his reflections:

"I should very much like to know how many telegrams, letters, and visits I should have received if all those who were vexed at my 'elevation' to princely rank had expressed themselves to me. Alas! I have not reached the heights of old Field-Marshal Wrangel, who said: "Was so-and-so vexed about me? Glad to hear it." I could not get away from the sense of my life's being a wonderful piece of legerdemain. And this was a fresh phase of the trick! What will the final one be? The only pleasure this phase could give me was the joy and pride of those I loved and who loved me; for I really do not feel that I put on my night-shirt that night, as a Prince, with feelings in any way different from those of the Count—though I daresay Richard Dohna did."[1]

He thanked the Emperor again on New Year's Day:

"The exceedingly gracious and kindly feeling expressed in the high distinction with which Your Majesty has favoured me fills me and mine

[1] Count Dohna had been made a Prince at the same time. He had angled for it in 1897, but had been refused. But now the Emperor had decided on it, so as not to make his friend's elevation too conspicuous.

with sentiments of profound gratitude. Fully to discharge the debt of gratitude will require the fidelity and service of many generations of my House. I put my trust in God, and beseech Him that these coming generations may never, as I shall never, grow weary in our service of gratitude.

"My wife is deeply moved by Your Majesty's revival of her much-loved name in the chronicles of my House.

"With fervent wishes for Your Majesty's well-being and happiness in the new century, I associate the request to be permitted to thank Your Majesty in person within the next few days."

He could not confide his inmost thoughts to the sovereign, but in a letter to the Empress he expressed them:

"Your Majesty will most graciously permit me to write a few words, under the impression made upon me by the high honour His Majesty's gracious favour has bestowed.

"During the long period in which I have had the happiness and honour of following, and taking an active interest in, the fortunes of Your Beloved Majesties, I have always received from Your Majesty such interest and kindly sympathy in my own fortunes that I feel impelled to say a few words to Your Majesty about this new turn in my destiny.

"I am filled with a sense of the beloved Emperor's graciousness. It is this *alone* which affects me. Your Majesty knows that worldly honours make no impression on me—*personally speaking*, indeed, this new dignity almost embarrasses me. But such a distinction touches the interests of future generations, and that being so, personal feelings have nothing to say. And how should I *not* have rejoiced in a favour so conferred ! Mine is not an easy life. Where there is a great deal of light, there is always a great deal of shadow. And God alone knows how deep are the shadows which He has appointed to me for my chastening. I have bent to His will without a murmur—but under the heavy pressure of care and grief, worldly things lose yet more of their importance in my heart than would in any event be so. All the brighter, all the clearer, however, do the kindness, friendliness, affection which I have experienced shine forth—and especially those shown me by him whose head wears the consecrated crown, and who amid all the stress of his burdened life yet finds time to display his kindness, his friendship, so warm-heartedly. *That* makes me happy. I repudiate the thought of recognition for my services, or for my having ruined my nerves and health for my sovereign (which I can with a good conscience declare I have done !). He who does not do his duty from an inward compulsion, as if it were a ' matter-of-course,' who does not put all he is at the disposal of his Fatherland, is not worthy to call himself a Prussian ! And so the idea of a ' reward for faithful service ' is anything but agreeable to me ; and thank God we still have plenty in our Fatherland who think as I do.

"But those gifts which flow from a warm heart, all kindliness and friendship—*they* are, as I have said, a refreshment, a divine essence which moves and delights us as do the gifts of the Divine One Himself. And the beloved Emperor—Your Majesties both—know so well how to give gladly, cordially ! May the echo of that gladness *often* float back to the dear exalted givers, together with the heartfelt gratitude I feel for it.

"Will Your Majesty be so very gracious as to convey my sense of gratitude to His Majesty? In these tiring days I do not propose to approach the Emperor with an effusion of feeling—his time is too much taken-up."

The already brilliant position of the Ambassador was not a little enhanced by this act of Imperial favour. On January 13 he was able to tell Bülow: "Here the affair has turned out to be a very practical and skilful political move. Nearly everyone regards my elevation as an act of Imperial courtesy to Austria-Hungary, and they are never tired of boasting about it."

This strengthening of his position was soon to stand him in good stead. For the relations between the allied States just now suffered some disturbance, and the Ambassador had a great deal of difficulty in averting lasting consequences.

It was of very great significance for the future that he now succeeded in approaching the heir to the throne, Archduke Francis Ferdinand, who was profoundly hostile to Emperor William and Germany, bestowed excessive notice on the Russian Ambassador, and very markedly avoided the German. During the Court-ball at the Burg on January 13, 1900, Eulenburg contrived, as if by chance, to come face to face with the Archduke, and engaged him in conversation. His charm did not fail him on this occasion. The ice was broken, a friendly correspondence began, and the hitherto so Russophil heir to the Hapsburg crown became in time a personal friend of the German Emperor's.

An opportunity of clinching this achievement

THE ARCHDUKE FRANZ FERDINAND

presented itself when the German Crown Prince paid his first visit to Vienna in April, 1901. In every way the sojourn was a brilliant success, but the most valuable of all impressions was that made upon the Austrian heir-apparent. Eulenburg wrote of this :

> "I told the Crown Prince, with respect to whose visit and social obligations the Emperor had given me a perfectly free hand, that after his call upon Emperor Francis Joseph he should go direct to the Archduke Francis Ferdinand and announce himself in person to Princess Hohenberg. I knew quite well that this would establish for all time the friendship between our Emperor and the Archduke which I had taken such pains to bring about. That night at the banquet the Archduke came rushing up to me with these words : 'I am deeply touched by, and very grateful for, the visit paid by the Crown Prince to my wife, and shall not forget it to him. Yes— he, a foreigner, knows what is the right thing to do, though *here* they have no conception of it ! I am very, very grateful.'"

Successes of this kind had to compensate the Ambassador for the difficulties thrown in the way of his superiors in the service, and the undermining of his own position. We know the kindred proceedings which marked the turn of the years 1898 and 1899. They were to continue, and in the end they contributed to the Prince's resolve to retire from official life.

In 1898 Holstein had contrived to get the French Military Attaché in Berlin, the Marquis de la Guiche, removed on the pretext of some indiscretion or another. He came to Vienna, where he was more dangerous on account of his great popularity in aristocratic society, and, moreover, because he was on the best of terms with Goluchowski, the husband of Princess Murat. So Holstein now pursued him in Vienna as well, and even discerned an opportunity for bringing down the detested Austrian Minister, and doing Eulenburg some harm. His pretext was the attacks to which the German Military Plenipotentiary was exposed in Paris during the Dreyfus case. Holstein managed to get this official recalled; he also managed—and this through the General Staff without consulting the Embassy—to make Austria, and Italy too, take similar steps, by way of proving their loyalty to the alliance. France could do no otherwise than retort by recalling *her* attachés, and M. de la Guiche was obliged to leave Vienna—to the great chagrin of aristocratic circles, who were sorry to lose the charming French couple and took Guiche's removal in bad part as a sign of servility towards Germany. The old Emperor had been persuaded to see it in the same light, so that when the Frenchman took leave he uttered the words "*Auf Wiedersehen*," whereby he made himself personally responsible for a speedy reversal of the measure. He now expected that Germany would follow his lead, and said so, very emphatically, to the German Ambassador. But in Berlin they would not hear of such a thing. Eulenburg was again between two fires. He had no doubt whatever that the whole proceeding had been foolish and fraught with danger. The joint recalls were in themselves a palpable result of someone's having put on the screw; and what made it the more desirable not to oppose Austria's desire to restore the *status quo* was that Germany and Italy could still, through their naval attachés in Paris, carry on as before, while Austria had no such officials. But nothing could have justified so wounding the Austrian Emperor's susceptibilities and making Goluchowski's position so difficult, for such a bagatelle. Goluchowski was just then being strongly opposed by the Czech aristocracy ; they wanted him to be replaced by Count Thun, which would simply have meant the end of the Triplice.

Holstein, on the contrary, saw in all this no more than the opportunity for getting even with Goluchowski for the slights put upon him thirty years before. That was why he trumped up a crisis. To that end he utilised another incident which just then took place. A Hungarian Jew named Recknitzer had, in Constantinople, undertaken an action on behalf of the English banks against the construction of the Bagdad Railway—as he said, on Goluchowski's recommendation. This was untrue, as was at once demonstrated. But Holstein, instead of clearing up the matter, used it to blacken Goluchowski as being a secret opponent of German policy in the East. His most flagrant proceeding, though, was to hand over to the Austrian Ambassador Szögyeny for his perusal certain reports of Eulenburg's on which the Emperor had made marginal notes, criticising in a disparaging sense the Austrian Minister's capabilities and achievements. Holstein knew that Szögyeny was a personal enemy of Goluchowski's ; and Szögyeny served up the notes, piping-hot, to his chief. Eulenburg learnt this from his own lips, but was obliged to give his word that he would not say anything about it.

Holstein's sharp practice was this time powerfully supported by the Emperor's military environment. Count Dietrich Hülsen-Häseler had for some time been among the Emperor's aides-de-camp. As Military Plenipotentiary in Vienna he had been far from a success, and therefore detested the Austrians. Why he detested Eulenburg also we shall learn later. Was Holstein acting in collusion with him? Eulenburg thought so, and was alarmed by the conjecture that the Foreign Office, hitherto the mortal enemy of A.D.C. politics, was now (when *he* could be injured) hand-in-glove with the wire-pullers. The Emperor's anger over the affair of the attachés was plainly to be traced to Hülsen's influence. This was reinforced by the tittle-tattle of others, and the effect was what may be supposed.

As representative of the German standpoint Eulenburg, with the Austrian Emperor, had gone to the limits of his power. He could not have said so much as he did had he not enjoyed the old sovereign's personal favour. With his own Government he interceded for a change of attitude. His suggestion was that Germany should utilise the approaching opening of the World Exhibition in Paris to reinstate the military representative in France as an act of courtesy, when the allied States could follow Germany's example. This wise counsel was met by a sharp rebuff—on March 27, 1900, he received the following trenchant snub:

> "His Majesty the Emperor has declared, on his own most exalted initiative, that he would regard the separate reinstatement of the Parisian Military Attachéship by the Imperial and Royal Government as a direct affront. The further handling of this question by the Viennese Cabinet will supply a test of the relations *between both realms*. Our most gracious Sovereign, now as before, sees in isolated Austrian action a *casus fœderis*.

" I will add for Your Excellency's strictly private information that His Majesty has heard from a foreign but reliable source in Paris that on the side of France every effort is being made to cause a rupture of the alliance on this question. The Parisian Government would regard it as a great triumph for itself and Your Excellency's French colleagues if it succeeded in obtaining the restoration of the Austrian Military Attaché, while we on our side firmly asserted the impossibility of again filling the post.

" His Majesty confidently expects that Your Excellency will, without endangering Count Goluchowski's position, succeed in making His Majesty's view prevail."

It was not difficult to divine the source of " the Most High's initiative." The minute was signed by Bülow. Eulenburg made a note on it : " So this bagatelle may possibly lead to a breach with Austria ! That Bülow should have consented to have anything to do with such dangerous folly is a proof of his dependence on Holstein. I am distraught by the political vista this suddenly reveals to me."

Of the concluding passage where he was told that he must succeed in producing the desired effect without endangering Count Goluchowski's position, he remarked : " And I *shall* succeed, because the Austrians listen to my counsels. . . . But I shall *not* succeed in quickly dispelling the bad feeling which so futile an exaggeration of this side-issue in great world-politics must necessarily arouse in the old Emperor and Goluchowski, both well-tried friends of Germany."

And he was right there too. By March 29 he was able to report officially that Count Goluchowski, as a loyal ally and in view of the German Emperor's personal wishes, had given his word of honour that his Government would let the question rest and would do nothing without Germany's full concurrence ; and that he hoped the magnanimity of the German Emperor would allow him to " do something to remove the painful impression inevitably left on Emperor Francis Joseph, who had taken so strong a personal part in the matter."

The real state of affairs was revealed by him in a private letter to Bülow, which the Emperor was to see. This letter, with the Imperial marginalia, we now give :

" Vienna, *March* 30, 1900.

" DEAR BÜLOW,

" Yesterday I had a talk with Goluchowski about the Parisian Military Attachéship, in accordance with the command of the Most High ; and I honestly strove to make the inevitable unpleasantness as little felt as might be. How far I succeeded in this I cannot as yet be certain. I have never doubted that the Austrians could be persuaded not to take separate action in this matter. The difficulty was to avoid displeasing the Emperor Francis Joseph. *That was what made it such a ticklish business.* From the moment the Austrians had told me that they would not act apart in the matter, they were bound to stick to their word—that is to say, they would always have been open to persuasion. My yesterday's telegram confirmed this view, and will doubtless have satisfied His Majesty. At any rate I don't know what more Goluchowski could have said. Separate action is now definitely precluded.

" Count Nigra will to-day or to-morrow say to Goluchowski that for Italy, whence the undesirable French Military Attaché has not yet been recalled, it would be impossible to consent to the reinstatement of the Parisian post. This step of Nigra's was advised by me, so as to divert at any rate a modicum of the bitterness from ourselves ; and I do not doubt that his quiet, persuasive treatment will have the desired effect.

" But I consider it my duty to give the following details of my interview with Goluchowski, in order to make the difficulties of the situation quite clear.

" The Minister received my communication with complete outward calm, but evident inward agitation. He was emphatic in saying that he did not desire to give any opinion on the situation in France and the hopes which might there be bound up with a rupture of the Triple alliance on this matter of the military attachés. That was beside the question, once the German Emperor had expressed a personal wish regarding the treatment of the matter. That wish was *sufficient by itself.* He, the Minister, had at first tried to divest the question of its political character, since he did not regard it as important in that respect. Once the political aspect became prominent, he could not possibly do anything but precisely what Germany did. To preserve the Triplice was more important than aught else. In comparison, nothing else signified.

" When our talk lost its official character, we began to discuss the matter more confidentially, more personally. 'I imagine,' said the Count, ' that Emperor William will not be able to reproach us with having shown no desire to meet him on this question, once we were informed of the attitude he wished us to take up. But my opinion is that the whole affair was not worth causing displeasure or a sense of wounded dignity to Emperor Francis Joseph. Do not forget that the venerable gentleman took a *personal part* in the matter, and that it must be very painful to him to withdraw from his position. However, I think Emperor William, in his magnanimous and sincerely amicable way, will find a means of dispelling that feeling.'

" In the further course of conversation Goluchowski said : ' Personally speaking, I am a cipher in this business. I deal with it purely and simply from the standpoint of the Triplice, which is such a cardinal necessity for us that nothing on earth will change my mind about it —not even the bad opinion which Emperor William has of me. If the Emperor says of my most loyally intended speeches in the Imperial Council that " they are nothing but phrases " ; if he considers my actions " feeble " ; if he says that I have tried to get up intrigues and that a sharp eye must be kept on me—I cannot alter it ; possibly facts will one day speak better for me ; but it *will not influence* my *conviction* of the necessity of the Triplice ! '

[Here the Emperor made a marginal note : " This is absurd ! Someone has been pulling the good Goluchowski's leg. Can the French have gone as far as this ? "]

" I answered that all this tale-bearing and misrepresentation seemed to me extremely disastrous, and that I could not imagine who could lend himself to such proceedings. Certainly it was not a friend of the Triplice.

" 'The sources are not official, it is true,' said the Count. ' But everyone knows that a great many things percolate from Berlin to Vienna. I am very well aware that those which influence the Emperor's opinion of me cannot possibly be official in origin.

"'Very assuredly,' continued Count Goluchowski, ' the tasks which I fulfil with full conviction are not made easy for me ! Suppose, for example, that the present question is brought up from a hostile quarter before the Czechs or Feudalists or various other enemies of mine, I am put in the position of answering extremely unpleasant—and, for our alliance, by no means desirable—interpellations in the Council or before the delegations. And if I then speak in favour of the Triplice, people in Berlin will say behind my back that " it was too late," or " is too lukewarm," or " ambiguous " or " tactless " ! However, I repeat that *nothing* will disturb me, because I am obeying my conviction.'"

[Emperor's notes at the end of this letter : " This is all the most utter nonsense ! Who can have dared to talk this sort of stuff to Golu I can't imagine—in this quiet dull winter, when I didn't see a soul to whom I could have spoken of him ! Phili must tell him that I had a good laugh over it all, and only wondered that a statesman of Golu's calibre could take such rubbish seriously. He must not lose his nerve. For I have never altered in my good opinion of him."]

This letter rendered Holstein's undermining abortive. The Emperor's eyes were opened, though he abstained—perhaps because he did not wish to be reminded of his own blunder—from thoroughly investigating the matter. Eulenburg had been able to avert the disaster only because he still stood so high in the Emperor's estimation, and likewise enjoyed the Austrians' full confidence, particularly that of the Berlin Ambassador, Szögyeny, to whom indeed he had appealed for help. He had been driven to such methods by Holstein's monstrous proceedings and naked treason. And Szögyeny stood by him further, in that he succeeded in dispelling the displeasure of Emperor Francis Joseph and Goluchowski. He managed to arrange that both should visit Berlin, and the visit was a brilliant success. The troublesome attaché-question was easily disposed of in a personal discussion between the two Emperors, the allied sovereign had an overwhelmingly enthusiastic reception from the ovation-loving populace of Berlin, and even Goluchowski basked in such sunlight that he went home more Germanophil than ever.

Count Goluchowski was certainly not the ideal statesman. Nor did Eulenburg think him so; and if he supported and shielded him, it was not from personal admiration or friendship, but from considerations of prudence. He knew that in Austria itself people had no illusions about the Polish Count, nor was he blind to the fact that just then there was a tendency to favour the Feudalist group represented by Count Thun. When the Minister of Education, Hartel, said that Goluchowski was lazy and superficial—too lazy to abandon the Triplice, but too superficial to perceive the danger in his flirtations with the Right—Eulenburg at once agreed, but remarked that Emperor Francis was an efficient counterpoise. To gain Goluchowski (so he wrote) one had to flatter his vanity, and especially when in Germany they had to proceed against the Poles. " Besides, *le dernier mot* with all our kind friends in Vienna is that we are envious and spiteful. If we happen to have a friend at the wheel in Vienna who is lazy and superficial, our best plan is to exalt his *vis inertiae* into a sort of shrine at which we worship. Then the *dernier mot* will die upon their lips."

The great question was how much the Ambassador's opinion counted for in Berlin. In the latest crisis he had had the last word with the Emperor; but it was to be foreseen that this would not be the end of crises. A Holstein does not so easily give in, and his influence was on the increase. The year 1901 was, indeed, the moment when, owing essentially to the mysterious influence which that morbid being had gained over the new Imperial Chancellor, the great opportunity was lost— that which, rightly used, would of all conceivable combinations best have ensured Germany's future— the opportunity of consolidating an alliance with England. Eulenburg, too, in this unfortunate year had clearer and clearer proof of Holstein's growing power. Not, at first, officially. Holstein had abandoned the open field, and turned to one where he could fight with unfamiliar weapons under the visor of anonymity.

In the newspapers which he influenced—and these were not a few at that time—there appeared malicious references to the frequent absence of the Viennese Ambassador from his post, to his many journeyings. The facts were undeniable, but only ill-will could have made them a reproach to him; for the journeyings, when they were not those of obligatory sick-leave, were taken in the Emperor's service as a member of his suite, and were anything but a rest or a recreation.

But what did the guileless newspaper-reader know about all that? It was easy to persuade him that such an important Embassy ought not to be left so often without its chief. And thus the Prince, who was sacrificing his failing strength in the service of the State, was stamped for the public as an idling, malingering diplomat. Only it was remarkable that in certain Austrian circles people were annoyed because this absentee-Ambassador mixed himself up so much in inter-Austrian matters ; still more remarkable that about the same time the rumour ran that he was to be transferred to Paris. With one accord the papers became as interested in his personality as though the fate of the universe depended on him. Not that he was without his champions. In Vienna the *Neue Freie Presse* bore witness for him, and in Munich the *Allgemeine Zeitung* definitely took up his cause. But, as always in such cases, the accusers had the advantage of priority, the defence only called forth more violent attacks, and no one could tell where the truth really lay.

Since the late autumn of 1901 the attacks had been reinforced by a personal quarrel which soon became public property in the shape of a lawsuit, and created a most painful sensation. Eulenburg had been from youth a friend of Count Bolka Hochberg, under whose management the Royal theatres were not in a particularly brilliant state. That was not so much the fault of the well-meaning and hard-working Count as of his secretary, a man named Pierson, who had got into financial difficulties by reason of extremely vexatious mismanagement. Eulenburg, who had cognisance of these matters, partly as a private individual, partly in his official capacity (a contractor in Vienna had applied to the Ambassador, hoping to get his money in that way), thought it his duty to warn his friend. But Hochberg took his secretary's part, informed him of the warning he had received, and Pierson instituted a libel-action. Eulenburg was thus, without any fault of his own, put into the most disagreeable of positions. It was out of the

The End of his Career 107

question for him to appear in court and prove the truth of what he had said. How could the Imperial Ambassador give the widest publicity to the complaints which in initiated circles were raised against the General-Manager of the Imperial Court Theatre —how could he formally indict a branch of the Imperial administration ? For a man of his way of thinking the impossibility was self-evident. He could not make known, even to private friends, that it was the Emperor, and none other, who— disturbed by his Lord Chamberlain's reports—had instructed him to warn Hochberg. Moreover, he was basely let down by a principal witness, a gentleman of very high position in the monarch's personal environment ; the man simply denied that he had said what he *had* said. The Prince, who even at this time was extremely ill, saw no way of avoiding the scandal but by a sacrifice of personal dignity. He prevailed on himself to make this Pierson a very comprehensive apology, which induced him to withdraw his action. This was, six years afterwards, when the Prince had fallen a victim to his persecutors, dragged into the Press by the hostile side. Till then it had been known only to a small circle ; but then it could be used against him, and it is quite possible that it did the Prince no good with the Austrian Emperor, who was likewise exposed.

At the same time, about the turn of the year 1901, there cropped up yet another crisis in the relations between Germany and Austria, which caused the Ambassador very great anxiety and trouble. In November, at Posen, there began the trial for riotous assembly of the parents and relatives of schoolchildren at Wreschen, who had refused to answer in German when under religious instruction. The accused were sentenced to severe restrictions of their liberty as having been concerned in a breach of the peace. This caused vast indignation among the Poles in Austria. The German consulate in Lemberg was attacked, there were high words in the Landtag at Cracow, and in Vienna on November 29 there was a demonstration in favour of the victims of Wreschen, which took place in the presence of the Polish Minister of Agriculture, Pientak, on the occasion of the annual festival in honour of the poet Mickiewicz. The Ambassador was obliged to make representations, but (as in other cases) he did this in a mild form. For him it was of the utmost importance that this unpleasant incident should not lead to a rupture in the Triplice—a danger which was the less to be trifled with because Austria-Hungary was just going through a grave Constitutional crisis about which the strictest secrecy was preserved. The Czechs and the French would have been in high feather if the German Ambassador had taken up an uncompromising attitude ; but that, in Eulenburg's view, was the best of reasons for doing the reverse. So he contented himself with obtaining an explanation from Goluchowski, which partially exonerated the offending Minister of Agriculture.

He defended his action in a private letter to Bülow of December 6 :

> " Though, personally speaking, I should very much have preferred to take strong action, after the monstrous proceedings at Lemberg and here —to bang my fist on the table like a lieutenant and rattle my sword—I believed it was above all things my duty to further the policy of the Emperor rather than that of our opponents. What a triumph for Messrs. Kramarz and Co. if I had shown my teeth ! Annoyance at my composure

The End of his Career

was plainly to be read on the countenance of my respected colleague Reverseaux" [the French Ambassador in Vienna]. "And as the same line has been pursued in Berlin, I perceive that H.M. and yourself share my view of the delicate situation.

"But if the policy hitherto pursued is to be in any way departed from, and if loftier (and to me at any rate unrevealed) considerations are to lead us *away* from Austria, I beg to be given a hint. I shall then undertake to make no end of a fuss, and proceed 'energetically' in these Pientak and Lemberg questions."

Bülow at first agreed, and suffered the "somewhat lame" Austrian explanations to close the incident. But the Emperor was not so easily satisfied. To the passage in Eulenburg's report about banging on the table he put a marginal note: "By far the best thing he could have done!" Eulenburg wrote again to Bülow about this:

" . . . His Majesty's unfriendly comment could not wound me so much as it might have done, because to behave like a Guards' lieutenant would have been to set all reason at defiance. I am so convinced that *nothing but composure and prudence* can avail in such situations that my beloved sovereign's annoyance cannot disconcert me. What a situation—to himself how surprising a one—I should have prepared for him if I had followed the prescription in the margin! . . . It takes a certain amount of self-control *not* to act upon that prescription. The feeling here is as bad as can be, all round. Worse than for a long time."

The incident seemed to be closed when Count

Bülow, on December 8, paid a tribute to the Austrian Government in the Reichstag. But appearances were deceitful. A month later the Imperial Chancellor made a long speech in the Reichstag which revealed the real state of German opinion. He took the fact of Italy's recent approaches to France as his text for a general review of the Triplice, and in the course of his analysis observed that Germany's situation and interests were different now from what they had been when in 1879 the alliance was consolidated. He concluded: " But if the Triplice is no longer an absolute necessity, it is still valuable in the highest degree," and so on. That was a definite cold douche for Vienna, and was there felt to be such. Everyone was offended by the speech; Goluchowski expressed himself with the utmost violence, and even on the Austrian Emperor the Imperial Chancellor's words had such an effect that in the ensuing audiences he never once inquired for the German Emperor, and when discussing foreign policy avoided mentioning Germany. Prime Ministers Körber and Szell expressed great anxiety about the consequences which might arise from a lasting coolness between the two sovereigns, and Goluchowski was most confidentially told, from a source very near to the throne, that there had been question of his leaving Vienna and of his probable successor, the Ambassador in Petersburg, Count Aehrenthal, a notorious Russophil. Thus did Berlin make public demonstration to the world at large of its dissatisfaction with Austria's attitude on the Polish question.

Eulenburg did what lay in his power to remove the bad impression. At a banquet for the German colony which took place at the Embassy on January 26, the eve of Emperor William's birthday, he proposed Francis Joseph's health in the following speech :

"It is an honour and a pleasure to me once more to be able to stand in this place and celebrate the noble, exalted sovereign under whose shelter and protection we enjoy our lives in this beautiful country. The link which binds this noble ruler to our Imperial Master, and which embraces the interests of our Fatherland and those of the realms of the Austrian-Hungarian monarchy, is so strong a one that I might call it infrangible. Those to whom that link is not a source of pleasure will not succeed in breaking it. But we whose *hearts* are bound up with it will not, and must not, be discouraged if sunshine occasionally gives place to clouds or rain. The lives of nations are like the lives of men—we cannot expect eternal sunshine. It is appointed to us to moderate our wishes in that respect. However, it has been said that the charm of life consists in *slight* variations.

"Our alliance is a well-built, a safe house, which can bid defiance to all unseasonable weather. It has become our *Temple of Peace*—nay, more—our well-loved *home*.

"But what is it that guards this home of ours, faithfully and affectionately, year in, year out? It is the friendship of the two noble monarchs whom we celebrate to-day. And so I know I am at one with you all when I ask you to join me in the aspiration : ' God bless, God keep the noble, faithful friend of our Emperor and our nation ! ' "

The Ambassador was able to report the success of this speech to the Imperial Chancellor :

"Vienna, *February* 6, 1902.

"At the Court Ball the Emperor shook hands with me very cordially, and said: 'When you dined with me on January 27 I had not yet read your speech. I thank you heartily for it. The speech gave me *very* great pleasure. You said the right thing at the right moment. What you said about "sunshine and rain" was just what it should have been. It has done a great deal of good. The speech has made a very good impression. Thank you very much for it.'

"I answered that these gracious words made me very happy—that it had always been my endeavour to serve our mutual interests. That had been the single aim of my speech. To this the Emperor replied: 'Yes, I know that you have our reciprocal interests at heart. I was *very much pleased* with your speech, and thank you very much for it, once more.'

"My impression was that the Emperor wished to identify himself fully with my words."

In Berlin alone there was, now as before, no perception of the delicacy of the situation as between Germany and Austria. Emperor William could not be induced to pay a visit to Vienna, which the Austrian Ministers thought highly desirable for the propitiation of their sovereign. Even the Imperial Chancellor was deaf to his friend's earnest admonitions, so that at last Eulenburg felt it necessary to give him an unusually outspoken answer, in which he took occasion to state his view of matters in general:

"... I am glad you are still of opinion that Goluchowski is *the best man* for us. Unfortunately he is not *nearly* so powerful as he was even a few years ago, and this is the result not only of the low estimation of his capabilities which prevails in every quarter, but also of the fact that Austrian feeling towards us has very essentially altered within recent years. The old adherents of the alliance do not wholly trust Goluchowski, and he yields too much to its opponents. So the more the alliance is debated, the more is Goluchowski.

"On reading this you will perhaps feel inclined to repeat what you wrote lately : ' I want to take the opportunity of warning you not to let your Viennese friends put you in too great a flutter. They mean well, but exaggerate flagrantly, all the same.' And ' the loyalty with which the Austrian side has treated the renewal of the alliance with us, surely proves the contrary of what you say in your letter. Have more self-confidence and phlegm ! ' And again : ' Don't be so easily discouraged ! Keep your nerve, and say to yourself that the Austrians need us more than we need them ! '

"To all this I must reply as follows :

"The renewal of the alliance is quite a different matter from the feeling in this country as regards Germany. Emperor Francis Joseph's principal reason for the renewal is that at his age everything new scares him to death. Goluchowski's is that politically he is too weak to be able to do anything else. The general feeling, too, is in favour of the alliance *as a practical necessity*—but there is no enthusiasm, no cordiality, no pleasure in it. Only a *very few* now feel and think in that way. I am neither discouraged nor a prey to official nerves (the moment I was conscious of any such thing, I should send in my resignation) ; but, quietly weighing developments, I see where these eight years have led us. If, after eight years' experience, I cannot be trusted to separate the chaff from the wheat in the political communications made to me *from every side*, the sooner I am sent home the better. Certainly there is plenty of talk in Berlin, but in Vienna the truth is surely more likely to be gathered.

"In 1894, when I came to Vienna, the year 1866 was buried in almost complete oblivion. Now it is the theme of angry discussion, and all the old hatred is revived in such discussions. Bismarck's *Gedanken und Erinnerungen* are chiefly to blame for this. The alliance with us, once regarded as a matter-of-course, is now debated in every quarter, though no one thought of doing so when I came to Vienna. The Slavs have gained immeasurably in power—I could not tell you how immensely; and in the Army, from the captain downwards, Slavs and Germans of the same regiment sit *apart* in the cafés. There was *no such thing* in 1894. The Clerical movement has culminated in even more outspoken spite against Germany since the 'los von Rom' ('away from Rome') movement. This calls for the closest attention, because the aristocracy, still so powerful, is startled out of its indolence and is therefore becoming more pro-Slav than before. The old Emperor is deeply involved in the growing Clerical movement—unwillingly as yet, but he is half-inclined to yield.

"The debate on the revenue has awakened some bitterness (chiefly directed against us) on account of the increasing agricultural distress. Of that, too, one never heard a word until a short time ago. Every economical measure which is found to be inconvenient, and which can even indirectly be connected with us, is attributed to 'the Germans'—*we* are the guilty parties, we the instigators, we the false friends.

"If you ask me whether people have to any extent lost confidence in us, I must regretfully answer that, things being as I have stated (a situation which is of course being exploited by our enemies with an energy and success that words fail me to describe) I cannot exactly maintain that confidence in us is what it was some years ago.

"In face of all this, what am I to think about our alliance? What, in such circumstances, does the loyal attitude of Goluchowski and the old Emperor avail me?

"The alliance is *not* going to break down, I grant—neither is the alliance with Italy. But, as regards Italy, *have* you—in spite of her renewal of the alliance—the same feeling as before?

"The remark that the Austrians need us more than we need them does not seem to me to exhaust the situation, in view of the actual state of affairs. At any rate it is risky, upon that basis, to proceed by pin-pricks (as certain influences in the Foreign Office seem to prescribe) or bludgeoning (such as occurred at certain New Year receptions). Surveying the situation depicted, I consider it so dangerous that I even ask myself whether it would not be more patriotic and more sensible for me to leave Vienna, if I am the principal cause of such pin-pricks as contribute to the general state of bedevilment.

"I do not think, dearest Bernard, that you can be entirely in earnest when you warn me against irresolution and 'loss of nerve.' For *you* can scarcely have regarded my *cautious* attitude in the very sinister Galician question as irresolution—though others may have chosen to do so.

"For the rest I quite agree with your remark: 'I often think of Achilles, whom our sovereign strongly resembles, and of whom Homer says: "His glory-loving heart knows neither fear nor retreat."' I assume that in this comparison you forgot the hero's heel. But what do you think would become of our alliance, if Goluchowski and Körber were much oftener to be dragged in effigy round the walls of Lemberg?

"As to the decision of again putting off His Majesty's visit, I bow to the considerations mentioned, which seem to me entirely reasonable. As this finally disposes of the question, it would be idle to point to the *symptom* of the general situation in Austria manifested by Körber's extreme anxiety for the visit, which is echoed by the *best* friends of the alliance. We must do without it; that is all.

"I should certainly not have anticipated a refusal or an evasion of the proposal—but once more I would draw your attention to the contending influences at Court, to which in certain cases the Emperor may yield when he happens to be in the company of those who are working in the opposite sense to ourselves. Clericalism, represented at the Burg by the Archduchess Valerie and her husband" [Archduke Franz Salvator] "together with the confessor Father Abel—to say nothing of their hangers-on—must necessarily be panic-stricken at the thought of our Emperor's visit. We must not forget that in those circles our sovereign is regarded as the *father*, the *supporter*, the *financier* of the ' Los von Rom' movement. These people *swear* to it—idiotic as it is! They know how fascinating our Emperor can be in personal intercourse, and fear the influence of such a nature on the old gentleman, whom they want to ensnare irretrievably, and *have* to a certain extent ensnared. No one likes interlopers!

"Forgive me, dearest Bernard, for having bothered you with these matters on your holiday! But it seemed to me important, because you will have an opportunity of talking them over quietly with your brother Carl—which I *earnestly beg you to do*. I want especially to bring Carl to your notice as a political intelligence! Now that I have lived with him longer, I can judge of him in that respect. I have seldom had a secretary who could compare with Carl as a diplomatist. He really surpasses them *all*. . . . I must mention just one thing more, which I have discussed with *no one* but Carl. But I regard it as a duty of friendship to warn you against thinking that you possess to a sufficient degree the confidence of Austria, or even of the Emperor, Goluchowski, or Szell. That is unfortunately *not* the case. You are not regarded as a pillar of the alliance, but as a subtle, far-seeing diplomat—so far-seeing as to look *beyond* Austria. You cannot have any idea of the effect produced by the speech in which you referred to the alliance. *Nothing* will efface the impression. On this ground I thought I ought to suggest your returning from Italy *by Vienna*. To-day, in spite of your refusal, I cannot but stick to my opinion that it would be *very* useful, indeed important, both for you and for us, if you could manage to come."

The Prince afterwards made some notes on the draft of this letter.

"Looking over my letter to Bülow of March 21, I can scarcely recognise myself in such a hard-hitter. But his of the 14th had annoyed me so much that I, too, let myself go. What enraged me was the impression I received of Bülow's having fallen completely under Holstein's influence ; and that was why I thought it necessary to define the situation in Austria as clearly and precisely as I saw it myself. *Without any reservations.* Hence I also considered it right to spare Bülow himself as little as I did our Government and even the Emperor.

" Will Bülow have understood that the letter was really to Holstein's address ? I think he is clever enough for that—but I doubt that he will have the courage to show it to Holstein.

" I know very well that no one can give anything like so truthful a picture of the situation in Austria as I can. But I also know very well that Holstein, who once wanted to destroy me through Goluchowski, is now intent on removing Goluchowski *and myself* through Bülow. Therefore I am loth to play Holstein's game by resigning—but this is a case of *vis major*. Month by month I grow more uneasy about Bülow's dependence on Holstein. What are they both up to ? "

Eulenburg fully confided his view to the Imperial Chancellor's brother, of whom he had spoken in his letter, and Carl Bülow wrote to him : " I subscribe to every word in your letter, except the remarks about myself."

We have not the Chancellor's answer to this composition ; he seems to have taken no notice of it. In his next letter he writes only of the necessity that Eulenburg should recruit his health, " so that you may live and work for many another long year for those you love, and utilise your brilliant talents in the way that makes you really happy." Eulenburg's services to the State, his work for Emperor and country, are ignored. To anyone acquainted with the calculated subtlety of Bülow's methods of expression, this is sufficient—it meant that, politically speaking, he had abandoned his friend. Was Eulenburg too independent, too powerful on account of his standing with the Emperor—or, as an enemy of Holstein's, inconvenient to Bülow? Eulenburg had long since taken the wink for the nod. From the beginning of the year he had familiarised himself with the thought of his retirement. What finally decided him was the now unmistakable breakdown in his health.

He had never been a strong man. In his early youth there had been some fear of lung-trouble. A winter on the Riviera dispelled that anxiety, but all his life his lungs were delicate and susceptible. A severe attack of typhus in Egypt in 1872, when his life hung on a thread, laid the foundation of permanent ill-health; it left a chronic weakness of the digestive organs which increased with years. Nor did he escape the usual accompaniments of this ailment, depression of spirits and hypochondria. Thus even the happiest period of his life, those first years in Munich, was often shadowed by anxiety about his physical well-being. Almost yearly there was some more serious illness. In 1884 he had an unusually dangerous attack of measles; in the same year a tumour on the neck, close to the artery, necessitated a hazardous operation. When not fully recovered from an illness, he went in the spring of 1886 for the first time to Prökelwitz, there to meet Prince William. He returned in very bad health and great depression of spirits. Only the gravest anxiety about an illness of his wife's succeeded in rousing him from his hypochondriacal self-tormenting, at that time exacerbated by the still undecided question of a change of profession.

The years after his appointment to the Embassy at Oldenburg and to the post of "travelling Ambassador" were a period of continuous physical, mental, and spiritual strain. His yearly visit to Carlsbad could never take full effect, because he never had time for the after-cure. Even the leave at Liebenberg, usually not more than two or three weeks in September, was no real relaxation, for then the management of the great estate, the arrears of the previous twelve months, had to be attended to. Gastein did him more good than any other place. Whenever he could take the cure there in August or September, he felt really restored to vigour. But the ultimate source of his illness was beyond all remedy—wearing anxiety about his Imperial friend, friction caused by the toil for him and the country of which the reader has had a glimpse, and the conflict he never ceased to feel between his own nature, craving to develop its artistic powers, and the official duties which obliged him to stifle them.

To this, as years went on, was added anxiety about his aging mother and her failing health. In January, 1895, she was seriously ill, while her son was torn between the conflicts raging in Berlin and an "absolutely overwhelming" social success in Vienna—it was his first winter as Ambassador. It was then that he seems to have had his earliest inkling of what had resulted from the incessant over-exertion which the last seven years had imposed on him. His health was so enfeebled that he no longer felt equal to the conflicting demands of his life. In a written soliloquy of that time we read :

The End of his Career

" Anyone else on earth would, I believe, have felt these three sensations to be sufficient reason for throwing in one's hand—throwing it in at Liebenberg !—and letting the affairs of the great world take their course, since they would anyhow, without my assistance, have gone as God willed them to go. If only the Emperor were not my friend ! But the duties I have to fulfil towards my Fatherland and my King are so rooted in my Old-Prussian heart that for me there could be no survival if I shirked them before my health was actually broken-down. And even more powerful than that stringent moral compulsion is the duty I have to fulfil towards my friend William von Hohenzollern, whenever I see him in danger—not less from the external abysses of intrigue than from those internal ones belonging to his own nature. I could not but despise myself if, fully conscious of such duties, I weakly stood aside. Anxiety about my dear mother's precious life torments and oppresses me. The Berlin intrigues infuriate me, and undermine my health by the endlessly increasing toil they impose upon me. The carnival of social life at Vienna unspeakably wearies me. The management of Liebenberg, my art, intercourse and correspondence with my friends, and the eternal craving to enjoy the society of my much-loved wife and children, the longing to live for them and the impossibility of doing so because of my burdensome life—*that* is the pang which grows ever more and more poignant."

Soon afterwards, in March of the same year, his life was further darkened by news of the hopeless illness of his Chief Ranger, who had been with him in the campaign of 1870 and by his efficiency and remarkable personal excellence had gained his master's friendship. To his mother he wrote of this news:

"You will understand that I can't enjoy anything now, or feel at all happy. This varied, rich, and in many ways delightful life seems like a mockery. How I envy those whose work consists simply in fulfilling, quietly and apart, their appointed task! But to be obliged to include in it the keeping-up of a social position—and such an onerous one as mine—that is corroding, heart-rending, gruesome as a dance of death. God laid a heavy cross upon me when he gave me a tender heart—perhaps that I might learn self-control. If, in my toilsome and responsible life, I *have* learnt it—perpetually involved as I am in grave political matters, perpetually awaiting the issue with an anxiously beating heart, while I carry on light conversation and show a straight face—well, the lesson may have its value, the lesson of 'holding one's-self in check' of 'getting the upper hand of things.' But oh, when the heart is sore! Then the machine of habit works on with its smiles and friendly speeches, and even its moments of oblivion; but once let the machine stop for a single moment—and the sore heart asserts itself, and one could cry out in horror against the glare of such brilliant unreality. For after all, the only real thing in life is the heart."

From this time forth that was the prevailing tone in his intimate communications. From Carlsbad, where he was sent in April, 1895 (and it was there perceived to be a most necessary measure), he gave his mother a résumé of his reflections: "I have

fallen upon evil days as I grow older. So much already reft from me—a changing world—and still too young to bear in patience what God sends me. I am far from being so resigned as I ought to be—wholly submissive indeed to the Will of God, but still with too keen a sense of vitality within me."
An entry in his diary for February 15, 1896, after the death of the Lord High Steward Prince Hohenlohe, who had been so attached to him, is extremely moving :

> "I called on Princess Constantine, and went alone into the death-chamber where the kind little Prince was sleeping his last sleep in the bed with its vast crimson silk hangings. He was smiling as happily as though he had never known a moment's suffering, as though he were dreaming of some wonderful bliss. The sight of that repose suddenly affected me so deeply that I felt an ineffable longing for my own life of terrible, tormenting unrest and crushing responsibility to come to an end, and such quiet sleep as his to fall upon me. I could scarcely tear myself away from that picture of utter peace. . . . When I left the house and drove in my carriage through the hurrying crowds, I felt all the weight of my paradoxical life and destiny descend upon me like a terrible burden—my envied life ! Ah, if all those who envy me could know how I envy *them*—remote from such glitter, peacefully circumscribed ! "

1896 was one of the most agitated and lacerating years in his life. After the long and excessive strain caused by the perpetual ministerial crises (it was in the May of this very year that Eulenburg, by the exercise of his utmost energy, succeeded in averting the Chancellor-crisis at Prökelwitz), and

the resulting fatigue of the Norwegian cruise came the Tsar's visit to Berlin at the end of August, and the beginning of the Oriental disturbances consequent on the Armenian atrocities in Constantinople. On the return from Norway Eulenburg had hastened to the Emperor at Cassel; thence to the Emperor Francis Joseph at Ischl, and on to the Imperial Chancellor (Prince Hohenlohe) at Aussee. Betweenwhiles he had managed to put in a few days with his family at Bad Neuhäuser near Königsberg. On his return thence to Vienna he wrote in his diary:

> "Those were blessed, splendid days! My Augusta, my happy children, my Mama, on the beautiful quiet sands by the Ostsee, no acquaintances, all to ourselves! What a spiritual abyss divides me from the world in which I stand—must stand—officially, in obedience to the dictates of friendship and duty to my country! Where is the man who could possibly harmonise the character of an Emperor who was the kind of friend *my* friend, who is the Emperor, is to me, with the piece of machinery we call a Government? I know no one but myself. But why had it to be I? Why did God impose on me this torment, this renunciation—on me, to whom what others strive for as their highest good is an almost unbearable oppression? Why did God give me this deep, this sacred sense of friendship? For I cannot reckon sense of duty towards one's country as an unusual attribute. That is rather something elementary."

He could take no further period of leave that year, and yet his health was so impaired that his doctor urgently insisted on a cure. Römerbad in Steiermark was chosen, for as it was in Austrian territory the Ambassador could visit it without being on leave ; but the choice proved a mistaken one. Gastein, as before, was the first place he felt better in.

Of late years there had often been talk of his exchanging the Ambassadorship for the Ministry of the Household. So long ago as the November of 1894, when Eulenburg had been barely six months in Vienna, Hohenlohe and Holstein had approached him with this proposal, of which Hohenlohe had also spoken to the Emperor. Eulenburg wrote of it to Bülow :

> " It is not a bad idea. I should have no special political bothers and no responsibility, yet would be empowered to advise, watch over, pacify His Majesty. That I should thus be in a certain degree the *spiritus rector* of the whole machinery of State is manifest, so long as the beloved Emperor honoured me with his confidence. My notorious journeyings would be fewer. . . . But you can imagine what a bombshell it was to me when Holstein, with his tragic airs, represented this as an urgent necessity. . . . I should very much have preferred to wait some years for the Ministry ; now I don't know what I ought to say."

Bülow's telegraphic reply is significant :

> " *Accepte seulement, si tu es absolument sûr que les sentiments de Sa Majesté pour toi restent les mêmes, en vivant dans la même ville, et que ton influence ne s'affaiblira pas par contact continuel.*"

Eulenburg thought the question so serious that he spoke quite frankly about it to the Emperor. He was ready to undertake the post, though at the moment it seemed to him in many respects a sacrifice. He believed, moreover, that he was quite fitted for it, and he would have enjoyed making his house an intellectual centre for Berlin society, an advantage lacking since the death of Schlemitz, a predecessor in the high office. But he thought it should be considered whether his recall from Vienna, after so short a time and so strikingly cordial a reception there, might not be a mistake.

He expressed this doubt to the Emperor, leaving the matter entirely to the Imperial decision, though he did not conceal from the sovereign that he would prefer the step to be postponed.

The Emperor seems to have acquiesced, for the matter was not further discussed at that time. When it was brought forward again in October, 1896, the situation had completely altered. Eulenburg himself would only too willingly have accepted the offer, but he saw that it was impossible. Of this he wrote briefly to Bülow on the 26th:

"The Imperial Chancellor had summoned me to Berlin to ask whether I should like the Ministry now that there were to be some changes. I decidedly refused, for I should not find it pleasant in these days between the drowning Marschall, whom I should have to rescue every week or so, and Hohenlohe-Holstein grabbing the Emperor's lead at the political card-table. Later we may talk of it again."

In his diary for October 16 the reasons for his refusal are more explicitly stated:

"The Chancellor asked me whether I would accept the Ministry. I was obliged regretfully to decline. The Emperor, even if he thought me indispensable in Vienna, would have yielded to my desire. But in view of the open campaign against unfortunate me—who, God knows, am not neglecting my Fatherland but toiling for it like a slave—I should in that position, which stands outside the political Ministry, be represented as the head of a camarilla, and finally fall a victim to intolerable hostilities. So, as I have said, it won't do—alas and alas!—and I found it very hard to refuse. How splendid it would have been to be close to Liebenberg and Mama, and how it would simplify the children's education! I feel more of a martyr than ever. My enemies think it good fortune, and are trying to spoil it by their hatred."

So he had to go on under the yoke, which grew no lighter with years. Even Bülow's entry into the Government, which did at any rate bring the longed-for relief from his trying office of mediator, was too late to restore the failing powers and health. The year 1897, indeed, marks an epoch in that respect. In the spring Eulenburg had had a long illness. Influenza had brought on an attack of an hereditary ailment—gout—which he had to endure, in addition to all the others, for the rest of his life. Simultaneous with his illness were the Eastern developments and the outbreak of the Græco-Turkish war. These claimed the Ambassador's full energies, so that he could not spare himself in any way, or find time for convalescence. Then came the serious crisis in Berlin which ended in Marschall's retirement. To this in the summer was added the very trying Norwegian cruise, and in the autumn ensued the final Chancellor-crisis. These exertions had been too much for him. In spite of Carlsbad and Gastein he was continually ailing. He complained of his own violence and impatience, to him inexplicable, a state hitherto unknown; but which any experienced doctor would at once have attributed to nervous exhaustion. Nor did it improve. A second sharp attack of gout in the spring of 1898 did pass off, but his nerves were seriously affected. Of the Norwegian cruise in that year he wrote to Bülow: " Morally speaking, I feel ever so much better . . . but my nerves have gone to pieces, and my body has had a bad time of it." However, he carried on somehow for about two years. Outwardly he showed no sign until things had gone too far. Anyone who had to do with him officially, or met him in society, saw as before the pattern of a dignified, perfectly self-possessed *grand seigneur*, equal to any situation and charming in them all. People had no suspicion of the ever-increasing strain it was to preserve appearances. All they noticed was that the Ambassador had changed his way of life. There could be but few of the former social gaieties. He kept as quiet as he could, confined himself to the indispensable duties of his official position, and left it in great part to the Princess to keep up social intercourse in Vienna. Nevertheless, in 1900 he was visibly worse. His family-doctor, Dr. Kanders, regarded his case as very serious. Nervous tremors, constant fainting-fits, pointed to organic functional disturbance, and his nervous exhaustion manifested itself in great indecision, which went so far that at times the Prince felt incapable of writing a letter and had an inexplicable horror of opening them. On the Norwegian trip, that summer, he for the first time ventured to speak to the Emperor of resigning, but was decisively overruled. The Emperor considered his friend indispensable for Vienna. However, after a renewed attack of serious illness a year later, the Prince was obliged to reopen the subject.

The End of his Career

His doctor reinforced his plea by a very urgent letter to the Imperial physician, Dr. Leuthold; but in vain. The Emperor still refused to believe in the necessity.

Then came the winter of 1901 to 1902 with its still more exacting demands. Eulenburg felt that he was no longer fit for his post, and with that had come the moment when he could answer to his conscience for insisting on the freedom for which he had always craved. On January 13, 1902, he turned to Bülow with a request to choose the most propitious moment for his retirement, and intercede with the Emperor to let him go.

"My state of health," he wrote, "is lamentable. I can find no other word for it. This is the simple truth. I am utterly worn out by ten years of terrible, exacting toil with our dear sovereign. Now I am in such a state that the slightest agitation causes me such misery that I could despair of my life. It is a serious nervous breakdown. If I want to be any use to my family, if I want to go on living, I *must* think of retirement."

Bülow at first thought the moment unpropitious, as the Pierson case was still impending, and advised him to wait. The Emperor, too, again showed little understanding of the truth. He would not even hear of long leave. Eulenburg reiterated his arguments to Bülow on March 8:

"Nothing will alter the resolve for which I have given you my reasons. . . . So I count on your faithful, proved friendship to tell me the right moment. Though indeed I think that that moment will be dictated by the Lord of Life and Death. I am so gravely ill that we shall have to bow to God's decree. . . . My doctor has left me in no doubt whatever about

K

my state. . . . You will think it only natural that I should cherish the ardent hope of spending the last years of my life—can I say years?—in peace among my dear ones, far from this unbearable existence. . . . Perhaps it is right that I should tell you what the doctor said to me. . . . He told me that it was his duty to give me the whole truth. My nerves require at least a year's complete rest, and I must begin that rest as soon as I possibly can. At my age there is no time to lose. If I do not follow his advice, I shall be a dead man in a few years. If I take this step now, it is possible that I may be spared to my family for a while; if not, that is out of the question."

Still Bülow would not come to the point. He reminded Eulenburg of his many enemies, saying that they could not get at him while he was in Vienna and Bülow in Berlin. One is tempted to call Eulenburg's answer prophetic:

" I know I shall be able to rely on you when I am out of office. It will be mine to ask it of you—if I am in a state of health to cope with events. That the Prussian country-gentry and their friends will empty yet another bucketful of poison and filth over the head of a broken, dying man, I have no doubt whatever. But it won't go on, if they see that I am really a match for them. Your friendly succour will not fail me in that hour—I know you too well to question that."

We could wish that the concluding words of this strikingly prophetic passage had been as well justified by after-events as the rest of it was. However, Bülow now made up his mind to bring the

THE END OF HIS CAREER

matter forward. He suggested asking for three months' leave, as a preliminary measure; the Emperor, now again most graciously inclined and full of sympathy, would be sure to grant it. A few days later Eulenburg was summoned in all haste to his mother's death-bed at Meran. She passed away on April 11, 1902, in her son's arms. Then the last link that held him to Vienna was severed—for there he had been near his mother during her regular long winter-sojourn in the South. Firm in his resolve not to return to office, he began his period of leave. On May 23 he wrote to the Emperor from Liebenberg, where he had again fallen a victim to a bad attack of gout. It was a kind of farewell letter :

"I repeat to Your Majesty that I can remain in the service *only* if my duties are commensurate with my strength. I will not do partial service where others could in the same position do *all* that is necessary. I will never deceive my faithful friend, and I know very precisely what I owe to my Emperor. The result of my cure will show me how I stand. At the present moment I am perfectly persuaded that it will do me no good. In this persuasion I appeal from the depths of my heart to Your Majesty, and cry to you : '*Spare yourself!* For God's sake, spare yourself for the Fatherland and all who love Your Majesty!' I have had terrible proof of the state that overwork, ceaseless thought and action, anxiety and want of complete rest can lead to in the course of time. Even the tenacity and self-control, which have seen me through so many years, have their limits. This warning comes from the bottom of my heart—I pray Your Majesty to keep it ever before your eyes. It is the prayer of a man who loves Your Majesty as few on earth can do."

With Bülow he had a long talk which still further confirmed him in his resolve to retire. Of this he wrote to him on May 27 :

"Despite all the gratitude and pleasure I felt during my talk with you, I brought away an impression of another kind which profoundly agitated me, and has had an abiding effect. It has made me feel quite sick, and—morally speaking—I shall never recover from it. Your anxiety to give me a clue which might guide me through the labyrinthine paths of my complex life and still more complex situation, showed me with appalling precision the many dangers arising from the frightful jealousies with which I am surrounded—dangers to which, in my enfeebled state of health, I am no longer equal. . . . I will not be a burden on your friendship, and indeed I am not now fit to endure the despicable everlasting see-saw between caprices and suspicions, attacks and fine phrases, etc. . . . Naturally I shall have the commonsense, being so ill as I am, to keep away from Berlin altogether for several years."

In the same letter he briefly summed up his whole official past. It is more than the cry of a spirit temporarily weary unto death; it embraces a confession of faith :

"In our last conversation at Berlin you said so truly : 'The Prussian genius is hard and ruthless. Subtle natures like yours . . . are not attuned to it.' I have known that from my youth. And I have also been well aware that only the very warm friendship of the most powerful person in the State—combined with good luck—could possibly have nullified the contradiction between my nature and the Prussian genius. The instant that friendship fell off in the smallest degree, the contradiction broke all bounds—and especially as luck failed too. *That* sweet little bird I used always to hear twittering in the bushes beside me ; but he has been silent for some years. I believe in luck, and nothing is more destructive to a human being than trying to force it. Wisdom has a fine ear for such singing, and I don't want to make the mistake of pretending that the bird is not mute. . . . In the light of my resolve, high office, politics, society fade away like Klingsor's magic garden at the lifting of the sacred spear, and give place to my music, my tranquil Liebenberg, the restoration to my family—all as words from Heaven to my ears. To how few does God grant such a rebirth—the possibility of return to one's true individuality ! "

The whole summer was given up to recruiting his health. Professor Renvers, the famous Berlin specialist, called in by the Prince's family, had declared that organically he was perfectly sound ; it was merely exhaustion of the faculties. He promised complete recovery in three months. When the customary Carlsbad cure was finished, the Prince submitted himself to Renvers' treatment, going on his advice to Sylt and thence to Gastein— but his fears were justified ; nothing did him any good. The former troubles—giddiness, heart-weakness, breathlessness, extreme irresolution— grew worse instead of better, and headaches and stomach-disorders were added. Renvers had been completely mistaken. There can be no doubt that the serious organic disease, afterwards diagnosed by all the doctors who investigated his case, was present even then—rheumatoid arthritis, which so often appears as a result of continuous psychical disturbance. There was no longer any hope of his restoration to health. A year's rest offered the only chance of his being able to lead a private life which would be at least endurable.

So the decisive step could be no longer delayed. On August 27, 1902, the Prince sent in his resignation to the Emperor. He had told the Imperial Chancellor, four days earlier, of this step, and had written as follows :

> " It causes me no regret of any kind, because I see you at the Emperor's side. I am even fully conscious of the ' providence ' that enabled me to smooth the way on which you now walk so securely. For me your emergence to power was a change ; for the Emperor and the Fatherland it was the hand of destiny. I never expected anything else, and knew it must be so. Therefore I take my departure without any sort of bitterness, any sort of sorrow. At the beloved Emperor's side I see the only possible man—and round your head there floats and waves the mysterious veil of your appointed destiny. May God immerse it in the flowing river of His bounty ! And I can the less feel any regret, or imagine any sense of loss, because the dual life which I was so long obliged to lead had never given me any pleasure. My faithful performance of duties in a very exacting office never had been able to give me any of the satisfaction felt by a man who is of one piece. The artist in me was always lamenting ; and it is he who now, when the door of active official service closes against me, stands

The End of his Career

cordially smiling me welcome. Whether my health will still permit me to grasp his hand is another question. But he does me the affectionate service of making pleasant to me what to others would seem an irretrievable loss."

On Bülow's advice the Emperor still withheld the final discharge, but granted a further three months' leave. When this too was over, came Eulenburg's release from the ambassadorial post, and the placing *en disposition*. The Prince would have preferred the full release, but he yielded to the Chancellor's view—with what sensations is revealed in a letter to Bülow of November 13 :

" How wretchedly ill I am is evident to me from the fact that I leave the service without one moment's regret. Not the least thought of missing it occurs to me. That strange experience shows me how terribly I must have suffered during the last years. What a plenitude of activities was mine, and how they ruled my existence—and yet I feel as completely apart from them now as though it had been an utter stranger who was concerned in saying good-bye to Vienna, in my resignation, and in the entire political past. I must indeed have been worn out ! "

He had only one urgent request to make. It concerned the private secretary who had been with him many years, and whose position in the service was owing to him. Now he requested the title of Court Councillor for this remarkably efficient public servant, who had still two years to put in before qualifying for it. His reason for this request is characteristic of him : " When I look back on my time of service, the thought of Kistler is inseparable from it; and I should not wish for any recognition and praise in which he did not share, having shared in my toil and been unwearying in relieving me of so many burdens. Unless he were rewarded, I should decline any praise or mark of gratitude for myself."

The Emperor manifested his favour by a decoration, and a telegram which said: " I have conferred on you the Grand Cross of the Red Eagle with the Oakleaf, as a mark of my high estimation of your most meritorious service. May your restoration to health enable me to call upon you for further achievements."

Now he had to bid farewell to Vienna. He made a grand effort to pull himself together for these visits. It is needless to say that his retirement was felt very deeply in the society where he had taken so distinguished a place. Count Goluchowski had written, on receiving the tidings:

> " I scarcely need to tell you how we all regret your departure! And our regret is increased by your being impelled to it by considerations of health. God grant that rest may completely restore you, and that you may again be permitted to place your distinguished services at the disposal of your Emperor and country, at no distant period. No one desires that more heartily than I, of whose sincere friendship for you, my dear friend, you cannot be in any doubt."

His personal farewells had to be reduced to their simplest form, for the Prince felt by no means equal to the larger ceremonies, receptions, etc. To a Viennese friend he had written: " I can't say how it grieves me to part from the dear old sovereign in Vienna, and especially from Vienna itself, which has been a real home to me." On December 9 he was received for the last time by the venerable monarch whose appreciation he had won to so unusual a degree. The Prince has described the incident:

"My farewell audience with Emperor Francis Joseph was a painful occasion for me. I was deeply affected by the thought of never again in my life beholding the dear old gentleman. We had, in the long years of intercourse here, grown personally very much attached to one another, and the confidence shown me by the Emperor was quite unusual. For he would discuss internal Austrian affairs with me—a fact which could not but astonish me, for his custom was to discuss internal questions with the Minister in charge of the particular department, and with no one else.

"It was evident that he wished to give me some special pleasure at our farewell interview, from the way in which he announced his intention of giving me a picture of himself. He said: 'I am very glad to give my picture as a keepsake, but it shall not be what is called "a likeness of the Emperor," for I intend really to sit to the painter for it, so that it may be a real keepsake.' I then begged him to add to the pleasure by not being painted in a Prussian General's uniform, but in the undress uniform he always wore when I sat with him in his study—and in the chair he always occupied during my audiences. The kind old man laughed at my request, but was touched by it, and understood what I meant.

"When I came out, and on passing through the parade-ground was once more saluted by the old bodyguard, and when on leaving the Burg the sentries called 'Pass' and stood to attention, the end of my official life was signed and sealed, and closed by the beat of drums. Any other man than myself would probably have been overwhelmed by the sensation. But the only thing that affected me was my good-bye to the dear old Emperor, whom I truly loved. For after all the physical and mental torment of this 1902 my departure was like drawing a deep breath, and my thoughts flew to Liebenberg, Augusta, and the children. May God in his mercy now grant me the rest for which I so fervently long."

From the quantity of letters which reached the Prince on this occasion we give, as a proof of how he was valued in his immediate circle, the words in which a youthful member of the Viennese Embassy replied to the news of his retirement. The writer was Count Brockdorff-Rantzau—to whom at that time no one would have attributed the part he was to play in future years. He wrote on November 23 :

" My more than insignificant position gives me no right to express what I feel on hearing of Your Excellency's inexorable resolve. . . . Though my time was too short to give me the opportunity of making myself as useful as I had hoped to do, it has at any rate, through the confidence Your Excellency was good enough to place in me, been long enough to impress upon me *for evermore* the *true* conception of the duties belonging to a profession in which it is the exception to meet with high-minded and sincerely independent characters."

The Prince himself (as those who have learnt to understand him will have guessed for themselves) had never had any illusions about the nature of his calling. He had been deeply conscious that circumstances may make it difficult to harmonise the claims of diplomacy with the dictates of morality; and when recalling his activities in that kind, he expressed himself plainly on the subject. "Politics," he wrote, "are essentially dishonest, and hence immoral." He recalled a remark of Caprivi's, who had said to him a year after becoming Imperial Chancellor: "Well, I certainly cannot say that one is bored in this establishment, for politics are undeniably interesting; but—have you sons? Then never let them become diplomats." And yet he testifies in his own behalf: "As a matter of fact, I cannot reproach myself with any political action for which I could not answer to my conscience as that of a decent man." He knew equally well that every action of a diplomatist could not be measured by the strict line of private morality. He held by the principle of the first man to systematise German statecraft, Justi (d. 1771): "As the most persuasive eloquence is that which is inspired by personal enthusiasm and yet can dispassionately control the expression of it, so the consummate statesman is he who can utilise the ingredients of his personal character, his inborn proclivities, in the part which he is called upon to play." As such an ingredient of his personal character, which he had utilised in his part of diplomatist, Eulenburg regarded the confidence which his various experiences justified him in feeling that he could inspire. "My habit of throwing this knack of inspiring confidence into the balance when grave political questions were under discussion, I could not, in the interest of the Fatherland, consider as wrong-doing. But was it not, nevertheless, playing false? At all events it was a form of play in which the better part did yeoman's service to the worser, and one's only justification to one's conscience was, and had to be, *the Fatherland.*" Eulenburg could not acquiesce in the current French saying which William II among others was fond of quoting, and which he wrote on the photograph of himself that he gave to Herbert Bismarck : "*A gentilhomme gentilhomme ; à corsaire corsaire et demi.*" Eulenburg remarked of this : " Though I have never been a *corsaire*, I must honestly confess that I was occasionally tempted to be a *corsaire et demi* when it was a question of spoiling some game that went against my country's interests. However, I can say with a clear conscience that I never abandoned, even then, the part of *gentilhomme*. For the *corsaire et demi* is not, as I think, called upon to enter the lists when the *gentilhomme's* blade can lay the *corsaire* low. So I should like the old French proverb better if it ended : " *et à corsaire, encore gentilhomme.*' "

A year before his retirement he had summarised the teaching of his career in a moment of grave introspection. "Very late, too late," he thought he had realised that his markedly artistic proclivities were not the true purpose of his existence, not " the thing God meant him for." In the compulsion laid upon him by his father to enter the service of the State against his own wish and inclination, he now was ready to acknowledge the divine dispensation guiding him to his real vocation in life, to which he had submitted, " though with a resignation which to my last breath will never lose the character of martyrdom. I have been obliged," he continued, " to take a very active part in the course of Prussian and German history at a very strenuous period. My part was rather to avert than to achieve, but I was always very conscious of being called upon for an arduous task—that most

arduous one of reconciling people to one another."
In this confession of faith he even found the way to satisfaction with his fate. "We must try to comprehend the Will of God, and subordinate ourselves, against our wishes, hopes, temperament and individuality, without a murmur, without allowing ourselves to faint by the way. It was not the Titans who took Heaven by storm ; it was the sage who gained it by a struggle. He who submits to fulfilling his duties, however irksome they may be, is the sage who reaches his Heaven."

MARTYRDOM

I
YEARS OF SILENCE

WHEN at the end of 1902 the Prince, physically a broken man, withdrew to Liebenberg, he was still yielding to the hope that the liberty gained at last would so far restore health and energy as to permit a return to his artistic interests. That hope was bitterly deceived. Not recovery, not even improvement, awaited him; his lot was to be continuous and ever-increasing suffering, and the story of his life from 1902 to 1906 is in essence the chronicle of a sick-bed.

After the first winter, a trying one in which he was mostly bed-ridden, the longed-for improvement began at last to show during the spring and summer. It enabled him to obey the Emperor's urgent request to take part in the Norwegian cruise in July—of course as a private person with no official duties, and surrounded by the most solicitous attentions from his Imperial host. Though in September he was not so well, he thought himself fit to accept the invitation to Rominten (against his doctor's advice) so as not to disappoint the Emperor. There he at once succumbed to muscular rheumatism, and after lying for a fortnight, feverish and in great pain, in his room beside the Emperor's, he had to travel back to Liebenberg in the Imperial saloon carriage. " The Emperor was inexpressibly tender and kind, and his simple humanity showed at its best." (To Bülow.)

On December 16 the Prince, sitting for the first time at his writing-table, was able to express his gratitude in a letter to the Emperor. A relapse quickly followed, and was accompanied by severe pleurisy and endocarditis, which brought him to the brink of the grave. The first signs of recovery came with spring, but the trouble was not eliminated; indeed, there remained a diseased condition of the muscles of the heart (myocarditis) and this was followed by thrombosis. The old ailments were of course much intensified. However, the annual cures at Carlsbad and Gastein did him some good; he was able to take part in life once more. But he was very ill both physically and spiritually. There were times when depression seemed to have completely overwhelmed him. In the summer of 1905, as also the year before, he was obliged to refuse the Emperor's invitation for the Norwegian cruise. He told him that unbearable despondency made him incapable of social intercourse or work of any kind, and was almost depriving him of the desire to live. At Gastein he again improved. " I don't know myself," he wrote to the Emperor from there on August 8. " I do feel like Philip Eulenburg now—and that must mean a certain degree of progress."

His only pleasures at this trying period were the extensive enlargements and embellishments which he was carrying out from 1903 to 1906 at his Liebenberg estate, all from his own designs. It gave him particular satisfaction to be able to defray the expenses of these costly architectural schemes out of the money he made by his compositions. The inaugural opening of the splendid music-room in November, 1906, at which the Emperor was present, was perhaps the last happy day of the Prince's life.

Meanwhile his health had suffered another shock. After a serious attack of bronchitis which he barely survived, his nervous condition became so grave that in the summer of 1906 he voluntarily underwent a rigorous form of treatment. A distinguished physician, Dr. Krull of Güstrow, managed to obtain some improvement by insisting on absolute rest and seclusion.

Need we give more explicit evidence of the unlikelihood that a man so seriously ill would, of his own free will and with no official obligation, have mixed himself up with politics, which he had never cared for? And yet this was the very reproach made against the Prince. He was said, from his seclusion, to have used his influence on the Emperor to pursue, as "irresponsible adviser," his own personal schemes; and to interfere with the work of the responsible organs of Government. The reader of these pages does not now need to be told how senseless was the accusation. To what end should the Prince have worried himself with political intrigues? During the many years in which he had had every opportunity to pursue private political aims, he had never been anything but the Governmental pilot with the Emperor; and now that as an invalid he was glad to be rid of the burden of political responsibility, was it likely that he would assume a precisely contrary part?

It was a matter of course that his personal relation to the Emperor should continue; and that the ambassador *en disposition* should now and again be in a position to express an opinion to his sovereign was equally natural. That was his right; in certain instances his duty. Anyone who makes it a reproach to him merely shows that he has no conception of such relations. In what manner and what spirit Eulenburg did this, future examples will demonstrate.

But anyone who has read so far will be convinced

beforehand that the Prince, after his retirement, adhered more resolutely even than in the past to the principle of saying and doing nothing to make difficulties for the Imperial Chancellor, whom now as then he regarded as the only possible head of the Government. Any calculated exercise of influence in the direction of any particular policy, or even very frequent advice to his monarch, is absolutely excluded from our survey. Despite his proximity to Berlin, the Prince saw the Emperor less often than of yore. The Emperor, indeed, occasionally complained of his friend's being so seldom to be seen. When on February 12, 1905, he came to Liebenberg for the Prince's birthday, he greeted the Princess with these words: " As Phili will never come to me now, I have to come to him! " In the following year the Prince actually avoided a repetition of this visit, by being away from home on his birthday.

There were legends among the public of a " Liebenberg Round Table," a close corporation of friends, among whom the Emperor was a frequent guest; they were said to exercise a most unhealthy influence upon him, and form a regular camarilla. That there was not a particle of truth in all this can be proved from an authentic source. At Liebenberg, as at other great houses, there was a visitors' book, and in it the Emperor's visits were conscientiously recorded. According to this, Prince Eulenburg received the Emperor as his guest on the following occasions: On January 15, 1903, the Emperor announced himself by telegraph and came (accompanied by only one A.D.C., von Kessel) for a few hours, in order to make the acquaintance of the eldest son's fiancée and her mother. On May 24, 1904, he was present at the young couple's wedding, for which there was a very large gathering. The Imperial Chancellor was there too. On February 12, 1905, there was the above-mentioned birthday visit. The Emperor was accompanied by four gentlemen of his suite, Hausmarschall von Lyncker, Count Soden, A.D.C., Admiral von Müller, and Physician-in-Ordinary Dr. Niedner. The rest of the company, besides the Prince's relatives and friends, consisted of Generals von Leszczynski, Helmuth von Moltke and Count Kuno Moltke, the Ambassador Baron von Varnbüler, and the author Genthe. From October 30 to November 1, 1905, the Emperor was one of a shooting-party, as so often before, at Liebenberg. In his suite were Master of the Household Count August Eulenburg, A.D.C.s Count Moltke and von Kessel, and Dr. Niedner. The other guests were General von Leszczynski, Baron von Varnbüler, Baron von Werthern (a neighbouring landed proprietor), Professor Schiemann, the Prince's relatives, Counts Kalnein and von Esebeck, and Headkeeper Nietsche. The Emperor's last visit to Liebenberg was from November 7 to 10, 1906. As he had a bad cold there was no shooting. Instead they had musical performances from the children of the house, and the conversation turned by preference on the enlargements to the castle, then just completed. The sovereign was accompanied by Hausmarschall von Lyncker, A.D.C. Count Moltke, and Dr. Niedner. Other guests were Count Arnin-Boitzenburg, County-Court Judge von Arnim, General Leszczynski, Baron Varnbüler, Baron Wendelstadt, and a Swedish family-friend, Frau Artwedson. Also the French Councillor of Legation Lecomte.

Such are the authentically attested facts. Where is the " Round Table " ? When did it sit, and who were the members ? Was Leszczynski, the laurel-crowned veteran of 1870, by any chance one of the political intriguers who formed a ring round the Emperor? Beyond those whom the Emperor brought with him, only one of the above-mentioned was present more than once—that is three times in four years; the Württemberg Minister of Embassy Varnbüler, of whom William II was particularly fond and whom he saw very frequently elsewhere. Among the A.D.C.s who usually accompanied him we more than once find the name of General von Kessel. The Prince had every reason to consider him one of his bitterest enemies. So the Liebenberg Round Table is finally reduced to a single name—that of Count Kuno Moltke, who was constantly with the Emperor at Berlin. *He* was at Liebenberg with the sovereign three times—three whole times ! That this man should have been regarded as the special instrument of Eulenburgian intrigue is simply ridiculous. So far as the charming, estimable, artistically gifted, but very simple-minded, fellow troubled at all about politics, he was as a rule of a different opinion from his friend. The few letters from him found among Eulenburg's papers show an almost continuous difference of outlook.

Of one name there is still something to say, because a legend is attached to it. Like a living spectre the French Councillor of Legation, Raymond Lecomte, haunts the history of these years. The story goes that the Prince had brought the Frenchman, whom he had known since the 'eighties (they had been together at Munich as Secretaries of Legation), into the Emperor's environment, in order to frustrate the Government policy in the Morocco question, and that he had succeeded in doing so. The Emperor was supposed to have been led by Lecomte to make certain

YEARS OF SILENCE 151

asseverations which the French Ambassador was soon afterwards able to make use of against the Imperial Chancellor. The absurdity of this tittle-tattle is manifest when we remember that the Morocco crisis was going on in the autumn of 1905 and came to an end in April, 1906—therefore long before the Emperor met M. Lecomte at Liebenberg! That meeting was the first and last to take place there. It had been arranged at the Emperor's express desire; he had known Lecomte since 1895 and wanted to hear his opinion, as a connoisseur of ancient architecture, upon the new buildings at Liebenberg. Lecomte, foreseeing the gossip, had come against his will, stayed but one day, and kept away from the Emperor as much as he could, talking with him only before witnesses, and never once of politics.[1] The Prince's correspondence with the Emperor is the best proof of his lack of interest in politics at this time. There is scarcely any mention of public events. The Prince thanks him for his gracious friendship, shows his interest in the Imperial family's doings, tells of his children, his own health—which he depicts as hopefully as was possible. Whenever politics are

[1] The truth about these incidents has recently been made known in unprejudiced and convincing fashion by the Imperial Court Marshal, Count Zedlitz-Trützschler (*Zwölf Jahre am deutschen Kaiserhof*, p. 173 *et seq.*, 1923). Not only is the history of Lecomte's invitation to Liebenberg related with perfect frankness and accuracy, but the fairy-tale about the frustration of Foreign Office policy is satisfactorily explained—it was the French Military Attaché who received from the Emperor the assurance that he would not go to war about Morocco. And Count Zedlitz speaks with like accuracy (p. 159) about the nature of Eulenburg's relation to the Emperor, saying that the Prince, who had now no political ambitions of any kind, " was henceforth seen only once a year at Rominten, and the Emperor once went to Liebenberg in the autumn for one or two days. For the rest, in the whole year, Eulenburg was perhaps once or twice invited to luncheon, and otherwise there was virtually no continued intercourse." Other judgments there delivered on the Prince are, however, entirely erroneous. For the reader they need no refutation.

touched on, it is as though between private people. On April 9, 1904, there is this : " Sincere good wishes for the Russo-Japanese War ... I am sorry to be out of it all, now that our harvest is ripening." On January 26, 1905 : " There is a good deal of sheet-lightning in various quarters of the sky. That is why my desires are in the direction of keeping the peace. May the *stability* which Your Majesty's wise political attitude ensures to Europe, be by God's help preserved." On March 11, 1905, he is made anxious by news from Russia : " Monarchical prestige in Europe will be seriously assailed if peace is not soon made, and order restored *tant bien que mal* in the interior. A Three-Emperor Alliance is more necessary than ever—but we must be careful. Just now it is extremely unpopular in Germany. We need reforms in Russia, and no fusillades, before an alliance can be made acceptable."

How little the writer was *au courant* with the course of secret negotiations is shown by a passage on August 8, 1905 (from Gastein) : " If President Roosevelt comes still more into the limelight, Europe may soon be having a dose of American policy which will take its breath away. Only a coalition of the older States can help us.[1] But how to gain France ? I do not believe in the mortal danger of an alliance between England and France, even if King Edward is *tout grisé* by the Entente, as the King of Roumania tells me he knows from eye- and ear-witnesses."

William II may well have smiled, reading his friend's recommendation of a plan which he believed himself to have already carried out—the

---

[1] This was an old idea of the Prince's, for which he had bestirred himself so long ago as the 'nineties. Unfortunately in vain. He had rightly divined the future.

covenant with Russia and France, supposed by him to have been made, at the end of that July, at Björkö!

We see, then, that the former ambassador was now practically no more than a newspaper reader, and not even a keen one. As a rule, he read only the *Lokalanzeiger*, occasionally perhaps the *Kreuzzeitung* and *Vossische Zeitung*. But of course he was a newspaper reader who, thanks to his experience, could read between the lines, and who also heard many things that did not come to the ears of others; yet who, while closely observant, stood somewhat apart and had no views of his own.

So the award of the Black Eagle, the highest distinction a Prussian King can bestow, must be attributed only to his past services. The Prince received it in person from the Emperor, when he met him in Berlin at a luncheon-party given by Prince von Donnersmarck.[1] Thirty years had then gone by since he, as a young Doctor of Laws and

[1] It was soon being said that the Order was the reward for a sumptuous publication to which the Prince had written a preface. This foolish babble was quite worthy of a Harden, who was the first to promulgate it; but it is amazing that a man like Hammann should not have been ashamed to report it (*Um den Kaiser*, p. 15). He even declares that the Prince was the originator of this "Hohenzollern Tribute." Not a word of truth in it! The Prince was, quite late in the transaction, asked for a preface, which with his usual good-nature he, though not very willingly, promised; for that pretentious kind of illustrated volume was not to his taste. He at any rate took care to have the proposed title *Deutsche Ruhmeshalle* (*German Pantheon*) altered to *Deutsche Gedenkhalle* (*German Halls of Remembrance*). The book, moreover, was not a "Hohenzollern Tribute," but dealt with the whole history of Germany in a very realistic spirit of scientific research. If the Prince is to be reproached for his preface, what must be said of the collaborators? There were recognised experts among them, men of all parties—for instance, Professor Hugo Preuss, to whom we owe the present constitution of the realm. That Hammann (following in Harden's footsteps) should connect the conferring of the Order with the book, is highly disingenuous, for he himself was concerned in its publication in the summer of 1906. He could easily have shown that this took place *after* the conferring of the Order.

Referendar, had entered the service of the State; and we know that he himself saw no reason to be elated when he compared then with now, and that he was very far from over-estimating his own deserts. He beheld in the Order simply a mark of the sovereign's friendship, and in that spirit he thanked him. To the Emperor he wrote:

"Liebenberg, *April* 7, 1906.

"At the luncheon-party to-day I could not tell Your Majesty quite all that I felt on receiving the highest distinction at Your Majesty's hands, and seeing the gladness that shone from your dear eyes because you were making *me* glad! Now that I am back at home I must try to express my feelings—here, where no sounds from the official world can reach me, and only your faithful old friend addresses you.

"I told Your Majesty in Berlin that I did not think I had earned such a distinction, and that I had never been susceptible to outward show—but that I *did* feel what it signified when the King of Prussia gave a subject the Order of the Black Eagle.

"I have always despised those who think they deserve any reward for doing their duty. Perhaps there may be some excuse for it in men whose natural propensities make duty a burden. But I am not among them. I regard myself as one born and bred to serve State and Sovereign. It seems to me such a matter-of-course that I will not waste words upon it, except to thank God that I *do* consider it a matter-of-course. But it is otherwise with the reward for it. Your Majesty will understand that I cannot see it as a 'reward,' since I take my services for granted; and that therefore I think no pursuit more despicable than that of Order- and Star-hunting.

" Nevertheless there are two sides to the public recognition by the sovereign of conscientious and deserving men, and these seem to justify it. One is political, the other personal. The former is not without its undesirable background, in that it turns to account the inordinate vanity of the human species. But the latter pertains to one of the sovereign's proudest prerogatives—for so he can testify to his friendship, can give pleasure, can rejoice the heart.

" This latter is what Your Majesty has done for me, and with what quite peculiar pleasure I well know, because our mutual relation is a peculiar one. In what way can *I* regard all great distinctions and marks of favour—I who possess so much more than all in possessing the friendship of my King? Their only effect can be that upon my heart, which feels that they proceed from the warmest, truest, kindest desire to testify to that friendship."

If nevertheless the ambassador *en disposition* was engaged in politics at this time, it was certainly not by his own desire, but by that of the Government, which wanted to make use of his occasional proximity to the Emperor and the personal influence he had upon him. Thus when in the autumns of 1905 and 1906 he was the Emperor's guest at Rominten, and there was very little to do, he could now and then attend to Foreign Office business. But he who had always observed the strictest etiquette in his intercourse with the Emperor did not now fail—when as a mere private individual he happened to be with the sovereign—to watch the signs of the times, and give the Imperial Chancellor full reports on all he saw and heard.

He sent Bülow a detailed description of the 1903 Norwegian cruise. His impressions were anything but pleasant. Many things which constant habit had made it easier to accept were now, after the two-years' interruption had increased his sense of spiritual remoteness, distressing and irksome. More acutely than ever he felt himself an alien in the Emperor's day-by-day environment, and the tone was repellent to him. To the Princess among others, he wrote of this.

" The sun has a warming and soothing influence. But it cannot dispel the anxieties which dominate us. The fifteen years of Norwegian cruising have not been without their effect on body and mind. Many things have grown clearer, many more exasperating. The contrast between the various ages and the convulsive gaiety of the company pains me most. All the guests are without exception men who have reached high office ; Princes, Excellencies, Privy Councillors, and Professors have developed out of Counts, Majors, and painters ; and they are all completely worn-out. But they retain sufficient energy to put up a show of hilarity, fun, even talent. So energetic are they that everyone does his gymnastics in the mornings. It very much disgusts me. I can't stand these Excellencies nowadays—for ever ducking and squatting ; nor can I stand puns and suchlike before nine o'clock in the morning. Sometimes I ask myself how the Emperor can, for he too is fifteen years older. And it is he who keeps the whole thing going.

" Sometimes I am overwhelmed by depression in the midst of the racket. But I know too that other energies are alive in me, and these make up for such a strange obligation of duty in this imperfect world of ours—spiritually speaking, I mean. I have suffered too long and too keenly in the calling that was forced upon me not to feel very distinctly what a blessing is emancipation, and what the power of a link which connects me with other and better, finer things than this kind of life represents, though it is regarded by most people as the acme of earthly bliss."

He was able to get the better of these external annoyances, especially as the Emperor was all kindness and solicitude for him. " I see," he wrote to the Princess, " at every turn how entirely he leaves me at liberty, and I have enough self-respect to take it as a matter-of-course. He knows very well that I am neither uncourtly nor obtuse." What troubled and tormented him was his perception that years had wrought a change in the Emperor which could not be observed without grave anxiety. The irritability and unreasonable excitement which had long ago been evident were not only much increased, but, though hitherto only displayed on special occasions, were now constant with him. Eulenburg, who knew his Imperial friend so well, could easily account for it. Political vexations, such as the recent very unfavourable General Election; added to these, the first clear signs of England's active hostility in her closer approach to Russia; worst of all, the complete lack of any personal successes—this, against the background of the continual restlessness which marked the Emperor's manner of life and was telling more and more upon his nervous system, had induced a condition which could no longer be called normal. The Imperial physician, Dr. Leuthold, confirmed this view, and gave it as his opinion that " we must have recourse to a stay in one of the spas, under a strict régime, if we want to obtain the rest which the poor Emperor requires."

The Prince, informing the Imperial Chancellor of this, commented:

"I confess to a fear that such a stay with two A.D.C.s *couleur* Scholl and Plusckow would not be of the slightest service—and this will, dear Bernard, increase your responsibility to an intolerable extent. Pray God for strength, for without His aid you will be driven well-nigh to despair.

"Your mask of optimism is well-chosen. The Imperial Chancellor, in the terrible state of opinion which prevails in every quarter of Germany, must not hang his head. But please don't overdo your part of optimist so far as to let this letter have no weight with you, as merely an outburst of pessimism on my part. My sole purpose is to give you a hint of the gradual alteration in the mental and physical condition of our dear sovereign. You used to rely to some extent on my perception, and it does not deceive me. Quite apart from Leuthold's confirmation; and he, as a doctor, must have made his professional observations.

"I am so deeply depressed that I am glad to be leaving the yacht at once. I often feel tears rising to my eyes. . . . It goes hard with me to tell you these things . . . but you will understand the *bearing* of my letter."

These impressions were confirmed by a stay at Rominten in that September. The Prince, seriously ill, confined to bed by a feverish attack, had a long and very earnest talk with the Emperor, of which he at once made a memorandum. He had tried to tell His Majesty the truth, with a frankness which not many would have ventured on, and which—we must lay stress on this—not many would have suffered. Among other things he said :

"During my long days of wearisome illness I have thought a great deal about Your Majesty —about you as a human being. A crown is nothing to me ; not so he who wears it, because of the responsibility laid upon him. There are certain Emperors and Kings who utterly revolt me ('So they do me,' remarked the Emperor). But the more remarkable the personality of him who wears a crown, the more danger in that crown for him—and for his realm.'

"'What do you mean by that?' asked the Emperor.

"I shall speak quite frankly. As a free man I have only my conscience to answer to ; and I say : *Your Majesty's individuality is gravitating towards that of the absolute ruler.* You are developing markedly in that direction. You are hard and inconsiderate—at the expense of the heart which belongs to you. Your contempt for your fellow-beings has increased. As you once said to me on a walk in Norway, your main characteristic is self-will. I will not dispute the justice of that view. But in any case, the line between certain actions of a ruler and the manifestations of his self-will is likely to be very hard to draw— if he really *is* self-willed. This brings with it impatience of contradiction and rejection of the good advice which others are anxious to give you. In a word : Autocracy at the expense of the autocrat's usefulness to himself—and to his people and his country. This all sounds very harsh ! But thank God I can modify it, and it is your personality which enables me to do so. As against your contempt for your fellow-creatures, you have a rare fidelity and capacity for attachment. Fidelity is always rare; in a monarch it is miraculous. For the monarch can always, when he chooses, plead the good of his State—*alias* his own convenience. As against your hardness, you have your heart. You should make more use of it. . . . As against your self-will, you have your intelligence. How easily *that* could avert the injurious consequences of an occasionally too conspicuous autocracy!"

The Prince did not feel that his remarks had been understood. Therefore, on his return home, he made use of the first slight improvement in health to write from his bed to the Imperial Chancellor:

"It gives me quite extraordinary pain not to have seen you for so long. Moreover, for many reasons I think I *ought* to see you. Also regarding impressions at Rominten. If it is at all possible to come for a few hours as soon as may be, I should be very grateful if you would."

The Chancellor does not seem to have taken the reiterated warnings so seriously as they were meant; at any rate nothing was done to restore the Emperor's nerves by rest and seclusion—which a ruler who wants to rule personally needs more than any other man. So things went on as they were for many a year, and it was a wonder they "held out" so long as they did—until one day the Prince's prognostications at the end of the last Norwegian cruise were really fulfilled. This was what he said on August 9, 1903, concluding his report to the Chancellor:

"You will find H.M. in no respect altered. Looking better or worse, according as the crossing was good or bad; feeling eager and happy at the thought of seeing you again, and confiding his political anxieties to you. Probably a little subdued compared to our experience of him, for he has a mixture of respect and fear for you on account of his more or less distinct consciousness that *he can't get on without you.* He will seem cheerful and good-tempered, will show his amicable side, and will appear as what (in the good hours which are getting rarer and rarer) he often is, and just as often is not—though always the interesting man and the interesting ruler. And you will—with a certain amount of justice—answer the question, 'How is H.M.?' with 'Going strong! The trip has done him good.' You will give this answer for some time—you could not *but* give it. And when you are in bed at night, with the lights out, you will probably torment yourself and wonder how much longer you will be able to say that.

"I do not by any means think that a crisis is at hand. It would only happen *soon* if troublesome or very grave political events should take the Emperor's overwrought nerves by storm. Nor would the crisis take (as so many fear—or hope) the form of mental derangement, but that of nervous prostration. The same kind of thing as I myself have been through."

What the Prince had seen and heard on this last Northern trip only confirmed his resolve to regard his retirement from the service, even though he might still be held *en disposition*, as final. He wrote to Bülow on July 29, 1903:

"Though after such severe suffering, so many moral pangs, I have at last opened a new chapter in my life, which despite reviving sensations of well-being I must probably regard as the concluding one, I am on the one hand unequal to renewing the experiences above described, on the other unwilling so to spend the evening of my days. I may perhaps be able still to do friendly offices for my friends; but to the poor dear sovereign to whom I was a friend I can show my friendship only by the *sincerest* compassion and sympathy, and even that from the seclusion which best suits my temperament. Nothing more."

Compassion and sympathy—no longer any word of joyful fellow-feeling. The mute remote spectator, who had once been a statesman standing at the hub of the universe, found no pleasure in watching the drama of German politics—found nothing but anxiety, daily increasing anxiety. He saw foreign relations being more and more endangered, saw Germany's whole position growing more and more uncertain by reason of the ever-swelling commitments of the Big Fleet—the deadly peril of which he had been among the first to realise, without being able in any way to prevent it. The Emperor would never have listened to his arguments, and even the Chancellor did nothing in response to his friend's earnest representations, though he could not deny that they were justified. Prince Eulenburg was always convinced that Bülow was no advocate of the Big Fleet policy.[1] None the less he had once received this answer to his urgent

[1] It is true that this is contradicted by Bülow's glorification of the German Fleet in his book on German policy. Nevertheless, it is shown to be accurate by his letters in August and September, 1908, which were published by Hammann (*Bilder aus der letzten Kaiserzeit*, pp. 57–59). Anyone who, as Bülow does in the second of these letters, gives the preference to Admiral von Galster's supplementary scheme of defence, can never have whole-heartedly accepted the guiding principle of the Tirpitz fleet-building plan.

arguments—that in such matters a sovereign had a particular kind of instinct to which others must bow the head. Eulenburg had no difficulty in translating this mystic utterance into sober prose. Bülow knew how gigantic the Fleet loomed in the Emperor's and the public's estimation, and was not the man to engage in mortal combat against it—a combat which might easily cost him his position, to which he clung as to dear life.

The situation at home offered still more serious features. From dangers abroad they might escape by retreat, though it were with losses or even humiliation—but still escape alive; the tangled skein of home-politics seemed, to his pitilessly searching eye, to offer no prospect whatever of a solution. In 1903 the Prince, for his own edification, drew up the balance-sheet in a memorandum ranging far and wide over the course of history. He thus reached the conclusion that the Prussian military and official State, which had done such great things in the past, was not suited to the tasks awaiting the German Empire in the future, because in essentials it was alien to the rest of Germany, and was opposed to the spirit of the age. The traditions of the Prussian Army seemed to him out of harmony with the naturally pacific temper of the German Empire, and the old uniform coat which had so well befitted the conquering Prussian State had, for all its glory, the look of a strait-jacket on the modern realm that stood for peace on earth.

"The Army," he wrote, "has become a castle-guard and has to do sentry-go, because we have not even yet contrived to win the hearts of the people. But is it the end and aim of an army to do sentry-go, when it has every right to dream of fresh glories? The Army will never look with anything but growing distaste on the 'civilian,' who was already sufficiently despised, and now is called upon to do great deeds for the social and economic State which the Army called into existence by its achievements. Trade, industry, agriculture, always controlled by the organs of Government—for except under the constitutional guardianship of Frederick William I and his successors, it were inconceivable that anything whatever should ever be done!—are to stagger the world by their achievements. That is the Emperor's dream. But *what* is to be achieved? Who are the men to achieve it? A fleet is built, because the future lies on the water. How is this future conceived? No doubt on the English model—but here we lack the millions as well as the personalities. The industrious German business-man is not of that kidney, even if we were in a position to protect him in any and every emergency. And we are not in that position. Perhaps the future of him who does bad business at home may lie on the water. But he will not be capable either of leadership or rule. No; true to his innate feudal servility, he will make no bones about accepting foreign domination. And yet we *might* have had personalities, talents, and energy! But they are all stuck in their barracks and offices, and never think of getting away from them—nor do their sons either. And who can blame them, so long as Prussia is a Prussian military State, and the tradition survives?

"So it boils down to overcoming the following difficulties: Prussian glory and Prussian tradition rest on the shoulders of the Army and an immense official class. We cannot abandon these great traditions without weakening our position abroad; we dare not lay a finger on our Army. But this tradition is our lion in the path, our fatality, if we want to comprehend the spirit of the age, or even get the better of it. That full-fed leech, the Army, and that monstrous cuttle-fish, Officialdom, are draining the people's heart-blood—its best, its noblest sons. They are sacrificing their native genius on the altar of the castle-guard and the sentry-box.

"But why should not the élite reform themselves? They are intelligent enough to understand the age. Are they dazzled by the glitter of epaulettes? I do not think so. But even the strong men of the State are not strong enough to break through the iron ring of tradition, supposing they were prepared to impose terms on the Throne, the Fatherland, and foreign countries. For tradition in Prussia has taken a form which, though utterly incomprehensible to other civilised States, does seem a symbol of the special Prussian contribution. It consists in the conception of honour which is peculiar to Prussia, and is by Prussia instilled into the German Federal States.

"These castes, which comprise the nobility as well, divide the population into people 'with whom you can fight a duel' and 'people with whom you cannot.' The foreigner is utterly unable to comprehend this classification, and if he *were* able, would be far from measuring its scope. The foreigner could never understand that, for instance, certain classes are obliged to exclude a man of talent, because he belongs to certain other classes; that the marriage of a man of talent with a woman of inferior or even only less exalted standing destroys his career; that when a young man of the class with whom duels *can* be fought enters a profession which includes those with whom they *cannot*, he cuts his own throat. The foreigner would exclaim 'Why, this is China!'

"But we have not the courage to break the ring

which clamps our best and noblest energies as in a coat of mail. For we should not like taking it on ourselves to disparage the circle to which we belong. The thought of the sneering smile on the face of the veriest booby who is nevertheless 'duel-worthy,' if we took but one step outside the rigidly-marked path of the duelling-class, would alone be enough to deter the most intelligent, the most emancipated of Prussians. And so this queer classification precludes any intercourse among the most valuable classes of the community, any common endeavour for the modern State.

"Against this castle, this fortified dwelling, which holds spell-bound the best men we have, and prevents us from turning our finest ore to account, two formidable enemies are slowly but steadily advancing: Poverty, which reduces the aristocrat to his shabby old garment of duel-worthiness; and the phalanx of the Fourth Estate, whose masses will soon level down, by ignoring them, these duelling and non-duelling distinctions. Prussianism, like a knight in bronze, stands on its lofty pedestal and watches the oncoming masses without stirring from its place. Confidently it looks up to the old iron pennon with its inscription: 'With God for King and Country!' But the Fourth Estate shouts: 'Eat, drink, and rule!'—and blows up the knight with a charge of dynamite.

"Tradition does not know what is lacking to it. It does not compare foreign peoples and States with its own Fatherland, and if it did, would but still more arrogantly lift its head. The system is slowly strangling the Old Prussian. The Old Prussian does not even notice that the strength of the Prussian tradition, the brilliant organisation, has become likewise the strength of the Fourth Estate, which like us all derives from Prussia—and which could teach us to understand the new age, even if an altered franchise and other palliatives had to be resorted to for the discouragement of social democracy, which is nothing but the youngest and most vigorous of Europe's sons, now awakened to self-consciousness.

"Such we are—and know not that we are! Who is going to tell us? We should believe no one who represented the sacro-sanct Prussian tradition as an obsolete thing, because we have the strongest army on earth and are greatly renowned. We are the disciplined, Hohenzollern-taught nation, and we are not intelligent enough to perceive the terrible thraldom in which we have been fostered. But what are we to do, to confront the inevitable catastrophe? Wait, until (say) Austria collapses and we have to fight her cause? Wait, until our leading statesmen get up a war, so as to distract attention from the colossal burden of debt and the social disaster, and give the military State some ground to stand on? Wait, until the Fourth Estate attacks *us*, and *then* try to destroy it? Destroy that Estate which will rise like a menacing phoenix from our burning? Or shall we disarm, stretch out a hand to the duel-forbidden, and put all our energies at the disposal of social life and the State? Who would venture on such eccentricity?

"So we shake our heads, we poor weak strong men—shake them so hard that one day they will roll off at our feet."

For an impotent looker-on it is torment to be a seer. It condemns him to the part of prophet crying in the wilderness. Prince Eulenburg was not, as one ignorant of the facts has recently said of him, a mute Cassandra. Our readers know that he spoke, and was not heard. It was with perfect right that he wrote, recalling the critical years before the opening of the new century, that the postponement of the necessary measures—while still there was time, while he was making his appeal to the Reichstag (as the reader knows), while the situation abroad and at home was not yet so desperate as in 1908 to 1909 . . . that that postponement was to blame for the World War and the Revolution.

" I saw the disaster creeping on us like a monstrous beast of prey, and suffered agonies from the obtuseness of German statesmen, diplomats, military authorities in every quarter, as also of the Prussians and—their unfortunate Emperor. For condemned as I was to utter impotence, and filled with such a sense of duty towards Emperor and Empire as had broken down my health, I drifted—I and my ideas—despairingly on the ocean of German incomprehension."

II
HOLSTEIN'S REVENGE

BUT once more the anxious looker-on was to be called upon for a brief period of active service to the Fatherland. This was in September, 1905 ; the Emperor was at Rominten, and Eulenburg was his guest there. They were awaiting a visit from Herr von Witte, who was on his way home after successfully concluding a treaty of peace with Japan, and was regarded as the coming man in Russia. In the preceding July the Emperor's meeting with the Tsar at Björkö had taken place, together with the precipitate signing of the Russo-German alliance, in which France was to have been involved. Bülow had tendered his resignation on account of the procedure by which the treaty had been obtained ; and it was only after much persuasion, in which Eulenburg joined, that he consented to stay. This had left a certain grudge in the Emperor's feeling for him—he no longer trusted Bülow as before. But he still believed in the future of the diplomatic success which he thought he had achieved at Björkö, and the question was whether he could gain Witte for his views concerning France. To all appearance he had brilliantly succeeded in this ; Witte seemed delighted with the new alliance and eagerly agreed to the Imperial suggestions, for which he proposed to work in Petersburg. It was arranged that, in order to keep inconspicuously in touch with him—for Witte was not yet a Minister, and at no time did he undertake the Foreign Office—he should direct his letters to Eulenburg, who would pass them on to Emperor and Chancellor, and answer in the sense of their instructions. This correspondence was in fact carried on for the next two months, but like the alliance itself was merely sowing the sands.[1] Even when he became Prime Minister on November 7, Witte was not in a position to overcome the dislike felt in Petersburg and Paris for the German alliance. His letters grew more and more evasive; and after March, 1906, the Björkö incident was a thing of the past. But for Prince Eulenburg it was perhaps the final sealing of his doom. His correspondence with Witte can scarcely have been kept secret from Holstein, and it is easy to imagine the suspicion and enmity it aroused in him. And now destiny ordained that a mere accident should add fuel to the flame of this malignant distrust.

The reader will remember the situation between Germany and France in the autumn of 1905. The Emperor's visit to Tangier and the fall of Delcassé had left strained relations, the question under discussion being whether and in what circumstances the German Empire would support the stipulations made by the French in Morocco.

The negotiations were prolonged by the attitude of the German Foreign Office, which was ambiguous and contradictory. In Paris it gave rise to the impression that Germany wanted war, which the existing French Government had good reasons for dreading at that particular moment, but which at no time did it desire, being more inclined to come to a durable friendly understanding with Germany.

[1] Witte's account of this in his *Erinnerungen*, though not wholly straightforward, is in accord with our own, which derives from authentic documents in the Prince's own handwriting. Witte had very good reasons for not admitting that he was then strongly attracted by the idea of an understanding between the Continental Powers, and therefore approved the Björkö negotiations.

That was why Secretary-of-Legation Lecomte, who understood Germany better than any other French diplomat and was her warmest friend, was hastily transferred to Berlin, where in earlier years he had held the post of First Councillor of Embassy.

As we are aware, Raymond Lecomte had known Eulenburg very well at Munich, and was a family friend. He seized the earliest opportunity—an accidental encounter in the street—of taking his old friend into his confidence. He told him quite frankly that there was some uncertainty in Paris about the views of the German Government, but that the impression given was of a design to force France into war. France did not want war, for which she could perceive no grounds; but she would accept it if it could not with honour be avoided.

Eulenburg did what duty dictated in such a case. Without entering into any discussion, for which he had neither the necessary equipment nor the authority, he listened attentively to the Frenchman's communication and went at once to his friend, General Helmuth von Moltke, who had at that time just succeeded Count Schlieffen as Chief of the Grand Staff. From him he learnt that the Staff was very far from desiring war. He then hastened to the Imperial Chancellor with the information he had gathered. Prince Bülow was no less surprised than himself, and joined in repudiating any thought of war. Eulenburg had the impression that this incident opened Bülow's eyes to the game being played behind his back by the Foreign Office—that is to say, by Holstein. He put two and two together when from that moment the Chancellor took entire control of the negotiations with France, with the result that all incitements to war were thenceforth at an end, that the international conference met at Algeciras, and that the Morocco incident was finally disposed of to the advantage of France.

That was all Eulenburg had had to do with the affair, nor had he said a word about it to the Emperor. His task was fulfilled when he had reported the salient passages in the Frenchman's communication—which no doubt was not wholly spontaneous on Lecomte's part. If Eulenburg's intervention really did influence the course of German policy, and was to be regarded as having contributed to preserve the peace, that was the business of none but the responsible organs of Government. Everything that has been said of his " irresponsible " influence on the Emperor and his wire-pulling against the official policy of the Empire, is pure invention. He could not have acted more correctly and loyally than he did.

But it is often our best actions which most injure us ; and Eulenburg had, without suspecting it, given an adverse turn to his destiny by his strictly orthodox procedure. The winding-up of the bankrupt Holstein policy towards France, which—not to Germany's credit—fell to the task of the Algeciras conference, resulted in the downfall of its originator. A letter of resignation, tendered by Holstein for the fiftieth time in the certain hope that it would as little as any of the others be accepted, *was* countersigned by the Emperor at the instance of State Secretary Tschirschky, representing Bülow, who was ill.

Holstein was at first beside himself. He naturally did not see that he had made himself impossible, that all experienced men in the Foreign Office had long regarded his removal as a necessity. Nothing but a spiteful intrigue could in his view have caused the downfall of him, the Omnipotent. Who

BARON VON HOLSTEIN

had done this thing ? His morbid imagination, thirsting for revenge, sought the criminal. It could not have been the Imperial Chancellor ; of him he was certain, for that man feared him too much. (Prince Bülow was clever enough to leave him under that delusion, and never let him know that he had been a party to the State Secretary's proceeding.[1]) So it could only have been a member of the camarilla, and a very powerful one, who could get such a thing done over the Chancellor's head—some personal enemy who had the Emperor's ear. Could it have been Eulenburg ? *He* had indeed disapproved the recent Holstein policy, and for this reason : the Prince held Holstein's chosen attitude towards France to be insanity at a time when the temper in Paris was more pacific, and less hostile to Germany, than ever before. He would have made no concealment of this in his conversations with the Imperial Chancellor, though he had never said a word about it to the Emperor. But Holstein's imagination had never needed more than a fly to see a whole herd of elephants. Soon he was absolutely convinced that it must have been Eulenburg who had put the thin end of the wedge into his Morocco policy, and thus was to blame for its fiasco. A correspondence with Witte, an old friendship with Lecomte—what more was needed to construct a detective story ? Of course it could have been no one but Eulenburg ! It was to *his*

[1] On the morning when his fate was made known to him, Holstein must have presented a deplorable and undignified spectacle. According to the description of a journalist whom he received, he was alternately sentimental—" They have taught an old man another lesson in philanthropy "—and foaming with rage : " So this is the end of it ! I am to be sacrificed for the mistakes they have made ! " But most of all he was tormented by the question of who had done it. " Can it have been Bülow ? " The visitor protested : " You cannot think that ! Do you think Bernard Bülow the man to stain his hands with your blood ? " " No, no ! I can't think that ! But who is it —who ? " He never thought of Tschirschky.

interest to bring Holstein down, and *he* had the power to make the Emperor acquiesce in the deed.

A fortnight went by, and in that morbid imagination the suspicion had become a fixed idea, and was to be reflected in action. We leave the Prince's memoranda to speak for themselves.

"*May* 1, 1906.

" By the morning's post I received a registered letter from Holstein, in which he said that for certain reasons it was dangerous to be seen with me.[1]

" Has he gone out of his senses ? But I feel it to be a matter of life and death, and I wired instantly to Axel Varnbüler, who is always exceedingly punctilious in affairs of honour, and betook myself by the next train to Berlin, with the letter in my pocket. Varnbüler despatched to Holstein the appropriate challenge : 'Exchange of pistol shots until disablement or death.'

" I went to the Foreign Office to give information of the proceeding, as I am *en disposition*, and therefore under the Office. Bülow is still laid by, after his slight seizure on April 5. Tschirschky is representing him. When I told Tschirschky about the challenge, he literally collapsed upon a chair. He said that this would be one of the world's greatest scandals—for God's sake and the Emperor's couldn't I withdraw the challenge ? I said I couldn't dream of doing that, and I went back to Varnbüler."

---

[1] The letter says : " After many years you have attained your end —my removal from office. And the base attacks upon me must be equally to your liking," and so on. Anyone acquainted with Holstein's methods will see in these words merely the involuntary confession that it had been his aim, throughout many years, to relegate Eulenburg politically. We shall soon see the proof of this.

"*May* 3, 1906.

" Two very unpleasant days. Holstein has chosen Derenthall (my old friend) for his second. Varnbüler has called in Hugo Reichach, who is an expert in serious affairs of honour. As no immediate answer came on May 2, between the 2nd and 3rd we sent Holstein a letter demanding an unequivocal apology. Holstein agreed to this, and to-day I received an apology from him which gets me out of my terrible position. Axel Varnbüler and Reichach consider the incident closed. I told Tschirschky so.

" I cannot say that *I* consider Holstein's attacks to be really disposed of. He will revenge himself in his wonted fashion. For he is in a tight place, socially speaking, with his deadly insult to me—and his instant retractation. Holstein's apology was thus worded : ' Prince zu Eulenburg having assured me, on his word of honour, that he had neither hand, act, nor part in my dismissal, and has been in no way concerned in any of the attacks made upon me by the Press, I hereby withdraw the offensive remarks made upon him in my letter.

' (Signed) HOLSTEIN.'

" As the two Berserkers, Varnbüler and Reichach, solemnly assure me that the incident is thus closed [1] to their complete satisfaction, I will try to feel at ease. But I frankly confess that it does not entirely satisfy *me*, bitter as it must have been for Holstein to have to write those words."

[1] This was a misapprehension which, as the Prince's memoranda show, was afterwards cleared up. Baron von Reichach was asked simply to advise on matters of etiquette, and did not take part in the subsequent discussions. In his book *Unter drei Kaisern* (p. 76 *et seq.*, 1925), he depicts the earlier proceedings as above, but makes the mistake of attributing to Baron v. Varnbüler the words : " Anyhow we must get him up as a hero." He himself, as he authorises me to say, was the speaker, and not Herr von Varnbüler.

"*May* 5, 1906.

"That the blame should be put upon me for Holstein's dismissal in the middle of April—or rather, for the acceptance of his resignation by the Emperor—is one of Holstein's crazy delusions. Surely he must know me well enough to know that I would not 'do him in,' having once been friends with him. But this only proves that his retirement has really driven him out of his mind. When (on April 17) lately I lunched with H.M. at the Palace he did tell me that Holstein had got his marching-orders. And this was the way he put it: 'By-the-bye, I have this day countersigned Holstein's letter of resignation. Even though he *is* your friend, we couldn't put up with him any longer He is really quite crazy now.' I told H.M. that for some years I had not been friends with Holstein, and that finally he had thought fit to defame my character. 'Really!' said H.M. 'That is news to me.' Thus casually did I hear of Holstein's dismissal—and I am supposed to have caused it!"

The Prince had once more proved himself a true prophet when on May 3 he had written: "Holstein will revenge himself in his wonted fashion." How, in his enforced leisure, the fallen man began to prepare that vengeance we learn from the letters he wrote between May and August of that year to the editor of a South-German paper. It is tolerably certain that they were not the only ones of their kind. In them he attacked the Emperor, the Press bureau at the Foreign Office, occasionally even the Imperial Chancellor, and fulminated against the *dii minorum gentium* who were supposed to be guilty of his fall—Hammann, leader of the semi-official Press, von Huhn, representing the

Kölnische Zeitung, and Stein of the *Frankfurt Zeitung.* He was making out a case for himself, and preparing the ground. He did not name the man against whom, in reality, the whole thing was directed; but he was bold enough to hint at the affair of honour, and did not hesitate to tell the exact contrary of the truth. " Our courts of justice," he wrote on August 16, " take no account of affairs of honour. . . . And a justly accused man does not venture on that field. A few months ago I took very sharp measures against a man considerably younger than myself—and no insignificant man, either—calling him among other things a despicable person. His response was to send me a friend who merely said to my representative that the subject of my indictment was ready to declare on his word of honour that he had never done anything, or caused anything to be done, against me in the matter I have referred to. I required that this declaration should be given me in his own handwriting—and I got it. Voilà ! "

The effrontery with which the facts are here distorted seems less amazing when we know that Holstein, when he wrote this, was not so very much afraid as he had been of an immediate exposure. If we compare the wording of his insulting letter with that of his retraction, we are tempted to ask why the latter was not given a more emphatic form. It had been urgently represented by the Secretary and Under-Secretary of State that this should not be insisted on; and as Holstein's superiors they were entitled to be heard on the question of the affair of honour, and were naturally most anxious that it should not come to a duel. Eulenburg had yielded, and contented himself with the words as they stood, thus bearing the brunt himself and sparing Foreign Office, Government, and ultimately the Emperor. Varnbüler wrote a full account of the proceedings, which explained and justified Eulenburg's attitude ; it was consigned to the archives, and Eulenburg received an attested copy. Soon afterwards the Imperial Chancellor asked the Prince to let him see this copy, for he was not yet well enough to go to the Office and examine the archives. Though repeatedly asked for it, he never gave it back—said it was not to be found at the moment, must have been mislaid, etc. These excuses accorded ill with the faultless order that reigned in Bülow's workroom ; but they did not alter the fact that the Prince was no longer in a position immediately to justify his attitude in the affair of honour, by laying the authentic account before no matter how rigorous a judge. Thus it was easy for Holstein to give currency to his shameless misrepresentations.

But these were mere preliminaries. When he despatched the letter we have quoted from, he had already taken a long step forward. On August 18, 1906, the astonished public was reading in Harden's *Zukunft* an open letter from Holstein to the editor, and Harden's answer to it. In these the precious pair, hitherto mortal enemies (the *Zukunft* had in the past sharply castigated Holstein's policy, and Holstein as usual had hated Harden beyond any other man on earth), shook hands and executed low bows to one another, like any knights of old after the combat. Eulenburg at once saw the drift of this comedy. His diary comments on it thus :

> " The tone of the Holstein-Harden campaign in the *Zukunft* opens a most disturbing vista. I see in it not only his revenge upon me for making him decline my challenge, but something more

far-reaching, more ominous, and I cannot conceal my anxiety.

"As regards myself, I remember Holstein's attacks on Harden, how he hated him, how extremely dangerous he thought him. And as regards others, I know that Harden offered his pen to the Emperor, and that the Emperor merely sent him a message through his A.D.C., couched in the form affected by those 'sublime' creatures: 'H.M. has no intercourse with anyone belonging to the Press, nor does he wish to have any'—whereupon Harden placed his pen at Bismarck's disposal against H.M. !

"What can such a pair be brewing now?

"I regard this Holstein-Harden alliance as an ominous fact—and I am not alone in this. Everyone who knows the two conspirators shares my views."

For some weeks nothing happened. At the beginning of October the Prince, a little better after the thorough-going cure at Güstrow, was with the Emperor at Rominten, attending to Foreign Office business. As always, he furnished the Imperial Chancellor with exhaustive reports. On October 5 he wrote:

"During my sixteen years of autumn visits here I have never known such an ebb in the political tide. You can't think how pleasant I find it! Though my health has apparently improved, I still needed rest, and our sovereign's good-tempered mood and countenance have sensibly contributed to my recovery. But, all the same, the three meal-times beside or opposite Their Majesties are a strain which I can only endure by spending the hours of digestion in bed. Even their cordial and friendly treatment cannot blind me to the fact that I have neither sufficient youth nor sufficient vitality to perform the duties of a courtier, even though I *do* go to bed to digest my food. One can't be an actor for more than a few days at a time. But I am full of gratitude for all the kindness and attention they show me. . . .

"Now I must tell you, for your information, of His Majesty's attitude when we spoke of you. The Emperor thought you quite up to the mark at Wilhelmshöhe; but not so well at Berlin.[1] To August Eulenburg he spoke very angrily indeed of that incident about the African railway line.[2] With me he talked quite quietly of it—as it were cautiously. I gathered that he attributed a certain lack of energy (of course I am still speaking of the African railway business) to the illness from which you had not entirely recovered. Yesterday, after receiving your report on the Brunswick question,[3] he said to me: 'Well, if Bülow puts his back into this, it will show that he's still what he was!' I have the impression that the railway tiff is passing off, but he is trotting out 'energy' on any and every occasion. One thing is certain, that he knows of absolutely *no one* who could take your place. I feel that, from the way he spoke of you despite this railway bother. But even that has its uses, and keeps him out of mischief! Undeniably he is much perturbed by the idea that you might be

[1] This refers to Bülow's fainting-fit in the Reichstag on April 5, in consequence of which he had been away from the Office for some time.

[2] In the summer the Reichstag had refused to vote supplies for a railway line in South-West Africa; the Emperor had, however, expressed his desire that it should nevertheless be constructed, and had shown some displeasure towards the Chancellor when this was not done.

[3] The question of the Regency in Brunswick was then under discussion in the Reichstag.

too ill to carry on—it worries him, he would think it disastrous. When I happened to mention your health to the Empress a few days ago (His Majesty sitting near us, reading) and said: 'Well, thank God it's all right now; but it would have been terrible indeed if Bülow had had to retire!'—His Majesty suddenly looked up from his newspaper and said: 'Yes, indeed—that would have been the last straw!' This spontaneous remark is very significant. But it is significant too of his nature that he describes anything that is not to his liking as want of energy—and now attributes that to your illness. I am giving you as detailed an account as I can. Who else would, if I didn't?

"I don't think Tirpitz has been working against you in any way. Hollmann and Müller were present at all the interviews. Hollmann gave me an account of them, and if a word had been said about you, he would *at once* have told me."

No one could have looked more carefully after the interests of a friend whose position was no longer secure.[1] And yet it seems to be a fact that Bülow had at that time begun to acquiesce in the ruin of the friend to whom he owed *everything*. Was he really envious of him, had perfidious insinuations had their effect, or did he pretend, for certain reasons, to regard Eulenburg as a secret enemy? Signs of a change of attitude on the Chancellor's part were noticed by the Prince's circle; he himself paid no attention to them, once he had given Alfred von Bülow, the Chancellor's

[1] Who can be certain how much the slight warning contained in this letter contributed to the remarkably sudden display of " energy "—not entirely accounted for by the occasion—made by the Chancellor in December, when the Reichstag was dissolved?

brother, the most laconic of explanations. Afterwards it became known what lies had begun to be told about him to Bülow. Eulenburg was said to desire his downfall and see him replaced by a "martinet" General.[1] Helmuth von Moltke, Head of the General Staff, was mentioned; others whispered of Count Wedel, the Ambassador in Vienna. The rumour was as foolish as could be, and its very senselessness points to Holstein, and no one else, as the man who set it going. Count Wedel had for years been one of the officers of the suite which Eulenburg considered so particularly dangerous and regarded with such great distrust; while of the intellect, education, and character of the man, whom he rightly held to be his personal enemy, he had by no means a favourable opinion. Of all conceivable candidates for the Chancellorship this was the last whom the Prince would have supported. And as for his friend Moltke, however he might prize him as an admirable and accomplished officer and honourable man, he knew only too well his incapacity for politics.

Meanwhile, as so often happens, the silliest gossip prevailed over the voice of reason. The idiotic tale was believed, circulated, and found its way into the Press in October. And when very soon after, on November 7, the Emperor paid his almost yearly visit to Liebenberg, the connection was clear to the malignant adversaries and all the ignorant and credulous outsiders—Bülow was to be brought down by the "Liebenberg Round Table." The Government speedily contradicted this—Prince Bülow's position was in no way endangered, he

---

[1] In Hammann's *Um den Kaiser* (p. 10) the reader will find the origin of this tittle-tattle. When the Prince's attention was drawn to the passage in question, he repelled the statements with utter contempt. "Nothing of that kind ever entered my head!"

enjoyed His Majesty's fullest confidence. But the
haste and solemn emphasis of these semi-official
statements was enough to reveal—either that the
Chancellor did feel his position to be menaced, or
wished to foster the belief that there were those
who desired his downfall. Moreover, there
appeared in the *Kölnische Zeitung*, which of all the
great newspapers was most closely in touch with
the Wilhelmstrasse, a correspondence which warmly
defended Moltke against the suspicion of having
aimed at the Chancellorship, but also made the
peculiar reservation that the writers did not propose
to discuss whether the " Eulenburg group " had
actually worked for Bülow's fall, since they were
not sufficiently informed of that group's views and
intentions. Finally, the Imperial Chancellor, in
a long speech to the Reichstag (November 14)
referred to the talk of a " camarilla " which
dominated the Emperor. Instead of denying its
existence, he merely said that that poisonous
foreign weed had never been planted in German
soil without great injury to Prince and people.
This double-tongued utterance as good as said :
" There *is* a camarilla ; the Imperial Chancellor
thinks so, and emphasises the danger of it ! "

A spectacle for gods and men ! Instead of
vehemently defending the Ambassador *en disposition*
(to say nothing here of the personal friend and
obligations of gratitude) against false reports, which
was the simple duty of any Government, the Chancellor openly and unmistakably offered him up.
Was the camarilla indeed so powerful that there
was nothing for the Government but " recourse to
publicity ? " It was like setting the hounds on the
man.

The Press needed no second indication. Rumour
had long designated Eulenburg as the source of

private intrigues, the man who brought undesirable influences to bear upon the Emperor. Now he was, in a trice, the publicly-denounced "irresponsible adviser" on whom the storm broke in full fury. An inextricable web of empty rumours, statements partly true and wholly false, imaginary accusations, and purposeful cabals was wound about the Emperor's friend. No one but had a stone to cast at the man who, seriously ill, a prey to anxiety, loyal to his Imperial friend and asking nothing more for himself than to end his days in peace, had from one day to another been turned into an enemy of the people. The insidious virus of the Holstein propaganda, administered for years in homœopathic doses, cautiously but unremittingly, had taken effect; public opinion was poisoned to the core. Many things combined to awaken enmities against the Prince, who had never done anyone any harm, and deliver him up defenceless to his adversaries. In the circles he belonged to, he had of old been aware of awakening distrust by his markedly different intellectual interests and his liberal turn of mind. As Caprivi's adherent he had excited dislike among the Agrarians; the false rumour of his having been guilty of the second Chancellor's fall had estranged the Liberals. He had almost completely lost touch with Prussian society through his long stay abroad and the long illness which followed. At Court he was hated by the monarch's immediate environment, where his personal influence had so often been found a hindrance; but among the great mass of the people the vexation felt with the Emperor was involuntarily directed against him, as the man who was always near the throne. The less people dared to attack the sovereign openly, to tell him all the anger in their hearts, the gladder they were to get at him through his best friend, to take that friend down a peg or two. Others again were ready to believe when they were assured that in the last analysis it was this friend, with his perverse counsel, his flattering insinuations, his general unsoundness, who should bear the blame for all that was displeasing in the Emperor's development. All without distinction, however, combined in the sentiment which, whether they confessed it or not, was the dominating one—a venomous, insatiable envy of the man who had the extraordinary luck to be called a friend by the Emperor. Thus was fulfilled in Eulenburg what a French historian observes to be the fate of all favourites: "*Les favoris sont jalousés par les courtisans et les ministres; ils sont haïs d'instinct par le peuple.*" With rare unanimity the Press of all colours demanded the head of the man whom not any of its readers knew.

It would be idle to give in detail all the senseless reproaches and imaginary accusations then publicly hurled at the Prince. Readers who have followed us thus far are aware of how much to believe in the statements that the Prince had " looked after all his friends," making one of the Moltkes Chief of the Grand Staff, the other Commandant of Berlin, and Herr von Tschirschky Secretary of State. Not a syllable of this is true.[1] The reader knows, too, that it was the contrary of the truth when it was

[1] He *was* concerned in the appointment of Moltke—unfortunately so little fitted for the post; but in a totally different sense. Moltke himself complained to Eulenburg that the Emperor wanted to appoint him against his will, and asked for advice. Eulenburg recommended him to refuse, and if that was no use, to make it a condition that the Most High should not interfere at the manœuvres. Moltke did so, and most unexpectedly the Emperor submitted (see Moltke's letters, published in 1923). So that if the manœuvres from 1905 onwards were no longer a farce (see Waldersee, *Denkwürdigkeiten*, Vol. III, pp. 219–266), Eulenburg should be given some of the credit. He had always regarded this point as most important. (*Aus 50 Jahren*, p. 285, et seq.)

said of the Prince that he was " an unhealthy out-of-date romantic and visionary," had always advised the Emperor badly, " had never been tired of insinuating to William II that he was born to rule alone, and being so incomparably favoured from above, could hope for, plead for, light and understanding only from that empyrean from whose heights the Crown had been conferred upon him, and to it alone could feel himself responsible."[1] For the reader will not have forgotten the frank words spoken again and again in the course of years to his Imperial friend by the Prince, and can testify that they were wholly concerned with enjoining reflection, moderation, caution, and self-control, coupled with earnest warnings against the Emperor's own temperament and his self-willed and autocratic tendencies. And the reader also knows that the sinister " Round Table" the " Liebenberg close corporation," under whose disastrous influence the sovereign was supposed to stand, existed only in the sphere of fable ; and he will be in a position to estimate all the reckless baseness of imputing to the man who was second to none in his sense of duty and responsibility that he had made the Emperor's friendly visits to his house an opportunity for bringing him in contact with a foreign representative, who in his turn made use of it to frustrate Government action through the monarch himself. Finally, to sum up, the reader will know where to look for the ultimate source of all these venomous lies ;

[1] These bombastic phrases (of Harden's) are evidently by way of imitating the style in which " Phili" was supposed to speak to the monarch. Of their success the reader will judge. As to who really were the flatterers that robbed the Emperor of the power to criticise himself, Waldersee's Reminiscences leave us in no doubt whatever, and quite justly. The late Professor Theodor Schliemann was witness on one occasion, when a military essay read before the Emperor on the disaster at Hochkirch concluded with the words : " Under Your Majesty's command, nothing like this could have happened."

nowhere but in the malignant imagination of a long-diseased and finally deranged intelligence—Holstein's. But into the chorus of the Furies in which—one blushes even now to recall it—a Maximilian Harden was leader, there soon entered a new and still uglier note. It was Harden who—first by veiled though transparent hints, but then more and more unmistakably and insolently—brought the hideous accusation of secret immorality and unnatural vice. Others took up the cry, intensified and coarsened it, and soon it was echoing all over the world: the Liebenberg Round Table, the camarilla, the Emperor's most intimate group, was a pack of degenerates, linked by mutual abnormal instincts; and the leader of that group, the worst of them all, was the Emperor's bosom-friend, Prince Eulenburg.

The martyrdom had begun.

III
PERSECUTION

CALUMNY is like the air. It may befall a human being to live guileless and unsuspecting throughout many a year in which, behind his back, the most abominable whispers are rife, until at last some accident reveals that malicious slander has spun its web around him as the spider does around the fly. Well for him if he can succeed in breaking free. Only too often the impalpable threads of calumny will prove to be inseverable.

Even in the 'eighties at Munich and Starnberg there is said to have been every kind of ugly gossip about Philip Eulenburg, who was then leading the happiest years of his life as husband and father. So, at least, it was afterwards maintained—with what truth, who shall now establish? Rumours are not to be tracked down when years have passed. Invisible and impalpable as they are, they can only be scented; and anyone who professes to have had, years ago, a peculiarly sensitive nose can never be put to the proof. Eulenburg, so it was said, had consorted with persons of doubtful reputation—nay, he had had a secret establishment in the city, to which he evidently resorted for questionable purposes. As to the first accusation—is there anyone to whom it might not happen without his being aware of it? Homosexuals are not branded on the forehead, they are everywhere; and in the free social intercourse of a city like Munich the most prudent of men may come in contact with such people, without having any idea of what they are. There *is* some truth in the talk of the extra establishment, only it was no secret nor did it serve any mysterious purpose—it was simply a workroom in which he could write without being disturbed. As the small family dwelling-place with its many growing children offered little quietude, and as his means did not suffice for a larger house or a regular studio, the Countess herself had persuaded her husband to take a room outside, to which she always had a key. When the Minister, Count Werthern, heard of this arrangement and placed a room in the Embassy at Eulenburg's disposal, the hired one was instantly given up. But Rumour takes no heed of such actualities; appearances are enough for her; and forthwith ready suspicion—readiest too in Court and diplomatic circles—puts a label on an unconscious man, which is seen perhaps by everyone but himself and those belonging to him.

Such rumours, if they were really current, may have been further fostered by what " people " said at Starnberg, where the Count yearly spent the summer with his family. The population of Starnberg had in the first half of the 'eighties been accustomed to the deplorable example of the crazy King Ludwig, who often stayed for long periods at the castle on the opposite side of the lake, when the soldiers from Starnberg would be commandeered for his pleasures. We cannot wonder if in a place where people were inured to such doings, many things were interpreted in a foul sense which elsewhere would never have been attributed to them. So that when these people saw the dignified Prussian Count show a conspicuous preference for a young fisherman as his helmsman, saw him go angling on the lake with him for hours at a time, besides employing him as an extra servant in the house, and in that capacity actually taking him at times on his journeys—to the usual vulgar sniggering was added the no less usual and vulgar jealousy of needy folk, and the arrow was full-fledged: the Count had an "affair" with Jacob Ernst, who was between 17 and 18 years old. In reality the Count—who at that time, as the reader will remember, was entirely absorbed in artistic ideas and plans—had found in this taciturn young man, with his unspoilt originality, a species of literary model which he studied until it gradually—despite a very unprepossessing exterior—became an object of affection. He got accustomed to Ernst, and Ernst was regarded and treated by the whole family as a member of the household. That was how it happened that some imes, when the rather modest establishment could not spare any other servant, he accompanied his master on his journeys. This was at the particular request of the Countess, who did not like her frequently ailing husband to travel alone. As years went by, Ernst became a factotum in the household; and when the Prince later acquired a villa of his own at Starnberg, he put him in charge of it. He sent for him, too, from Liebenberg, there to improve the fishery in the neighbouring lakes, which had been much neglected. Ernst did this with great success, for he was highly skilled in his calling.

Of all the talk and gossip, whatever form it may have taken, Eulenburg would not have thought it worth his while to take any notice. Sensible people would never have bothered their heads about it, and Jacob Ernst in time became respected and looked-up to in his own class. And as to the Prince, there are enough surviving witnesses to the unique position he held as Secretary and Minister in Munich—respected, loved, admired in every circle, at Court, amongst artists, and in society of all shades of opinion, as never Prussian representative had been before him. How should that have been possible, how should the Bavarian Government have so strongly desired him as Minister, how could society have received him with open arms, if there had been a stain on his reputation?

Slanderous rumour would have left him alone, if he had been a Herr Müller or a Herr von Dingskirchen. But with the Emperor's friend it was otherwise. Since envy and hatred lifted their heads against him in every quarter, rumour was fastened on and circulated; and so what was perhaps whispered in Munich drawing-rooms and blasphemed about in Starnberg taverns gradually gained currency as coins of the realm, secretly passed from hand to hand and more or less gladly accepted. Nobody had a fact or a proof to offer, but who asks for these in such cases? Rumour feeds on its own excrement.[1] And in this case there was, besides, the fact that the rumours were surreptitiously spread from so authoritative a quarter —the Foreign Office itself. For there can be no doubt whatever that the spider was located in the Wilhelmstrasse.

Finally it got to such a pitch that the Berlin

[1] It is, alas! undeniable that the sinister gossip was spread by Friedrichsruh, and not only by the questionable hangers-on of the Bismarck family—Harden, Schweininger, etc. That Herbert Bismarck once owed his escape from the sharpest pangs of conscience to the wise and sympathetic counsel of his friend, that that friend's advice and influence had saved the House of Bismarck from many a trial—nay, perhaps the German Empire from catastrophe—this, at Friedrichsruh, since Herbert had been in the shade and Eulenburg in the full blaze of Imperial favour, had been as entirely forgotten as were the words once addressed by the same Herbert to the same Eulenburg: "We are such old friends and so sure of each other's mutual loyalty, that you are one of the mighty few people whose bare word I would take for anything."

Criminal Inspector von Hüllessen, urged thereto by tale-bearing of every description (which was afterwards shown in the Courts of Justice to be wholly without foundation), included the name of Philip Eulenburg in the secret register of persons suspected of homosexual tendencies.[1]

For years Eulenburg had had no sort of inkling of all this. The first hint he received was in 1897, when Bülow gave him to understand, under the seal of the strictest confidence, that in the secret archives of the Foreign Office there existed a protocol concerning a conversation between Eulenburg and Imperial Chancellor Hohenlohe, according to which he was supposed to have confessed to having been, in Vienna, the victim of blackmail by the superintendent of a bathing-establishment, and that it had cost him 60,000 marks (or crowns).

The facts were as follows. In 1896 Eulenburg had had to listen to one of old Hohenlohe's usual lamentations about want of money. As he knew that the venerable gentleman had lately fallen into the hands of blackmailers in Paris and had been bled white, he tried to console him by saying that he, too, knew what it was to be hard-up. Owing to his frequent removals, he had been at the loss of about 60,000 marks in a short space of time, and the State would really have to re-imburse him. Moreover, the letters of a woman of the aristocracy had recently been stolen from him, and he had had to pay heavily to get them back. Hohenlohe must have retailed this conversation to Holstein, probably in a confused and distorted form. Holstein, even then at odds with Eulenburg, had long been accustomed to keep the German representatives abroad under observation by spies and agents, who

---

[1] It should be mentioned that in this there might easily have been some confusion of identity. Eulenburg had the misfortune to possess a near relative who was not guiltless in that respect.

PERSECUTION

of course furnished him with the sort of information he wanted, whether true or false; and so the gossip formerly rife about Eulenburg had reached him with the additions that might be expected.[1] Holstein now had a protocol drawn up, and himself countersigned it. His co-signatory was the Viennese bath-superintendent—an idea which he borrowed from some one else. For about that time a similar case had actually occurred in Vienna; only the victim was not the German Ambassador, but Archduke Ludwig Victor, the Austrian Emperor's brother, who was thereupon banished.

The statements contained in this singular " protocol," in which a perfectly innocent conversation was misconstrued into a confession of guilt, were now spread by Holstein in Foreign Office circles, with the piquant addition that Eulenburg's disbursements had been made good from the Imperial resources. This is the proof promised to the reader that Holstein, since 1896, had secretly, and apart from any occasional attacks of friendly feeling, been working against the Prince as only a deadly enemy can.[2]

---

[1] Harden represents himself as having heard the following from old Schlozer: " He had agents and spies in every city. Their communications formed the material for secret reports whereby the Emperor was to learn what his Ambassadors were about. These fellows, once they knew what their employer wanted, naturally collected all the backstairs tittle-tattle that was going. And it was on testimony of that calibre that people like ourselves were kicked out of the service like thieving maid-servants." Though we have only Harden's authority for this, it has the accent of truth, and many could testify to the facts stated. (*Zukunft.* August 18, 1906, p. 239.)

[2] A portion of these facts is told by v. Treschkow, in his *Fürsten und andere Sterblichen* (1922), p. 125, *et seq.* One is really ashamed to mention the book, for its contents belong to the kind of literature purveyed at railway bookstalls, and places of ill repute. Nevertheless, we shall be obliged to have frequent recourse to it. The historian must not be too fastidious to take the truth where he finds it, and v. Treschkow, at one time Criminal Inspector, was in possession of good information, however vulgarly and carelessly he may have set

As Bülow's communication was confidential, no steps could be taken. But at any rate Eulenburg had been warned, so he had no difficulty in parrying Holstein's next lunge. In July, 1900, in Norway, the Emperor one day told him that he was glad to be able to give him, at the Imperial Chancellor's suggestion, 60,000 marks from the Privy Purse as compensation for the expenses of his removals. The Prince at once refused, saying that those losses had long been got over and that his circumstances had improved. He wrote in the same sense to Hohenlohe on July 29. If he had accepted the Imperial beneficence, he would unconsciously have set his seal to the Holstein protocol. But even without this Holstein would not have refrained from taking the final step—which was that he himself gave the Police President of Berlin confidential information against Prince Eulenburg as being suspected of homosexual practices.[1]

it forth. The above-mentioned facts he had partly from the Prince himself, partly from Hammann. Hammann's conjecture that the protocol may have been removed along with other documents by Hohenlohe on his retirement cannot be verified. From what Bülow hinted to Eulenburg, it must have belonged to the secret archives, which probably even Hammann never saw.

[1] The incredible fact was imparted to the Prince, on the instructions of Police-President v. Borries, by von Treschkow, who visited him at Liebenberg on January 31, 1908, for the purpose of warning him. Treschkow himself gives an account of this visit on p. 152 *et seq.* of his book, but says nothing of the real reason for it. Holstein's name was, of course, not mentioned by him; but " the high official at the Foreign Office " of whom he spoke could be no other, and von Treschkow preserved an embarrassed silence when the Prince asked him straight out if it was not Holstein. The only uncertain point is the date of the denunciation, but it certainly took place at a time when Holstein was still in office. It does not seem to have had any influence on Hüllessen's list (in 1900, Hüllessen took his own life). That was based, so far as Eulenburg was concerned, on the gossip of subordinates. But we must point out emphatically that the police had to observe secrecy towards all parties regarding confidential information of this description, the Emperor alone excepted. So that the denunciation might, if information was demanded by the Cabinet, come into the

Thus was " official material " prepared, so far as might be, in case of any action being taken against the Prince. To bring this about, and that in the shape of public legal proceedings, was the aim of the literary attacks which Harden, at Holstein's instigation, now began, and which were seconded by a respectable group of newspapers—these also, or at any rate some of them, inspired and inflamed by Holstein.[1]

It may seem surprising that Harden, when in the autumn of 1906 he opened his campaign against the " Liebenberg Round Table " and the " effeminate camarilla," should have so persistently directed his shafts against the practically harmless and rather obscure Count Kuno Moltke, and left Prince Eulenburg in the background. There were good reasons for it. He had no tangible material against

Emperor's hands—as it undoubtedly did—without the accused being able to express himself in any way on the subject. Even before the Court the matter did not come up, for the Prince disdained to lift the veil, by doing which he would have compromised the Police-President and exposed the Imperial Foreign Office in all its naked hideousness.

[1] Hammann thought it his business to contradict the statement made by me in a former work (*Die Aera Bülow*, p. 138) that Holstein was the instigator of the Harden campaign. His arguments are worse than threadbare. A counter-contradiction is rendered unnecessary by the testimony of the author, Olden, cited in Treschkow's book (p. 184). Treschkow wrote in his diary for June 27, 1907: " I was much interested to hear from Olden, who sees a great deal of Harden, that *His Excellency Holstein is almost daily in Harden's company*, and advises him."

The reader, on his side, will be much interested in Treschkow's entry for June 20: " To-day I was with Privy Councillor Hammann, who told me that the Imperial Chancellor is very anxious to be further informed about the Eulenburg affair. The Prince (Bülow) thinks it is *Excellency von Holstein who has supplied Harden with material, out of hatred for Eulenburg.*" According to this, Hammann himself on June 20, 1907, at Bülow's suggestion, told the Criminal Inspector the very thing which in 1922 he rejected as utterly impossible, in a tone of lofty superiority. But the reader will have plenty of opportunity to estimate the degree of reliance to be placed on Hammann's book, and its author.

the Prince, all he had was Holstein's calumny—while he thought he knew a great many things about Moltke which could be made good use of in a court of justice. Count Moltke had for some years been most unhappily married to an extremely hysterical woman, who made his life such a hell that on the urgent advice of his friends he had set himself free by a painful divorce case. This lady—she had married again and was now Frau von Elbe—was Harden's source of information regarding Moltke and his relations with Eulenburg; he intended her to be his sensational crown-witness in the courts. By means of her depositions the Prince too could be exposed.

The Prince himself showed complete indifference to the first moves in the Press campaign. No doubt he was indignant at the attacks on his supposed political intriguing; the other kind of insinuations he could not make head or tail of. Long inured to misunderstanding and calumny, he thought it best that he should bear the brunt of the whole thing, as he had done before now. He saw quite clearly that there could be no convincing refutation without revealing things which the public had no right to know. Political considerations imposed silence on him. In this, he was merely acting on the Emperor's own suggestion. When Eulenburg had complained of former attacks from the Press, the Emperor had said, very emphatically: "How *can* such things be treated seriously? We should only make ourselves ridiculous. Why on earth do you read such stuff?" Apart from his own constant suffering he was at that time (November, 1906) in great anxiety about the health of one of his daughters, and had on this account, just as the persecution began, proposed to spend the winter with his family near the Lake of Geneva. So that

MAXIMILIAN HARDEN

he did not make any objection when his friend of the Vienna days, Baron Berger, then director of the Hamburg theatre, tried of his own accord to persuade Harden (whom he had known from youth) to suspend his attacks, which were, as he represented, quite aimless—since the Prince really had nothing to do with politics and was going abroad immediately. The Imperial Chancellor also advised the Prince to get out of the line of attack for a while. So the departure was arranged for, and a notice sent to the papers. Eulenburg told the Chancellor this on December 10, and added: "What I don't like is that my enemies will feel that they have succeeded, and will probably begin again when I come back. But you know that I always follow your advice. There is something terribly depressing about the sense that I am fleeing the country to protect myself from the venomous envy of my fellow-countrymen, to whom I have never done the smallest atom of harm, for whom I have worked to the destruction of my health. It would fill a different kind of man with the profoundest bitterness. But I know that God sends such trials—and so I may have deserved them, though I am not conscious of any wrong-doing."

He had spoken openly of his feelings in an earlier letter to Baron Berger:

" My only protection, such as it is, against this bombardment is not to read any paper but the *Lokalanzeiger*, as I have done since I retired, that I may have some idea of what is going on in the world. But as an old friend I don't mind confessing to you that I am profoundly wounded by this dead set against me. You understand me, and *know* how I longed for liberty, for return to the interests of my family, of my Liebenberg, and how hard-hit I was when, being so mortally ill, I could *not even* be allowed to enjoy the repose I craved for. And now I am supposed to be the arch wire-puller, the "Chancellor-maker," the miscreant who is making the Emperor an absolutist! Really the world is *too* crazy. But what good would it do, if I declared on oath that since 1902 I have had absolutely nothing to do with politics, that on the rare occasions that I see the Emperor I never talk about politics, do not write to him, and for the rest have been from my youth up denounced by my circle as such an extreme Liberal that this rubbish about absolutism is really too stupendously absurd! But, as I say, what good would it do?

"Yet it may well fill me with bitterness to think that a man who ever since 1886 has honestly suffered and striven cannot even be left in peace like anybody else, but must have his grave dug for him with all the dirt and filth that can be scraped up. No, my dear fellow, it is no joke to be the Emperor's friend. But would it not be shameful to want to repudiate the best that is in one—one's fidelity—merely to save one's scurvy skin? A good conscience is always worth having!"

In that letter to the Chancellor the Prince had seen aright. His adversaries took his departure as a sign of fear, Harden felt he had won the first round, and when the Prince returned to Germany in the spring, the fun immediately began again. On April 27 the *Zukunft*, which till then had been silent, printed a most infamous attack, this time with an unconcealed reference to abnormal sexual life.

The Prince did not see it. Iller than ever, he

had vainly sought improvement at Wiesbaden, and since April 20 had been at home in bed with severe neuritis in the legs, feverish and in great pain. But worse than any physical suffering was the profound sorrow that weighed upon him as a result of domestic misfortune. He had been wounded in the most sensitive of all places, his love for his children, and was now a heartbroken as well as a suffering man. This must be borne in mind if we wish to judge his subsequent attitude aright. He had never been one to fight very willingly in his own cause, or to take up a matter hastily; now his energies were so exhausted that it was only by a great effort, and at the urgency of his friends, that he pulled himself together for defence. Stunned and inwardly indifferent, he would probably have preferred to yield fatalistically to his doom. Many years afterwards he recalled that time—the Christmas of 1906—when his family happiness was destroyed, and said that he was comparatively unmoved by all that had afterwards befallen him.

In this frame of mind he had written on April 5, 1907, to his old friend, General v. Lesczcynski:

" My health is still so bad that Berlin of all places would be far too much for me. . . . The attacks to which I had been exposed in the Press, are now to some extent over. But the feeling that a fresh storm may break out fills me with uneasiness, because I am physically too reduced to be able to act with the necessary energy and at the same time preserve my equanimity. . . . I have never been among the strong characters who can take the bull by the horns. Unfortunately! But it is God's will that an admittedly artistic nature, such as mine is, a nature as sensitive as the horns of a snail, should be involved in complications that are enough to break one's heart. No doubt it is meant to wean me from my devotion to the beautiful things of this world, and prepare me to leave it.

"To this chapter belongs also the inward battle against bitterness. I have worked indefatigably and faithfully for King and Country —worked till my health gave way. . . . But my reward has been mud-slinging and this hunt to the death. Well, I still love my Fatherland, and try to do good to my fellow-creatures—but with a very sorrowful sense of ' *You must.*'

"Though I was not among the strong characters, my artistic temperament did enable me to solve many difficulties in the sphere of actuality with a subtler instinct than that of others. Now the poor hunted deer has had a shot through the heart, and is cowering in the thicket. But his friends all cry: 'Up with you! There's no help for it. You must leap the ditches as you used to do!'"

Against the Press persecution it would perhaps have sufficed to arm himself with patience and—contempt. Harden and Holstein, however great their influence on the public, were not, in the Prussia of that time, powerful enough to bring down the Emperor's friend. For that stronger hands were needed, and these were not wanting.

We shall not here tell of the plot formed by those nearest to the sovereign in order to separate him from his friend. The Prince had had his enemies in that quarter long enough. Not for nothing had he fought against the pernicious influence of Court Generals and A.D.C.s. They could not get at him so long as the Emperor was true to his friend.

But it could not have escaped their notice that of late the friendship was not quite what it had been. The domestic calamity which had befallen the Prince had cast a shadow on that intercourse also. A short memorandum of the Prince's dated in the autumn of 1907 runs as follows:

"In my intercourse with Emperor William I for the first time missed a certain warmth, eagerness, sympathy when it fell to my lot to be obliged to tell him of the sad event which had troubled my domestic happiness. . . . The Empress showed me quite a different side of herself; she was like a warm-hearted friend, trying to console, and her sympathy for my pain was such that tears ran down her cheeks, despite the great coronet she wore, decorated with the Black Eagle Order.[1] For it was the Investiture of that Order, and I, as one of the Knights, was obliged for my sins to be present. The Emperor had undoubtedly been influenced by certain persons whose aim it was to put the blame for the episode on me. Though my faithful old friend General von Lesczynski had brought about a slight change of mood, and the Empress, too, had smoothed him down a little, there still remained a something which in monarchs is fraught with danger—a feeling that certain things are 'unsuitable.' Afterwards I heard through Kuno Moltke of something Doctor Ilberg had said—Kuno told me naïvely that the Emperor had spoken feelingly of me and my affliction, but had added ' Quite apart from that, there's something particularly horrible about such things occurring

[1] The Prince had made a grand effort and come from Territet to Berlin, because the Emperor made a great point of investing him ceremonially with the Order which had been conferred on him three and a quarter years ago.

in one's most intimate circle.' I think the ground was not unprepared for the rupture which was afterwards to be so decisive ; and I am inclined to believe that my enemies made good use of the feeling I speak of."

The Prince knew the men who were working against him, for a member of that very group had warned him. Their names will not be mentioned here, with the exception of one which has already been given by the other side—that of the Chief of the Imperial Military Cabinet, Count Dietrich von Hülsen-Häseler.[1] This man had been Military Plenipotentiary under Eulenburg at the Viennese Embassy, where he—an unmitigated Berlin-type with a wife to match—was, to put it mildly, not much of a social success. After some time he was transferred to the Emperor's immediate proximity as A.D.C. and there did remarkably well for himself. But a letter which Eulenburg wrote to the Emperor on that occasion found its way into the Cabinet archives, where Hülsen afterwards came across it, and took it in very bad part.[2] Ever since

[1] Von Treschkow, pp. 172, 201, 207, *et seq.* He died during the critical days of the November of 1908, from a stroke at Donaueschingen while taking part in a cabaret entertainment where he appeared dressed as a ballerina before the Emperor.

[2] Treschkow's account of this (p. 207 *et seq.*) is partly untrue, partly distorted. The letter in question—of September 1, 1897—thus refers to Hülsen : " As to Hülsen's appointment, I may mention that Your Majesty has raised a married couple to the heights of bliss. Hülsen, whose appointment to the command in Vienna I gratefully acquiesced in, and with whom I have got on and worked so well that I shall miss him very much indeed, was nevertheless always intent on getting the command of a regiment, so as to be eligible for service at the front. He knew himself well when he wanted that. Such a Berliner cannot really live and thrive anywhere else, and there he will develop into an original of the first rank. His outrageous scurrility, which makes us Berlin folk split our sides, is quite incomprehensible to foreigners. Though for that reason Hülsen was immensely popular in military circles, his individuality as a whole was not appreciated here. This depressed him, and made him ill at ease ; and so he detested the

then the Prince had had a deadly enemy in the Emperor's suite.

This man and others of his kidney contrived that the Emperor, who till then had known nothing about the public attacks on his friend, should on a certain day—May 3, 1907—have his eyes opened. He was handed the two last articles in the *Zukunft*, together with a whole collection of press-cuttings, and was also informed of the city- and casino-gossip resulting from them. The indictment had been drawn up with subtle skill, for among the persons attacked were two whom nothing could save—General Count Hohenau and a certain Major Count Lynan. Their offences against Article 175 of the Criminal Code were notorious. This to some extent confirmed the suspicions against others named in the same connection, though in these cases it was no more than rumour; and Prince Eulenburg, in particular, had never had anything whatever to do with the two offenders. His acquaintance with Count Hohenau was quite superficial; Lynan he did not know at all. But the Press was manipulated so as to make it appear that what was dealt with was a corporate body of degenerate persons, and this caused the desired sensation. The Emperor never believed in the shocking accusations against his friend; to that we now possess public testimony from the best-informed quarter.[1] But his military suite managed to impress upon him that Eulenburg had not sufficiently " shown fight "; and the result was

Viennese and life in Vienna. I am heartily glad of the good fortune Your Majesty has bestowed on this distinguished and remarkably clever man. In Berlin he will, to the joy of all his friends, develop into a show-cactus, with glittering, somewhat prickly foliage. The shrub does not do so well abroad."

[1] See Count Zedlitz-Trützschler, *Zwölf Jahre am deutschen Kaiserhof*, pp. 170, 237.

that through an A.D.C.—a personal enemy of his—the Prince was harshly called upon to justify himself for having taken no action against Harden's attacks, and to say whether he was " conscious of innocence." The Prince gave his word of honour that he was innocent, and announced that he would take legal steps immediately he had read the article, of which he as yet knew nothing. The interval, unavoidably employed in the harassing business attendant upon the institution of legal proceedings, was successfully exploited by his enemies in the Most High's immediate environment. When at the end of the month the Prince was able to notify the Emperor that legal steps had been taken, his letter crossed a second and still harsher minute, this time signed by the Imperial Chancellor, containing further rebukes and the categorical demand that he should either exculpate himself or leave the country (May 30). Eulenburg repudiated the accusations, point by point, but at the same time emphatically requested that he should be permitted to leave the service—a request which was at once acceded to. It was his definite official " fall " —and, what was worse, his condemnation in the eyes of the world. It had been sufficiently remarkable when the Government preserved an obstinate silence concerning these attacks on an official of the highest rank, and a highly-placed General ; but what doubt was left when the Emperor broke so suddenly and so harshly with his intimate friend of many years ? Not only must there be " something in it," but worse must lie behind. For public opinion the Prince was as good as condemned beforehand. It is easy to imagine his feelings when he saw thus shattered in the twinkling of an eye the bond of friendship which had linked him throughout twenty years to the sovereign for whom he had sacrificed so much. But he was not so very greatly surprised as one might suppose. He wrote to a woman of rank who was a relative of the Emperor's : " I could always say that he was true to me, but I always made the inward reservation that, despite our more than twenty years of good friendship, everything might come to a sudden end."

But even now he did not think only of himself. To his cousin, Count August Eulenburg, he wrote between May 8 and 9 :

" I have been in bed here for the last three weeks with neuritis in both feet and knees, suffering *tortures*. So I cannot come in person. And in this state I have to fight one of the most hazardous of battles. . . . The enclosed correspondence will show you that H.M. has been so misguided as to thrust his hand into this wasp's nest, which is really designed as a fight against, a scandal involving, *himself*. . . . The plan of campaign is as clear as daylight to the initiated. I am to be done to death, and all the venom, all the filth, is to bespatter H.M. : ' So *that* is what his best friend was ! ' . . . I am sick to death of all the abominations and vulgarities that are poisoning my life. But I am prepared for false witness, bribery, *every* kind of infamy. . . .

" They intend to lay me on the rack. That is beyond a doubt. H.M., through *my* downfall, *my* shame, is to be privately and publicly branded, shot through the heart. . . . If the police were to form a cordon round Harden's various pigeonholes and take possession of every scrap of writing they found there, they would have a fine haul ! Baron Berger, a friend of Harden's from youth up (who last winter *ex se* intervened with him on my behalf) told me that Harden is so besieged by members of the Court, the military, the nobility, and officialdom, all dying to twist my neck for me, that he doesn't know where to turn for visits, letters, and material of every kind. But who would have the pluck to make such a domiciliary search?

"Bülow told me that there was no end to the warnings he received from every side about my intrigues! It is enough to drive one to despair when one is ill, and only asks to be left in peace! ... They will stop at nothing. I know that. There are such things as criminal natures, and the campaign is conducted by one of them. ... All I can do is to pray for God's protection. I feel utterly powerless."

The most obvious method of defence was to lodge information with the Crown Prosecutor. Both the Prince and Count Moltke took this step, but without avail; the Crown Prosecutor refused to institute proceedings, on the ground that no public interest was involved—he who was so very much to the fore whenever a servant of the State, were it only a watchman, seemed likely to have his hair curled for him! Here the complainants were an Ambassador and the Commandant of Berlin—but it was of no public interest. Even the request for a disciplinary official investigation was refused; those attacked were told that they must themselves "vindicate their honour." Count Moltke had recourse to a private lawsuit after Harden had declined his challenge, and the military authorities had refused the disciplinary investigation. The Prince was counselled against this by his legal adviser and old family-friend, Privy Councillor Laemmel of Neu-Ruppin, who wrote: "The ultimate issue of such a proceeding would be that Herr H. would certainly be punished on the ground of libel pure and simple, or else for having made a libellous assertion which was 'incapable of proof'; but his good faith would be acknowledged, and the Prince's name would not be cleared of suspicion." He advised instead that the Prince should make a personal statement based on the accusations brought against him by Harden. This was done while the result of the other steps was being awaited. On May 31 the Prince, before the legal authority of his district of Prenzlau, made a statement on his own account regarding the moral delinquencies, and added a request that his whole former life should undergo investigation. The investigation took place; it lasted fully two months and yielded—no results whatever. The legal proceedings began on July 28. Harden, invited to give evidence, refused his testimony. He was legally entitled to do so, being still the defendant in the Moltke case, for the two actions were regarded as practically inseparable. From this point of view also it was unfortunate that Count Moltke had allowed himself to be persuaded to the trial in court. That that was a fatal mistake was only too soon to be demonstrated.

At the end of October, 1907, the case came up for hearing. The Prince was, legally, merely a witness; but was actually to be the real defendant. For more than three months, throughout the whole summer, he had been confined to bed with neuritis. His general health had been seriously affected by this. On May 17 he had had to tell Laemmel: " I grow worse every day. Can scarcely stir at all. Great pain. The doctor, to whom I am obliged to speak of my distresses, because I detect very serious symptoms—of a mental kind—urges my removal to a sanatorium. He fears for my reason and my life, unless I am completely shut off from the outer world." But the Prince would not entertain this idea, lest it should have the appearance of a flight from justice. Then he gradually grew better, and a stay at Gastein brought real improvement. But he was still very far from well. It is natural enough that in such circumstances even the best conscience in the world should leave a man shrinking from a public examination. Moreover, the Prince's intuition, which so often enabled him to foresee the course of events, now warned him of what he had to expect. On August 6 he wrote to his friend Varnbüler: "I have nothing to fear from the truth . . . but distortion of the truth, false witnesses, perjury, and the like I *have* to fear. Those who are against me in this have criminal natures. I do not forget it, and it enrages me." For a while he had thought of drawing up a document, and having it printed and deposited in the Prussian House of Lords, wherein he should give an account of the part he had played in politics. But he deferred this until the lawsuit should be over.

Meanwhile his health again grew worse. A bad attack of feverish bronchitis was added to the rest. On October 14 he told Laemmel: "The lawsuit seems to be taking a still graver aspect. I am absolutely bedridden with bronchitis, nervous exhaustion, and severe pain—this since yesterday morning. Quite incapable of giving evidence at Berlin, unless I get very much better. And how should that be possible!" Three days later: "Dr. Genrich has advised me very strongly against appearing as a witness, and tells me that he would have to forbid it even if I very much desired it.

He says that my health has suffered seriously from all I have gone through, but that I *may* survive it. The excitement of appearing in court would eventually lead to a crisis which might mean the end, or else a breakdown of the most melancholy description—therefore he most decidedly forbids me to go." Finally, on October 21, two days before the appointed date : " It goes ill with me. Lately I have had bad attacks, which make me very anxious indeed. What a life ! And one has to keep up one's courage somehow. If it were not for God and my dear faithful friends, I should lose the vitality which always gives me more strength than I care about having."

On October 23 the proceedings in the Municipal Court of Berlin were opened. They surpassed the gloomiest anticipations. A young, inexperienced magistrate, with a butcher and a dairyman as his sheriffs, from the first lost control of the proceedings ; Harden and his solicitor, Crown-Solicitor Bernstein of Munich, took the reins, and Count Moltke's defence completely broke down. The procedure from first to last was one monstrous scandal. The result was that Harden was acquitted, and loudly cheered in the streets. He had more than attained his aim—he figured as the Saviour of the Fatherland, who had emancipated the Emperor from a group of morally disreputable and politically injurious personages. His opponents were covered with infamy.

But the triumph of the wrong was too flagrant—it produced a reaction. Man's instinctive sense of right and decency had been too brutally assailed. The entire German Press united in the utmost disapproval of the procedure—it had too painfully revealed the lapses in German penal jurisdiction. From many quarters there arose a demand for the

P

intervention of the Crown. Even the Government bethought itself of what it should have done from the beginning—it ordered the Solicitor-General to take up the matter, and he lodged an appeal.

The Prince had, against his doctor's advice, caused himself to be brought to Berlin in the hope of still being able to give evidence before the court. But he at once fell seriously ill again, and was obliged to keep his bed. It was out of the question for him to appear in person. There remained the possibility of a domiciliary examination on commission. Incredibly, the idea was abandoned, though the case (as was to be expected) very soon went dead against the Prince. Not only did Bernstein accuse him of abnormal practices, but there appeared a witness named Bollhardt, a one-time cuirassier, who declared that he had been debauched by him ten years ago in Count Lynan's house. The evidence was palpably false, for the Prince, who had never been at the place designated, had then (1896 to 1897) been about fifty years old, while the witness described him as a young man between twenty-seven and thirty. Hence a confrontation was imperatively called for—yet none took place. Bollhardt *was* sent in charge of a policeman to the Prince, in order to establish the identity of the person in question ; but under the condition that no one present should utter a word. The Prince would not agree to this remarkable procedure. He rightly refused to see the man, unless in the presence of a commission of justice. And the matter was allowed to drop ! The examination of witnesses was closed, and the suspicions were left unrefuted. The Prince would take no further steps, beyond laying a statement of the facts before the President of the House of Lords, his local County-Court Judge, and other high function-

aries. No one but will agree with his conclusion :
" I cannot find words for my indignation with this
court of justice, which can destroy the honour and
reputation of irreproachable witnesses." How right
he had been to prepare himself for false witness !
Two days before the verdict, on October 27, he
wrote to his cousin, Count August Eulenburg :

> " Alas ! I am still alive. I am going through
> tortures ! They who condemn me for not bring-
> ing an action against Harden in the summer, but
> merely appealing to the Crown-Prosecutor, ought
> to understand *now* why I acted as I did. This
> scandal, which touches all of us monarchists, is
> the aim of everything Harden has done. Thus,
> and no otherwise, I foresaw the future—and I
> knew, too, for whom I should most agonise.
> Agonise so deeply that I scarcely know if I shall
> ever stand upright again, though I declare a
> thousand times before God that my conscience is
> clear. Well, others have suffered as badly before
> me."

The Crown appeal in the Moltke case made it
more urgent to attempt something of the same sort
in the Prince's favour. His friends were eager that
he should take similar proceedings against Harden
and Bernstein, for assertions made by them in
open court. These were instituted and followed
up by the Crown. The Prince's consent had been
given ; he expected no good to result, as we see
from a letter to General v. Leszczynski :

> " I have cited not only Bernstein but Harden
> to appear before the High Court of Justice, and
> the proceedings have already begun. There was
> a lot of writing to be done. Personally speaking,
> I think I have made a mistake. But I did not

want to seem stubborn towards friends to whom I have every reason to be grateful. You are among them.

"If public opinion does not acknowledge the right of a reputable person, who has proved himself useful to the State, to ignore such people as Bernstein and Harden ; if justice does not, of its own accord, take steps against outrages of the Press which make one think of mad dogs, and clap such 'National reformers' into prison or fine them heavily—which they would really dislike . . . if, in a word, a country has not the sense to be able to distinguish between *personal criticisms* and filth—why, one's best plan is to go one's way. The ridiculous and senseless prejudices which drove Kuno Moltke to bring the appalling lawsuit that has scandalised every well-disposed member of the community, are an illustration of my meaning.

"And now it is my turn to afford the sneering world, at home and abroad, a like spectacle ! . . . I bow to the Will of God, who lays upon a decent man the heaviest trial he could be called upon to endure. Christ has shown us how we ought to bear disgrace."

He could not always preserve the noble composure expressed in those concluding words. On December 12 he wrote to Laemmel : "I have nothing to fear from any of the witnesses subpœnaed, but it seems as though the big guns would be brought to bear upon me again. I no longer believe in ' getting off easily ' ! They want to drive me to suicide from sheer desperation—and their tactics are very shrewd. I shan't be able to bear it much longer, despite my faith and all the friends I still have."

Meanwhile the Prince had had another opportunity of appearing before the law as an "incriminated witness"—the term is indeed appropriate. A despicable creature named Brand, a writer—that is to say, a gutter journalist—and a champion of homosexuality,[1] had been misguided enough to accuse Prince Bülow of that offence in a pamphlet. Bülow caused the Crown Prosecutor to move in the matter; an action ensued, which of course ended in the man's being sentenced, and among the witnesses cited was Prince Eulenburg. This time (November 6) he had been able, by a great effort, to appear before the court; and those present could convince themselves that Prince Eulenburg was an elderly man, in very bad health and visibly suffering, who nevertheless could give his evidence with perfect lucidity and self-possession. He denied on oath all that had been attributed to him in the first Harden case, both the political intrigues and the perverse tendencies and practices. The general impression was favourable to him, a change for the better in public opinion seemed to be beginning. A respected paper, the *Nationalzeitung*, wrote at that time:

"It is difficult now to understand how the Crown could have declared the Count Moltke case to be of no public interest, and there can be no doubt that we should have been spared many of the painful episodes of recent weeks if that case also had been handled by the Court of Correction."

[1] An anomaly in our German administration of justice:—The paper edited by this man glorified the offence menaced by Article 175 of the Criminal Code. Nevertheless it was allowed to appear, and the editor was unmolested.

The long-awaited proceedings before the Court of Correction began on December 19. They ended, as is known, on January 3, 1908, in Harden's being sentenced to four months' imprisonment. The chain of evidence he had forged against Count Moltke was torn to pieces, the Crown witness, Frau v. Elbe, revealed as an hysterical liar of the worst description; even the " expert " in the first case, Dr. Magnus Hirschfeldt, who had contributed so much to Harden's success, now ate his words—there could not have been a more dramatic defeat. Prince Eulenburg, though still ailing and, as we know, depressed beyond all measure, had made the most strenuous effort to appear. He was not only concerned to give evidence for his friend Moltke, but was anxious to speak for himself as well, and did so. The judge, at first recalcitrant, yielded to his prayer and put no hindrance in his way. His evidence, his whole demeanour, made such a strong impression on the Crown Solicitor who represented the defendant Harden that in his peroration he definitely eulogised the Prince. But unfortunately all this took place behind closed doors, for this time the public was, very properly, granted no admittance.

During this examination there had been an incident which inaugurated the bad turn soon taken by the Prince's case. He had at once, as in the Brand case, denied on oath that he was guilty of any immorality punishable by law. When it came to Bernstein's turn, as the defendant's advocate, to put the question whether he was prepared to confess to other immoral actions which did not come under the criminal code, but were the outcome of abnormal diseased sexual impulses, his answer rang out clear and resolute : " I have never practised any abominations." And when

Bernstein spoke more plainly and said in so many words exactly what he meant, the Prince—evidently overwhelmed with disgust—answered with loathing and indignation: "Don't you call that an abomination?"

Here we interrupt our narrative for a moment in order to account for Bernstein's behaviour. He at that time believed himself to be in possession of proofs—or what he considered to be such—that the Prince's evidence was contrary to the truth; but he neglected to warn him that (still according to Bernstein's conviction) he was in the act of committing perjury. The serious reproach which by the standard of honour prevailing in his profession he thus incurred was more than he could obliterate during the trial by jury in the summer of 1908. All along the prevailing impression was that his purpose had been to draw from the Prince a declaration on oath of which he assumed that it would be proved to be untrue.

The Prince could have no suspicion of this, and at first felt a certain satisfaction. The day afterwards he, just come from the court, wrote a pencil note to Laemmel: "It went really very well yesterday. I was able to speak plainly. Unfortunately I am worse than ever. Violent bronchitis along with all the rest. So I can't write any way but this." And next day: "To-day, as also the day before yesterday, I was for six hours in court—it was terrible. But I was able to answer precisely, steadily, and (according to my own feeling) very effectively. Apparently this case of mine has gone dead against Harden."

But the favourable impression was transient. It had all, indeed, been merely the prologue; the drama was still to come—his own case against Harden and Bernstein; and the intense strain on his nerves was soon followed by the inevitable reaction. The Prince felt that his strength was no longer equal to the agitation that would still have to be gone through.

His condition grew worse and worse in the succeeding weeks. On February 13 he wrote to the faithful Laemmel in utterly hopeless mood, asking what good it had done Count Moltke to gain his case? He was a broken man, notwithstanding. "And I can hope for nothing better, at the best, for they will never let me out of their clutches until I am morally and physically done-for. I have no strength left for reaction. Then will come the moment of complete exhaustion, but not complete indifference—and the latter would be better. The former means despair and madness . . . I am suffering more than I can express in this battle between reason, utter and agonising failure of memory, and sudden attacks of total oblivion. . . . I still continually fear that my state will drive me to put a very tragic end to it."

Meanwhile the investigation against Harden and Bernstein was dragging its weary length. The Crown Solicitor Isenbiel, who was conducting it, kept the Prince *au courant*. It was with his consent that on January 31 von Treschkow was sent to the Prince with information of Holstein's secret denunciation. We can form some idea of the effect of this on the sufferer's state.[1] In addition, he

[1] His feeling is expressed in the letter which he sent von Treschkow on February 2, giving more detailed information, and which Treschkow prints on p. 157 of his book. He considers the tone to be "whining, unmanly." The reader will judge whether that description suits such a passage as the following: "It is absolutely infuriating that a man of sixty, ill and wretched and in need of help, cannot even be left alone with his misery. . . . Truly, nothing fills me with greater indignation than the baseness and petty-mindedness of my colleagues, for they alone have given rise to these suspicions. . . . They want to ruin me socially, in order to get at the Emperor, and my own colleagues con-

now fell ill with influenza, attended by painful catarrh. A worse torment was the endless delays in the proceedings against Harden and Bernstein. On March 12 he wrote to Laemmel : " The delay is terrible. I am tormented by the thought that there will be yet another fiendish trick with bribed false witnesses before we have done with it ! " He thought he foresaw more plainly than ever how things would go, and now regretted deeply having let himself be persuaded into legal proceedings. On March 31 he expressed himself on this point in a long memorandum for his friendly advisers. Nothing of importance had as yet resulted from the investigation. In the last Harden case Bernstein had cited as witnesses who would incriminate the Prince the Jacob Ernst of whom we know, and another man from Starnberg ; but neither had had anything to say. A third witness named Riedl, likewise cited by Bernstein, had hitherto been sought in vain. The Prince thought that Bernstein was keeping him in hiding, so as to use him with devastating effect at the critical moment.

" Harden's and Bernstein's ideal would be to have me arrested for perjury (as a witness in the last case) at the close of the proceedings. They won't succeed in that, but they *will*, by means of witnesses like Riedl, raise the question of perjury, and that will be enough, goodness knows. . . . We must not forget, either, that this case is what Harden *was working for;* Moltke's was only the

duct the siege with such unbounded stupidity and short-sightedness as not to perceive that they are sawing off the bough on which they themselves are sitting. My sympathies have been, throughout my life, with a cultured, artistic, serious-minded middle-class. My instinct seems to have led me aright, for now I find in those circles, remote from revolting jealousies, much sympathy for the position in which fate has placed me."

sauce for the dish. The same crass stupidity that drove Moltke to the courts has been displayed here too. First the compulsion, then the lamentation over the fresh disgrace—but now it is too late. Bülow has no interest in getting me out of it; he will not feel himself stronger than 'headquarters' and a short-sighted monarch, prey to utterly futile Generals. The case will last a long time, and stir up endless dirt. I am to be victimised, and so are all who have stood by me. If I do not appear at the bar, I am condemned from the first day; if I *do*, they will unharness Bernstein and all his wild horses, and slay me in the gutter. So the matter stands, and yet God will not suffer me to die."

In the meantime Riedl had been found after all. He had (as Isenbiel informed the Prince) made incriminating statements against him before the police authorities in Munich. Isenbiel had instantly made inquiries and found that there were thirty-two previous convictions against the man; he declared that in his opinion Riedl's evidence " deserved no credence whatever." " I do not consider that it will form a sensational or in any way disturbing element in the case."

He was mistaken. Even as he wrote, the " element " was in preparation, and twelve days later proclaimed itself. The Munich *Bayrische Kurier* printed, in the early days of April, a paragraph which was reproduced in other papers:

" The Moltke-Harden-Eulenburg affair is likely, within the next few days, to take an extremely surprising turn, which will be instrumental in giving Harden a triumph of which he himself does not dream."

This extraordinary announcement had the following background :

On March 25 an obscure Munich paper, the *Neue Freie Volkszeitung*, had had an article headed " Harden and Prince Eulenburg" in which this sentence occurred : " There is a queer story going the rounds among the populace, according to which Harden got a million from Prince Eulenburg to hold his tongue and make no disclosures." On this Harden brought a libel action against the responsible editor, Anton Städele, who afterwards stated that the article had not been commissioned, but refused to give any information as to its origin. Without questioning his evidence, one is nevertheless unable to resist the suspicion that there was some connection between the plaintiffs Harden-Bernstein and the article which formed the ground of their indictment. How else could it have been known in Munich a few days afterwards, and several weeks before the proceedings, that Harden would triumph over Eulenburg, when all that was in question was whether Harden had received hush-money—an imputation which in itself had all the appearance of being dragged in by the hair? Until proofs to the contrary are forthcoming, it is impossible not to assume that the article was written to serve as a war-cry. It was meant to give Harden the opportunity of coming forward with his " material " in a quarter from which the Prince was absent and in which Bernstein ruled the roast. The scheme, as was soon evident, had been most cunningly devised, and was carried through with corresponding effrontery.

On April 21 the case was heard before a Munich Municipal Court. Harden appeared with Bernstein at his side ; the defendant, strange to say, alone and undefended. Under the leadership of

Bernstein, who—as in the first Moltke case—quickly seized the reins, the evidence taken was from the first directed not against Harden or Städele, but against Eulenburg. Bernstein put into the witness-box the estimable Riedl with his thirty-two convictions, and from him obtained the statement that the Prince had, in 1882, been guilty of indecent, though not legally punishable, relations with him. Then Jacob Ernst was called; of him Riedl had stated the same thing. At first he denied everything. But when, after the luncheon interval, Bernstein—in a cross-examination lasting a full hour, and upheld by the judge—pressed him hard, and actually threatened him with instant removal to the bridewell, he got more and more terrified, and finally made a full confession.

Riedl's evidence was worthless, as that of a degraded wretch who was, moreover (as afterwards appeared), addicted to indecent exposure.[1] The Prince had, at the beginning of the 'eighties, often employed him as boatman, and when he fell into bad ways had vainly tried to influence him for the better. That was all. Riedl's own story was so revolting, the language he put into the Prince's mouth smacked so strongly of the pot-house, that it was utterly impossible to believe a word he said. Much of it, indeed, was easily shown to be false. How he ever came to appear as a witness has never been satisfactorily explained. His own assertions were not substantiated afterwards. Riedl was a false witness, a second Bollhardt. But Ernst, a respectable and an older man—how did *he* come to testify against his one-time master and benefactor, exposing himself in the process? If he spoke true, Prince Eulenburg had made a false statement on

---

[1] At the Berlin trial by jury an instance of exhibitionism was proved against him.

oath on December 21, 1907. Oath for oath. Which had sworn falsely—the Prince, who had declared that he had never committed any abominations, or Ernst, who represented himself as the victim of an abomination?

Jacob Ernst had always been a nervous sort of man who easily lost his head; he had besides been for some time much addicted to strong drink, was suffering from heart-disease and—was hard of hearing. The scene of his examination was later so depicted by an eye-witness that it is difficult to resist the impression that he was forced into his admissions by intimidation and moral blackmail. As he left the court he shouted frantically: " Now you can believe what suits you! " Next day the Prince's second son, Count Siegwart, just back from a journey, met him and—knowing nothing of what had passed—stopped and spoke to him. Ernst, who looked utterly wretched, gave almost incomprehensible half-answers to all his questions. " Yes—but can't you read the paper? It's all in that! " Then after a short pause: " Yes, that swine, Bernstein, did threaten me with gaol. And there was some sort of a fellow there that said he had been present when it happened. What was I to do in that case? You'll never lay eyes on me again! " And he rushed away. The Count thought he was not quite in his right senses, and that he intended to leave the place and commit suicide.[1]

It is manifest that in his agitation, combined with his deafness, he had thought to understand that there was anyhow an eye-witness to what they wanted him to admit. The suggestive force of

[1] So Count Siegwart was to have stated on oath at the trial by jury. But it was not in the depositions, for the case had to be broken off before that stage.

Bernstein's threats—one knows such men, who can make simple, ignorant people say anything in court by merely looking at them—so worked upon the unhappy Ernst that he believed the only way to save himself from gaol was to state what he was wanted to state. That thereby he made the Prince seem guilty of perjury he probably did not know, or at any rate forgot for the moment. What he himself thought of the accusations had already been expressed in a letter to the Prince of August 26, 1907, at a time when the public attacks were already going on, but before Ernst had been mentioned in connection with them. He tried in this letter to console his former patron :

> " Could you ever have believed, my lord Prince, that any people in this world could behave like that to such a good man as you are ? I couldn't. I would have hoped the contrary. I have known you for a long time, my lord Prince. You have never shown me or my family anything but kindness, and never been the slightest trouble to any of us. Don't be afraid—it will be all right. I made someone explain the paragraph to me—it is simply shocking to say such things about you. Such a normal healthy man as you are. I will close now, hoping you will get the better of the scandal, which is not worth powder and shot, etc."

And so Ernst's evidence, too, was unworthy of credence, extorted as it was by illegitimate pressure. How was it possible, how was it allowed, that this should happen ? The layman, going by his sense of right and his sound common-sense, is frequently unable to understand the demeanour of an experienced judge. If ever that was so, the procedure in the Städele libel action is a case in point. Quite apart from the influence permitted to be exercised on the conduct of the case by the solicitor on one side—the plea on which the case was brought was completely ignored! What had the objective guilt or innocence of Prince Eulenburg to do with the question whether Harden had or had not been libelled by the *Neue Freie Volkszeitung?* What was the purpose of taking evidence on imputed proceedings which, if they ever took place, had done so twenty or twenty-five years before? What end was served by proving them? If the defendant, the editor Städele, had tried to prove them, *he* would have had the right. He might have been seeking to prove that Harden had indeed been bribed. But it was no such thing. Städele made no attempt to defend himself; rather, he soon vanished completely from the proceedings. Instead, Harden was allowed to bring evidence for his not having been bribed. Where else in the world is it customary to allow the plaintiff to furnish proof that he has been grossly libelled? And, moreover, such proof was not now needed; for had not Harden already laid his material before the Crown, had he not cited the same witnesses who were now examined? That being so, would it not have sufficed to establish the fact? Why did the judge permit the repetition, in this second suit? But even if we could excuse that degree of indulgence—what authority had the Munich Municipal Court to examine the potential value of Harden's material, and the trustworthiness of his witnesses? And that in a most distressing cross-examination extending over many hours, and with difficulty to be distinguished from a moral torture-chamber? Was it not known in Munich that this matter had long been under investigation, and that the same witnesses had already been subpœnaed? How came a Munich Municipal Court to insert its clumsy hand into the mechanism of the Prussian High Court's procedure? In that respect the Bavarian judge had notoriously overstepped his province. We shall not enquire here whether he was within his strict legal rights in his unusual procedure. Here we are concerned with moral rights, and to that question the answer cannot be in doubt.

The judge who conducted the case, County-Court Judge Karl Maier, subsequently stated that his purpose had been to bring the truth to light, as against the unscrupulous concealments of Prussian justice. Thus he was, by his own confession, consciously overstepping the limits of his authority, and conducting the examination with his mind made up, instead of as an impartial judge. For that we might allow that there were at all events extenuating circumstances. But for something else there is no possible excuse. If he turned the case against Städele into one against Eulenburg, how would he account for not having taken the consequences of his action, and done Eulenburg the elementary justice of summoning *him* also, that he might confront him with the other witnesses? If that had been done, the whole case would inevitably have taken another course. But as it was, it ended by the absent Prince going forth from it a branded man, without one word having been uttered in his defence.

If it had been the aim of Harden and Bernstein to institute proceedings in which the Prince was accused in his absence, and condemned without being defended, they had got what they wanted. The Prince *was* condemned—condemned unheard. It was the moral equivalent of assassination, and—it is terrible, but it is the truth—a German judge lent his hand to it.

IV
PUT TO THE TORTURE

WHILE the knots of his doom were being drawn closer and closer, the Prince was lying in bed with a serious attack of neuritis, accompanied with fever and great pain. He was alone ; all his family were away from home. He had followed the proceedings only in so far as Laemmel reported them—a solicitor in Munich had been commissioned, on Laemmel's own initiative, to attend the court. Thus the Prince had learnt by telegram, on the night between April 21st and 22nd, that the case seemed to be taking an unfavourable turn. What had actually happened he read next morning in the newspaper. One of his attendants found him in a dead faint, and brought him back to consciousness. Under the first impression he wrote in the course of that day to his son : " The situation is terrible. They are destroying me. One cannot fight any longer against criminals. Now they have corrupted even those whom I thought utterly loyal. Nothing can surprise me now." But he had, immediately after receiving the first news, telegraphed to the Crown Prosecutor, begging that he might be confronted with the calumniator.[1] His wire crossed one from the Crown Prosecutor, requiring him to exculpate himself.

[1] The words of the telegram, received by Herr Isenbiel on the morning of April 24, were : " Heard last night from Munich that a certain Riedl had incriminated me before the Municipal Court. Urgently beg you to institute proceedings which will give me the opportunity of confronting the man."

The proceedings before the Municipal Court had, as was to be expected, reverberated loudly throughout the entire Press. The victors saw to it that this was kept up. Bernstein did not fail to give the eager reporters plenty of fresh material; Harden was gloating over his triumph. The Prince, on the contrary, declined to receive the thronging journalists.

Only they who lived through those days can form any idea of the amazement and horror that overwhelmed the respectable classes of the community—and not in Germany alone. But only a few voices were raised in public criticism of the actual events.[1] The prevailing impression was that conveyed by the Munich proceedings—the Prince's case seemed hopeless, he was condemned beforehand. " And so the Emperor's best friend of many years is really an unclean, disreputable man, and a perjurer into the bargain ! "

The Prussian Government offered a far from edifying spectacle. It had now completely succumbed to the pressure of public opinion, which from the beginning of these lamentable developments had overawed it. That it should soar to

[1] An article in the *Tägliche Rundschau* of April 23 deserves mention. It was keenly critical of the procedure at Munich. " Of the legality of this " (so it ran) " let jurists speak. To the layman it appears that the many anomalies of the Harden affair have received a remarkable addition. For we can recall no similar instance of a case still *in nubibus* . . . being prefaced by an insignificant libel suit so closely approaching a trial for perjury, in which the incriminated party himself was in no way represented." Hans Delbrück, in the monthly number of the *Preussiche Jahrbücher*, expressed himself more forcibly. He spoke of " yet further incomprehensible lapses of justice in the handling of the case," and asked : " How could the Bavarian judge permit such an examination to take place, such accusations to be raised, without the incriminated person's being on the spot and in a position to defend himself ? For the case which was to be decided these witnesses were entirely irrelevant. . . . The suit was manifestly brought for the sole purpose of enabling Harden's witnesses to give evidence. How could the Bavarian judge connive at such a thing ? "

such heights as to establish by a really impartial enquiry whether things had gone as they should in Munich, who the incriminating witnesses were and what their evidence was worth—in short, that it should not regard the accused as guilty before he had been enabled to defend himself in strictly legal fashion . . . this was not to be expected. But the behaviour of Crown Prosecutor Isenbiel was more than surprising. True, he was in a peculiar position. In the second Moltke case he had paid the Prince a striking tribute, and now he would have to proceed against him for perjury ! Another man would perhaps have drawn back, and left the case to a colleague. Not so Herr Isenbiel. He imagined that he could cause the zeal of his defence in December to be forgotten by now displaying still greater zeal in persecution. Nobody who knew the man was surprised.[1] To them it was manifest that himself, his office, and public opinion were all that really signified. And he soon caused it to be announced in the Press that he was unaware of any weakness in his position. " At all events," he declared, " I am conscious that the High Court has in no way neglected its duty, nor have I observed in my superiors any sign of a contrary opinion."

The Prince did not think so much about himself; his thoughts were for others, above all for his own family and their descendants. "You poor dears," he wrote to his son on April 25, " how you must be suffering on my account ! That is the torment which will destroy me. What to me, personally, is all this baseness, these lies ! A pure conscience is my shield." For their sakes he was ready to accept the battle which he regarded as already well-nigh lost. Seriously ill, in physical agony, almost daily

---

[1] Treschkow gives us the verdict of high legal circles : " He is as changeable as a chameleon. He can take every side in turn."

subject to distressing swoons, at times incapable of any mental effort, he was upheld by the consciousness of innocence—even when the faithful Laemmel lost all control of himself, so deeply did he sympathise with his friend's suffering. " I survive only because I am innocent. Otherwise it would long have been over." So the Prince wrote on April 29.

Some days afterwards the first examination took place. A commissioner, accompanied by a police-surgeon, appeared at the Prince's bedside. The examination lasted from 7.30 to 9 p.m., was very courteously and considerately conducted, and yielded no results. The Prince's letters were examined, some were taken away. On their departure the two gentlemen let fall some remarks implying that they themselves regarded their errand as a concession to the Press. The Prince commented in his diary: " What a fate! I am slowly inuring myself to the idea that I am completely done-for. How could it possibly be otherwise? I am being done down by false witnesses, Press, Government, Jewish gold. I see no hope of rescue. God gives me inward tranquillity, beyond what I can account for!"

The incriminating witnesses were now to be confronted with the Prince; everything depended on the result. He had no doubts whatever about it. " If the witnesses stick to their ridiculous depositions, it is not impossible that the court will decide to place me under arrest. All for the public eye, of course—so as not to give rise to any appearance of partiality! I am indeed in every sense the victim of my position—of the Emperor's position!" His legal advisers refused to believe in this possibility, but did not seem sure of their ground. " I myself," said the Prince, " have had such frightful experiences that *everything* seems possible to me. I know that I am a *victim*. History tells of similar, and worse, instances . . . and mine is a *political* case. No private person, whatever name he bore, would ever have to endure what is happening to me . . . I am prepared for what is to come, and feel strangely composed. I feel distinctly that God is comforting me, upholding me in this battle . . . and I know beyond any doubt that I am the innocently sacrificed victim. How often such a thing has happened before now ! Who am I, that I should complain ? It is melancholy to be elected to such a fate, but it is the Will of God."

On May 5 there was a further examination, quite unexpected, of four hours' duration, after a very bad night. The police-surgeon was struck by the deterioration in the invalid's health. A few days later this was made still worse by a violent attack of angina pectoris, after a long interview with his defending counsel, Herr Wronker. And yet he forced himself to write down a general survey of the situation, which is overwhelming in its merciless lucidity :

" My reputation has been destroyed by the current attacks in the Press, and my family irretrievably and terribly injured. What can be done to improve the situation in any degree for them ?

" What would be the effect of suicide ? I am afraid it would seem like a confession of guilt, and that would not do any good.

" Flight abroad—that, too, would seem a confession of guilt, and make still further difficulties for my unfortunate family.

" Be sent to a lunatic asylum—again a confession of guilt, even if mitigated by the fact that many would think the loss of my reason entirely explicable by my unspeakable sufferings. My family would be sorely distressed at the thought of my being in a madhouse, and my reputation would not be restored.

"Death, apparently in the course of nature (I could procure the means, easily enough). This would not alter the immediate situation, as regards public opinion. I should be said to have gone to the grave, to have died *a tempo*, 'with all my sins upon my head.' My unhappy family would be in no wise bettered.

"The trial for perjury comes on. Arrest hangs over me—whether it be prison, or the prison infirmary, or (at best) permission to remain at Liebenberg under official supervision. The situation would then be worse as to reputation—yet not really worse, since mine is already irretrievably gone. My family will go through agonies, at any rate until the court gives judgment.

"The case *qua* case. The disgrace of being involved in such proceedings is irremediable. But the disgrace I am now enduring is no less. My family will not feel it any more keenly when the case comes on, for after all that will be merely the torture of suspense. But it is not so bad as the perpetuation of my disgrace, were I to remove myself by suicide, flight, the madhouse, or death.

"Say I am acquitted. Some voices will be momentarily silenced. The suspicions will gain currency once more. The disgrace as a whole will remain. My enemies will renew the attacks. Fresh witnesses will be bought; a fresh case begun—the same game! My family will go through all the stages with me. Nevertheless acquittal, if I could depart this life immediately afterwards, would be a relief. But acquittal is not to be hoped for. My enemies have got the halter round my neck, every one of them—all too damnably. I must not reckon on acquittal. Only in another world will justice be done me.

"Say I am sentenced. That is to say—innocently sentenced. No measuring the frightful sense of disgrace that would weigh upon my family, whatever their consciousness of my innocence.

"The question now is whether, for the faint hope of acquittal, I should accept the possibility of condemnation—that is to say, expose my family to the risk of suffering still greater disgrace than that they now have to endure, or rather, would have to endure if I escaped by suicide, death, flight, the mad-house? To answer this question is a task too difficult and responsible for me alone. I shall have to turn for counsel to my legal advisers and my sons—in other words, to the friends who still are faithful to me.

"In this matter, my death is nothing, absolutely nothing, but a single factor in the problem. As a martyr in prison I should only feel as if I were acting a part. In truth I could face that too, after all I *have* undergone—but not when I think of my family."

On May 7 the witnesses were at last confronted with him. Needless to say, Riedl merely repeated what he had said before. Ernst had a moment of vacillation. Conscience seemed to smite him: "But what else can I say? I'll be gaoled if I say anything else." So he cried in great agitation.

But he, too, finally held to his depositions. To be sure, he could not then do otherwise if he wanted to escape gaol.

Then the blow fell. The sentence of arrest was pronounced. The judge could not help it, for the Royal Prussian Ministry had, at the behest of the Prime Minister and Imperial Chancellor, Prince von Bülow, ordained that the Ambassador *en disposition*, Prince zu Eulenburg, should be placed under arrest. The measure was afterwards upheld, though the Prince offered sureties in half a million marks. The reason adduced was the danger of leaving the facts in obscurity.

The only question was how to effect the arrest. The doctors—the Prince's family physician, Dr. Genrich, was also present—were extremely uneasy about it. They refused to permit the Prince's removal except under the strictest precautions. They strongly opposed any idea of conveying him to Moabit prison. Finally a compromise was come to—to incarcerate the Prince for the present in the public hospital of the Charité. Next day (May 8), after three (!) constables had, all the night through, kept watch upon an invalid who could scarcely stir for pain, the removal took place under the escort of the doctors. The Prince lost consciousness during the transit. But the police-surgeon had tears in his eyes when he was obliged to order the sick man to be taken down to the motor-car in waiting. " I can't help this—it is terrible ! " he gently whispered to him. To his colleague he had said in confidence that he had official instructions which it made his heart bleed to be compelled to carry out ; had it not been for these, he would never have agreed to the proceeding.[1]

---

[1] That from the first the case was conducted under pressure from high quarters has lately been established by the statement of Professor Georg v. Below in the periodical *Deutschlands Erneuerung*, January, 1924, p. 17. The Professor was enlightened on this point in 1911 by the lawyer who had been employed as Commissioner of Oaths in the case.

The Prince spent nearly five months (to September 25) in a narrow, gloomy room at the Charité—a suffering man, almost daily obliged to have recourse to powerful sleeping-draughts, cut off from the outer world,[1] cheered only by frequent visits from his family, and no doubt also by the fervent sympathy of the doctors and nurses. He quickly won all their hearts. Even the constables who were to be his warders were completely on his side. One of them would not be deterred from giving the defending counsel useful hints for the benefit of the accused. The effect of the Prince's personality on those around him is strikingly manifested in the letter from the matron, Sister Bertha Nitschke, which with her permission is reproduced in the appendix.

How indeed could he have borne his martydom without such sympathy? That he could not have done so we can guess from the diary which amid all his torments he still kept up, and which gives us a sort of summary of his physical and mental anguish. Hasty notes, merely to record events; then reflections, outpourings, scribbled on loose leaves with no particular aim or purpose—they unfold a picture of suffering in body and soul with which no pen could compete. They are the most speaking witnesses to the character of the martyred man, and at the same time the strongest proofs of his innocence. We refer the reader to this document, which we give, slightly abbreviated, in the appendix; and will now proceed to summarise the

---

[1] " Our criminals are better off; they can have a walk every day—are obliged to be in the open for half-an-hour. That is not the way here. The Prince spends day after day between four walls; he never comes out." So said the police-surgeon, Dr. Hoffmann, on July 4, before the jury, when he was trying to obtain permission for the Prince to drive out once a week on Sundays.

events which followed.[1] The business of investigation was prolonged until June 5. Harden furnished the incriminating material. He had obtained the names of several new witnesses; many of them were confronted with the Prince—they were miscreants of every type, some even handcuffed criminals. The Bollhardt of whom we know was among them, now under sentence of imprisonment. All these witnesses proved useless, for none of them recognised the accused. The zealous Crown Prosecutor had collected no less than 145 accusers; their number fell to about 12, the rest broke down. Had the case been conducted without prejudice, this would certainly have been taken into account, and the remaining witnesses subjected to severe cross-examination. But the Crown Prosecutor had his orders. "Interests of State" demanded that so highly-placed an offender should be proceeded against with the utmost rigour—else certain newspapers might accuse the Government of favouritism. So, on June 5, the Prince was indicted for perjury, and given the brief grace of eight days in which to prepare his answer to the very voluminous material.

On June 29 the proceedings before the jury at Moabit were opened. The public was from the first excluded, which did not, however, prevent the newspapers from getting plenty of information. Reporters besieged the court, pounced on the witnesses who had been examined, crowded round the jurors; and anything they managed to snap up was given the due sensational colouring, or freely supplemented by invention. So that what was known at the time was for the most part either false or malignantly distorted. It was the pack in full cry—on the court, the Crown Prosecutor, in-

[1] The papers were found in a sealed envelope among other documents a year after the Prince's death. They had never been read till then.

dividual witnesses even, and above all, the accused. Seldom has it been made more difficult for a jury to decide quietly and without prejudice on its verdict.

We shall leave this ordure where it belongs, and follow the shorthand report. The reading of these 1,250 folio pages, closely typed, leaves anything but an agreeable impression, nor do they form a glorious page in the history of German administration of justice. Neither the presiding judge nor the Crown Prosecutor did honour to their callings. County-Court Judge Kanzow, specially lent to the criminal department for this occasion, did not know how to conduct the proceedings as the importance and the nature of the case demanded. It is true that as regards forms and ceremonies less is expected from a judge in Germany than in many other countries. But a president who—to take only a single instance —speaks of the "precisiveness" (*Präzifität*) of the evidence, is by any standard a somewhat surprising specimen. Nor was he a striking example of decorum. He cut bad jokes, was "easy-going" one moment, and the next unnecessarily acrimonious and violent, so much so that the defence once threatened to throw up the case. All through he never kept a firm hand. True, there were difficulties on account of the imperative necessity to spare the accused, who was too ill ever to be able to follow the proceedings for more than a few hours at a stretch. But that very fact should have caused the taking of evidence to be as brief and succinct as might be. Instead, it grew steadily more and more diffuse; endless repetitions, foolish trivialities, futile questions of procedure, and personal squabbles ran away with precious time, and wearied all parties. The worst feature was that the President, for all his anxiety to appear impartial, was never able to conceal for a moment—and sometimes did not even attempt to conceal—that his desire was to see the accused condemned. His summing-up was unmistakably prejudiced. He actually had the effrontery to remind the Prince that such and such rumours were current about him. Since when has rumour been evidence, and the accused obliged to defend himself against it? The old, eternally valid legal principle that every one be held innocent until his guilt is *proved*—that cornerstone of all criminal jurisprudence seemed to have been forgotten by this learned judge.

Fortunately the jury was an excellent one. More than once, when the pedantry and mechanical routine of the hearing had given a crooked turn to the case, sound common-sense spoke from the jury-box and put matters in their true light. During Riedl's examination it actually happened that a juror took a hand, and acquitted himself better than judge or Crown Prosecutor. The latter was decidedly the greatest failure of all in his part. Evidently he had only one aim, to get the accused condemned. One knows how easily a Crown Prosecutor may stake his reputation on obtaining that result—knows, too, that his career may depend on it. But Herr Isenbiel's behaviour exceeded all recognised licence. Touchy, aggressive, pedantic, recklessly prejudiced, he fell upon every witness who spoke in favour of the accused, while for the others, however questionable their character, he fought like a lioness for her young. The notorious scoundrel Riedl was, if possible, to be whitewashed into a person of blameless reputation; and when a Munich police-official, from his own experience, cast doubts on his credibility, Isenbiel and Kanzow rivalled each other in the violence of their wrath. The four masons from Munich to whom Riedl had first told his filthy lies, and who now appeared as witnesses, showed finer instinct—they said with one voice that they had not believed a word of the miserable braggart's tale, and had simply laughed at him. There was no mistaking the fact that the Crown Prosecutor's behaviour was not a little influenced by his fear of the Press. Did he not contrive, during the final sitting, when it was a question of life and death for the accused, to deliver a tirade—which filled two pages—against the newspapers which had accused him of excessive leniency towards the Prince? And this in proceedings from which the public was excluded!

And as to the indictment concocted by this zealous official of the Crown! Only about a dozen of the 145 accusations had survived—in other words, Harden's material was reduced to its square root. But even after this purgation it presented a sufficiently sorry spectacle. All the tattle of the drawing-rooms, taverns, and servants' halls was garnered in and turned to account—mere nothings, distorted by envy and hatred, were solemnly registered as " grounds for suspicion." Had not the Crown Prosecutor's demeanour during the proceedings been sufficient to prove the reverse, one might have imagined that his indictment was drawn up with an *arrière-pensée* in favour of acquittal. It was supposed to throw a bad light both on the Prince and his orderly in the war of 1870 that the latter should afterwards have been in his service as a forester, and in consequence have gained a position of trust. But it had been the Prince's father who gave the man the forester's post, and kept him on because he had deserved so well in his service! Again, it was highly suspicious that the Prince should have made a business loan to a Berlin hairdresser who had attended him for years; that in his invalid state he should, on exceptional occasions, have shared his room in an hotel with his escort—once a servant, another time one of his officials. The authorities had made a veritable anthology of such malignant absurdities. Even the Prince's friendly relations with the late Nathaniel Rothschild were solemnly investigated, in case . . . ! One feels ashamed to repeat such things ; and ashamed even to have heard that the Berlin Criminal Department denounced the Prince before the court as having, when Ambassador, come every week to Berlin from Vienna for the purpose of visiting a disreputable house. And still more ashamed does one feel to read that among the most circumstantial depositions was one taken from a man who had frequently been convicted of fraud, forgery of documents, larceny, and embezzlement. What is the evidence, what is the oath, of such a creature worth ? How much more rational, in that respect, was the Old German procedure, which permitted only a free man's equals to give evidence against him !

Despite all the Crown Prosecutor's efforts to make the most of his incriminating material, despite the connivance of the presiding judge, the whole edifice of proof completely broke down. Not the smallest positive *fact* could be proved against the accused. The rumours current about him in Munich, Vienna, and Berlin were revealed as idle gossip of which not a word was true.[1] The police of Vienna and Munich had no information whatever, those of Berlin had merely heard the tittle-tattle. In homosexual circles, which were closely watched by the police in all these places, the Prince had never once been seen, nor could any

---

[1] There were many indications that the Prince's name had been used by another person.

intercourse with such men be proved against him. When a contrary statement was made, it was shown to be baseless. On the other hand, a great number of witnesses from all classes of society—high officials of State like the Master of the Household, artists from Munich, Baron Albert Rothschild of Vienna, quiet people, members of the Prince's household staff, servants, officials (all of whom volunteered to give evidence)—appeared in the witness-box and unanimously paid him the highest tributes, saying they had never heard anything but good of him. Even a one-time official who had proved to be unsuited to the diplomatic career and had therefore renounced it, but who now satisfied his rancour by retailing back-stairs gossip about his rivals—even he was obliged to testify that the Prince was the kindest of men, and that he would be grateful to him as long as he lived. Of the persons who in the course of time, and often for years, had been in his service, not one had a bad word to say of him. To them all he had been the best and kindest of masters, who looked after his dependents like a father, had an attentive ear, and always an open hand, for each and all. In his house, in his environment—such was the testimony of all these people, who knew him well—the air was clean. All that resulted from those many days of investigation was what the Munich case had already furnished—the depositions of Riedl and Ernst. Even the Crown Prosecutor had finally to acknowledge this. "As I have said from the first, and repeated again and again," he declared on the tenth day of the proceedings, "it is to Riedl and Ernst that we must return—on their evidence rests the entire case." He certainly had *not* said it before, but had given a quite contrary impression by his demeanour; now, driven into a corner, he played his last card, for all his other incriminating witnesses had broken down.

So everything turned on the production of Riedl's and Ernst's depositions, and the value that might be attached to them. The Munich proceedings were retraced, judge and sheriffs were summoned to Berlin, and had to submit to stern criticism of their proceedings by the defence. To this they were unable to give any satisfactory reply; even Bernstein, the head and front of the Munich judicial assassination, was hard put to it—the Crown Prosecutor actually made a stand against him. But he was shameless. His first examination extended over three days and lasted six hours in all, and even afterwards he was repeatedly put in the box—as though he were the Crown witness in the case! Yet he was never able to speak from personal knowledge of any incident whatever.

When the hearing had lasted 15 days, it was evident that all but one incriminating witness had broken down—even Riedl, though the Crown Prosecutor (who in the beginning had taken his measure correctly) now made the most strenuous attempts to rig him out as an irreproachable witness.[1] Jacob Ernst's evidence was the sole remaining prop of the prosecution's demolished edifice. But his demeanour in the witness-box was most extraordinary. Instead of speaking frankly and directly, as one who was relieving his conscience, he seemed reluctant, stricken, frightened, and by no means sure of his ground. It was only with great difficulty that he could be got to answer at all; and when he did, it was merely to repeat

[1] The last shred of importance was reft from him when in the course of the proceedings it was revealed that he had been before discredited as a witness, while at the same time it came out that he had tried to blackmail the Prince.

what had been asked of him. Of his own accord he said nothing at all, but made no resistance when the judge or the Crown Prosecutor put into his mouth the words they wanted. Sometimes, too, he flatly contradicted himself, or went against known facts; and when a question was inconvenient he would give incomprehensible replies or refuse to answer at all. To the defending counsel's question whether he had confessed to the supposed delinquencies with the Prince, no answer could be extracted from him. He showed unmistakably as one of the many simple-minded people who are helpless in the witness-box, and with whom a clever cross-examiner can do what he likes. If a solicitor of Bernstein's calibre, indulgently supported by a judge (as in Munich) had had the handling of Ernst, it is ten to one that he would have made him take back every word of his former evidence. Instead of this, Ernst's memory had been remarkably enriched since the first hearing. He now knew a great many things about which, even during the preliminary investigation, he had either said nothing or lied. Whence had those additional recollections come to him? It was established that in the interval Bernstein had got at him; the latter had reluctantly to confess it. Who else would have spoken to him about the case?[1] These supplementary "reminiscences" concerned one point in particular, and it is a point which demands some attention. The Prince was accused—not only of perjury, but of attempting to induce another to perjure himself. He was said to have tried to get Ernst to hold his tongue. The prosecution relied on two documents which had

---

[1] It was the same with Riedl. Here, too, Bernstein had to confess that he had " warned " the witness before he came to Berlin that he was " to tell the truth."

R

been seized at Liebenberg and Starnberg. The first has already been given here—it is the letter in which Ernst expressed his indignation at the persecution which was then going on. The Prince was said to have made Ernst write this letter, that he might have it at hand to prove his innocence. The statement is too foolish to need serious refutation; but we may add that the letter in question was *not* at hand when the trouble first began, nor was it found for some days.[1]

The second document was a letter from the Prince to Ernst of December 22, 1907. The date is enough to prove how deeply the writer must have been affected by the legal proceedings of the day before, when he had had an encounter with Bernstein and had heard him mention Ernst's name among others. Was it not natural that in such a frame of mind, when sending Christmas greetings to his former servant (as he did every year), he should have given vent to his anger and agitation over the base misrepresentations into which this man, too, had been led? In that connection he wrote: " Besides, if anything of the kind ever *had* taken place, it was such an old story that there could no longer be any question of punishment"; and added that it was evident his enemies were solely concerned to bring disgrace on " me and you and every decent person." Only prejudice could read into these words anything more than their literal meaning—that it was base to drag into the light things which, even if they had been true, were long gone by. The Crown Prosecutor and—judging by his conduct—the Presi-

---

[1] The Prince to his son, April 25, 1908: " Anyhow, I have letters from Jacob, who must have been got at. Unfortunately I have destroyed some which would absolve me; but yesterday I did find one that really makes it all right." It was the Princess who produced Ernst's letters. See her statement in Appendix II.

dent of the court seemed to be of a different opinion. They even thought it peculiar that the Prince should write so long and friendly a letter to Ernst. " A Prince does not write to a fisherman in so confidential a strain ! " That not all Princes conform to the Philistine's notion of such exalted people (children cannot imagine a king without a crown on his head, and yet a real king very seldom wears one) ; that after such an experience as that encounter with Bernstein, a man would write to an old acquaintance and right-hand man, though he were only a peasant, rather differently from the way he otherwise might ... such reflections were beyond the capacity of the gentlemen in question. But though the subtle perceptions of legally-trained casuists could detect a guarded hint behind the Prince's words, what probability was there that the simple-minded fisherman on the Starnberg lake would be able thus to read between the lines ? And even if he had been, in what word or syllable was there even the faintest indication that he was to say anything but what was within his knowledge? In face of this masterpiece of interpretation, the dispassionate layman's intelligence retires in disorder. No one can help reflecting that, as the saying goes, two lines of his handwriting might be enough to ruin him.

There is a parody of this kind of administration of justice, familiar to all the world—the trial scene in Dickens's *Pickwick*, where the note ordering " beefsteak and tomatoes "[1] is made to prove a promise of marriage. If Messrs. Isenbiel and Kanzow had wanted to illustrate this from real life, they could not have done better than they did.

Qui nimium probat, nihil probat. ("He who tries to prove too much, proves nothing.") That applies

[1] Chops, not beefsteaks. [Translator's note.]

to the whole case. The prosecution was its own condemnation; the more it sought to prove, the less it could be believed. The question indeed was as simple as could be—oath against oath—and which was to prevail? That of Prince Eulenburg, or that of a deaf, scared, feeble-minded fisherman who was given to drink? The answer does not need support from the principle: *In dubio pro reo*—that is to say, " when in doubt, favour the accused." The nature of things spoke loudly in favour of that accused. False witness on Ernst's part is explicable. But it is perfectly *in*explicable that a man in his thirties, in the midst of his young married happiness, and subsequently the father of eight children in ten years, should have been addicted to a vice the practice of which makes a man incapable of procreation. Such a thing is impossible.

The reader has had abundant testimony to what the Prince really was. Hence he will feel it to be equally impossible that the man who all his life found his happiness in intimate communion with wife and children, and sought and found his best support in steady faith in his God—whose relation with his worshipped mother could not be surpassed in depth and tenderness—who in the most trying circumstances never failed to show so strong a sense of duty and so sensitive a conscience as are rarely to be found—is it not impossible that a man like this should not only be the victim of abnormal tendencies, but should have debased himself for their gratification?

It has pleased some people to represent him as an effeminate character, a womanish type of man; and the picture has found general acceptance. Such are the superficial thoughtless judgments of the world, even when proofs to the contrary are within everyone's knowledge. That Philip Eulenburg was an ardent sportsman, mountaineer, and swimmer—attributes which scarcely suggest effeminacy!—might be ignored. But his writings! An author's works inevitably reveal his nature. And of what does Eulenburg write by preference? Of woman's love, and deeds of heroism. And again, the best things he did, his stories for children! Only the pure in heart can strike the note which captures childish hearts so marvellously as it was given him to do, in literature as in life.

And if children loved him, women adored him. Not without reason do we attribute to the female sex a sure instinct for true manliness. Philip Eulenburg was always, in age as in youth, a favourite with women. And they were not the least admirable who honoured him with their friendship—she above all, whose stainless image has, in her calamity, become so dear and sacred to the German nation: the last German Empress. Early and late, she gave the Prince her unrestricted confidence, and (her own son testifies to it) " she was a great judge of men." [1]

But there is a witness whose name carries more weight than even hers, whose testimony annihilates all doubt—his own wife. It is by her own desire that we here lay this testimony—which is in essentials what she was prevented from saying in court—before the world at large. The reader will find it in the appendix; and when he has read it he will agree in this verdict—that he who throughout a long life, and after death, could so charm, so bless, a noble-hearted woman was a whole, a sound, a clean-living man.

The proceedings had dragged on for more than a fortnight. The incriminating material was

[1] Crown Prince Wilhelm. *Totenwacht.*

exhausted, the most important witnesses for the defence were still to be heard ; but already the scale had sunk in the Prince's favour. Acquittal was as good as certain.[1] Then, in a trice, the whole thing collapsed. What had been feared from the first came to pass—perhaps the most poignant incident in this terrible human tragedy. The accused was no longer fit to stand his trial ; the case had to be adjourned.

By a superhuman effort the Prince, invalided as he was, had accepted and led the battle for his honour. All the saddened resignation, the gentle submission, of the preceding weeks had fallen from him when he appeared before his judges. Calm and resolute, he had spoken day after day, for hours at a time, morning and afternoon, with wonderful clearness and confidence, to the surprise of the

[1] When in my earlier book (*Die Aera Bülow*) I stated this, Otto Hammann sought to refute it. He had no personal knowledge, and does not name his authorities. I have every reason to doubt their testimony, for (besides what everyone who was interested in the truth could at the time discover for himself) I can call upon two unassailable witnesses. Privy Chancellor Dr. Hoffmann, who as police-surgeon attended in court, gave me on October 9, 1922, his written opinion on the Prince's illness, which had made it necessary to adjourn the proceedings. He wrote in conclusion : " In 1908 I regretted it the more, because according to my firm conviction (in a trial lasting many days one often comes to sense the feeling of the jury, or can deduce it from many indications) the case would have ended in acquittal." And a member of the jury, who had eagerly taken part in the examination of witnesses, told me on September 18, 1922 : " In my opinion, a verdict against the Prince was out of the question. The only prominent witness against him was Ernst, and he was so extremely vacillating and uncertain. No one could be condemned on the evidence of such a witness." To these have been quite recently added two important statements. Count Zedlitz-Trützschler says (on p. 171 of his book) that the Imperial Court physician, Dr. Ilberg, who knew the Prince very well, was convinced of his innocence and regretted that the Prince had not been well enough to see the case through, for he would certainly have been acquitted. And Professor v. Below heard from the investigating judge himself that " the jury intended to acquit the accused." What are Hammann's unauthorised statements, when set against these !

doctors and the defending counsel.¹ He was complete master of the situation during the earlier weeks. But as time went on—how could it have been otherwise?—his energies became exhausted, for it had been only by an almost miraculous expenditure of will-power that he had sustained them.² Nature takes her revenge in the long run. On the twelfth day (July 13) it happened that the accused fell asleep during an interval in which the court had withdrawn for consultation. Moreover, the blood-poisoning from which he was suffering had grown very much worse. On July 7 certain symptoms which had appeared days before (swelling and increasingly acute pain) left no room for doubt that thrombosis in the right leg had set in—a result of his daily transits from the Charité to Moabit, which now became positively dangerous to life. The invalid had to refrain from the slightest movement, was not allowed to leave his bed. On July 13 he was carried into court on a stretcher, and was unable to sit upright. He got through that day, though in great agony; but the proceedings had to be stopped before the usual time.³ The doctors then categorically declared that they could not permit any further transits to Moabit:

---

[1] What has hitherto been publicly stated about his demeanour in court is in contradistinction to the truth. This is especially the case with Treschkow's statements. They are mere hearsay, and shown by the shorthand notes to be entirely untrue.

[2] Dr. Hoffmann stated so early as July 4: "Another man in the Prince's condition would probably have been pronounced unfit to stand his trial; for few could have had the energy to stand upright as he did." And on the 16th: "The gentleman has immense reserves of energy, and, when in court, is usually upheld by his great indignation."

[3] One of his defending counsel, Dr. Chodziesner, said: "His Excellency is in terrible pain. I continually hear him groaning under his breath. It is getting on my nerves." Nevertheless two further witnesses were examined, till at last the Prince said: "I can't follow properly any longer." The proceedings were broken off at 3.20; they had been intended to continue till 4 o'clock.

"The accused is not fit to be moved; he is in constant danger of his life." Would the case have to be adjourned? If so, the entire proceedings were invalid, the whole thing would have to be gone through again. The accused most decidedly objected to this. So an unprecedented step was taken—on July 14 the court was transferred to the Charité!

It assembled there on the 16th, in the committee-room of the hospital. The proceedings went on as before. But it was clear that the extraordinary force of will which the invalid had been able to display was no longer within his capacity. He who had hitherto borne the chief burden of the defence on his own shoulders—lucid, precise, ready-witted —now began to fail. He could not keep his attention fixed. At times he was near falling asleep. Next day he was so much worse that there was no deceiving himself any longer—he was in great pain, high fever, sometimes not quite conscious. As afterwards appeared, pneumonia was setting in. The doctors roundly declared that he was not in a state to follow the proceedings. The Crown Prosecutor himself applied for adjournment; with heavy hearts the defending counsel were obliged to acquiesce. The court withdrew to consider its decision. After an hour's discussion the presiding judge announced that the proceedings were adjourned.

In the laconic notes by which the Prince, in his diary, tried to record the proceedings, we get a striking picture of these events. We give the essential passages:

June 29. 11.45-12.30. Beginning of my evidence. Went on without a pause after the accusations had been put to me. 12.30-1.45. Had a fearful attack. 1.45-2.30: Answered accusations; no pause. Dead-tired.

June 30. 11-12.45. As yesterday. No pause in examination; then half-an-hour's interval. 1.45-3. Continuation and hearing of witnesses.

July 1. 11-1.30. Spoke without pause in answer to accusations. 2-3.30. The same. Had another attack during the interval; worse at end of day.

July 5. (*Sunday.*) After a week of overstrain, alarming symptoms. My leg is swollen.

July 6. 2-3.30. Riedl in the box. Horrible ordeal for me—however he involved himself in contradictions and untruths. Taken very ill when I got back. . . . Newspapers full of the Pierson affair. Shocked at the baseness of Richard Dohna and B.M.—if anything can shock me now.[1]

July 7. 11-1.30. Examination of Jacob Ernst. *Terrible* day. Every word seemed to tell against me. But my innocence upheld me. 2-3.15. After the interval Riedl in the box again, but nothing of importance came from him. A bad day. Perhaps *decisive*. God be

---

[1] Prince Dohna, who had felt personally aggrieved by a change in the management of the Court Theatre, because the amenities he enjoyed behind the scenes were thus disturbed, had blamed Eulenburg—quite baselessly—for it, and had written him a furious letter, accusing him of perfidy. His brother, Count Eberhard Dohna, managed to explain and restore friendly relations. That insulting letter appeared in the Press during the case. Prince Dohna played—to put it mildly—an ambiguous part. Called to account by telegraph, he denied having anything to do with publishing the letter. On the other hand, the paper which first displayed it maintained even in 1921 that it had been supplied with material against Eulenburg by Prince Dohna. The Crown Prosecutor proposed to use the letter as incriminating evidence against the Prince, but desisted on being informed by the accused that he could produce numerous witnesses in his favour, and in particular would be obliged to call upon the Emperor for his testimony.

merciful! I feel very low physically, and then these indescribably base attacks by Harden, Richard Dohna, in the press. It seems as though my cup were full.

July 8. Rogati and Schopf, police-sergeants, declare Riedl to be a credible witness. Police-Commissioner Seuffert (Munich) says quite the contrary. He is attacked for this by President and Crown Prosecutor. The proceedings more and more *one-sided against* me. Apparently the Government has given the word.

July 9. Violent headache—my leg still more swollen.

July 10. My leg is alarmingly swollen. I am *terribly* afraid that I may become unfit to stand this any longer. . . .

July 11. A day of rest. The doctors anxious about my leg. I am more and more afraid of being unfit to proceed.

July 13. An appalling attack—frightful headache. My right leg swollen worse than ever. The doctors think the transit dangerous for me. I came home in a state of high fever, as bad as can be, and feel that my energies are exhausted.

July 14. Very ill.

July 15. A little better.

July 16. A little better. I am taken down to the committee-room—along with my bed and other articles!! There I am now lying, ill, wretched, with the court and jury and witnesses round me, and the room in a swelter of heat. They *besiege* me with questions—apparently they hope to make me contradict myself, in my feeble state.

Here the notes break off. Who, reading these laconic entries, can escape the conviction that the proceedings ought to have been adjourned much sooner—if, that is to say, they should ever have been begun? It was not the doctors' fault. They had repeatedly wished to protest against the continuation, and had only been dissuaded by the Prince's appeals and representations. And when it could not be avoided any longer, it was the Prince who opposed the adjournment. "I have no idea," he stated to the court, "how far the rights of an accused person may extend. But from a full heart and with full conviction I protest against the step that has been taken, both as regards the prosecution and the defence. My health is a matter of complete indifference to me. And I do feel strong enough to go on. An innocent man contends for his honour and his innocence. What is life to him? The proceedings are now to be adjourned. How can I tell whether I shall live to see them resumed? I am a sick man, I may go under, and then the grave will close over one who has not heard the verdict of his judges. On this ground I oppose the adjournment, and repeat once more that I feel strong enough to go on."

So spoke the man of whom the public was persuaded to believe—and to this day obstinately persists in believing—that he contrived by simulating illness to escape from judgment!

Let us now glance at these singular legal proceedings. There have not been wanting voices, abroad even more than in the Empire itself, to find great fault with them. An Austrian legal expert (Victor Rosenfeld) wrote an annihilating criticism of the whole trial, seeking to prove that in Austria it would have been impossible: "A tragi-comedy, scarcely to be exceeded in horror."

He thought it disgraceful that " a dying man should be called upon to defend himself against such accusations," and equally disgraceful that the court should have assembled at the Charité. The skilled criminal lawyer, Conrad Haussmann, gave a similar verdict : " Nothing like this shocking trial in the hospital has ever been known before." But the aptest was delivered by the Crown Prosecutor, Herr Isenbiel, himself—unwittingly, in his hopeless obtuseness. In clumsy phrases, dripping with false sympathy, he declared that the accused's deplorable state of health " had by itself made normal procedure impossible, and would perhaps have made a just verdict no less impossible—so suffering a man would scarcely be condemned by any jury ! " In other words : It could not but be repugnant to the instincts of right-thinking men to sit in judgment on a man so sorely afflicted. By what right, then, were proceedings begun of which every unprejudiced mind knew the result beforehand ? The defending counsel weightily supplemented Herr Isenbiel's remarks. He said what the whole proceedings show to have been true : " When a man who is incapable of defending himself is put on trial, justice becomes a farce, and the proceedings a form of torture." So it had been from the beginning. When evidence conflicts with evidence, oath with oath, the final issue turns on a single question : Which has the stronger nerves ? When a man has to speak from an invalid-chair, and finally from his bed, to his judges and accusers, when he cannot confront them as one in sound health, upright and face to face—that man is not fit to stand his trial. The Prince's marvellous energy, his mental and moral superiority, might for a while prove deceptive, but they could not alter the facts. Could he have faced the witness Ernst as a man in full control of his faculties, instead of as an invalid to whom any excitement might be fatal, threatened every moment with severe heart-failure and fainting-fits, the examination of that witness might well have demonstrated the truth. That alone was enough to make the whole trial a farce; and had the Prince been condemned, there would certainly have had to be an appeal.

But the farce was a torture as well. When proceedings are so prolonged that the accused, after a final fruitless effort, has to say, " I cannot follow properly any longer " ; when two days' interval has to be granted that his exhausted energies may be restored for the renewed ordeal—one is reminded of the Italian tyrants of the Renaissance, who tried the experiment of torturing a man for 42 days to see how long he could survive. Had not the torture-chamber been abolished in Prussia by Frederick the Great? If it was now revived, the explanation is simple enough. This was not a genuine trial—it was a *political* suit, and in such suits Justice from all time has veiled her face. The suit originated in politics, symbolized by the hatred and revenge of a fallen official, by the envy and detestation of ambitious rivals. And political, too, was the motive-power that kept it going—fear of so-called public opinion. That fear impelled the Government and its organs—Imperial Chancellor, Ministry of State, High Court of Justice—to institute proceedings, and condone incidents which in their barbarian defiance of all fair-dealing would never have been tolerated towards an ordinary member of the community, and which the most justice-loving nation in the world could only have looked-on at because for many years it had been taught to see in the accused the source of public misfortunes.

The proceedings were adjourned on July 17, but the accused remained under arrest. His astonishingly wiry constitution enabled him to overcome the acute pneumonia, but his general condition was much aggravated by the continued arrest. His letters at this time show that he himself had abandoned all hope of a favourable issue. He thought it unmistakable that the Government, in its extraordinary infatuation, had resolved on his ruin. He was struck by the remarkable similarity between his fate and that of his ancestor, the great Prussian statesman Eberhard Danckelmann, who had likewise been the friend of his king, and had fallen a victim to envious intrigues. Indeed, he even asked himself whether it might not be the Government's intention to let him die a prisoner. Their behaviour was so inconsistent that anything might be predicted of them. On the one hand, the Crown Prosecutor was urging the immediate reopening of the case; on the other, he made that impossible by refusing a temporary release from arrest, which was absolutely essential to the restoration of the Prince's energies. Imprisoned, he could only grow worse and worse—so the doctors firmly maintained. A lengthy diagnosis, dated September 14, and signed by the director of the Charité, Privy Councillor Kraus, and the police-surgeon, Dr. Stoermer, most emphatically stated that it was impossible to say when the Prince would be capable of standing his trial, and that if he remained under arrest he would steadily grow worse and worse. Notwithstanding this, the Crown Prosecutor persisted in his application for removal to Moabit prison.

This time the judges thought better of it. On September 25 the Revisional Chamber of the Supreme Court released the prisoner from arrest in consideration of bail to the amount of 100,000 marks —this, lest he should take refuge abroad. On the same day the Prince was permitted to return to Liebenberg.

There he gradually grew better, and regained courage and hope. His desire was to re-open the proceedings so soon as his health enabled him. In the spring he thought himself sufficiently improved, provided he could obtain permission to take the cure at Gastein which had formerly proved so beneficial. Then began the second act of the tragedy, more disgraceful even than the first. We leave the Prince's diary to tell the story :

"On the urgent advice of my family-doctor I was to take the cure at Gastein. The doctors sent by my desire to examine me at Liebenberg, when interrogated by me had nothing to say against it. I myself was anxious to take the cure, because Gastein had always done me quite extraordinary good after severe attacks of gout and neuritis. The preceding year (1908), though I was ill, I had been prevented by the legal proceedings. I was particularly desirous to get well enough to have the case re-opened.

"I reported to the authorities through my legal representative, Herr Wronker, and gave them every information concerning my escort and my address. On the day the authorities received these details, I began the journey to Gastein by easy stages. My representatives had told me that the authorities could have no possible objection to make, the more so as when I was released from arrest my movements had not been restricted. The Crown Prosecutor noted on the application : ' I have no remarks to make.'

"On May 22 I started, and reached Gastein on the 25th. Some days after my departure the customary persecution began in the sensational Press, with the statement that I had fled to England.

"The Crown Prosecutor wired to the Mayor of Gastein asking whether I had arrived there, and was told I had. The Crown Prosecutor then demanded a written declaration that I was in Gastein, which was immediately forwarded. The Crown Prosecutor next applied suddenly to the Penal Court, requesting that my bail, which since 1908 had been to the amount of 100,000 marks, should be raised to half-a-million. The Court refused the application. The Crown Prosecutor complained to the Supreme Court, and demanded either my re-arrest or the increased bail.

"The decision of the Supreme Court was conveyed to me in the afternoon of Tuesday, June 8. I was given until the 12th (Saturday) to deposit the sum, this to be in cash or Government stock, or possibly on the security of a bank recognised by the Supreme Court, under the very stringent conditions imposed by the court.

"I proposed to return without delay to Berlin, thus making it clear that I had no intention of leaving the country, but also in order to escape the heavy bail, which I could not at such short notice procure in Gastein. The doctor who was attending me positively forbade my departure, which on examining me he declared to be dangerous to life. Nevertheless, I refused to stay. He gave me a written statement in which he refused to take any responsibility.

"Next day, the 9th, I left Gastein with my wife. My doctor would not be deterred from accompanying me as far as Salzburg, fearing as he did for my life. He took me to Dr. Schenk's sanatorium there for the night.

"The police who had kept me under constant observation in Gastein followed me throughout the whole journey ... I am in fact a prisoner, though I have given the authorities no reason for making me so. I abandoned my intention of spending the following night in Prague, for I was so very ill that it was quite possible I might be confined to bed there if I did. So I travelled all night to Berlin, arriving on Friday, the 11th, very much exhausted by the sudden interruption of the cure and my great agitation of mind. The police followed me to my house in Berlin.

"My representative informed me that the Crown Prosecutor, in view of the great difficulty of raising so large a sum within twenty-four hours, had declared himself willing, on cash payment of the 100,000 marks by the following morning (Saturday, June 12), to make no further demand or take any steps in the Supreme Court until that court had considered and decided on the new situation presented by my return to Berlin.

"My representative made an application to the Supreme Court, asking that the decision to demand the half-million bail should be rescinded, I being now present in person and having shown myself ready to meet the wishes of the authorities by interrupting my cure and returning immediately of my own free will.

"It was a Saturday. All the banks were closed at three o'clock p.m. No business would be done on Sunday. It was a practical impossibility to sell securities or obtain ready money before Monday or Tuesday. By dint of

s

the greatest exertions the capital sum was collected from my son and some business friends in the course of Saturday; but owing to Saturday and Sunday intervening, there was no means of obtaining the money in the form required by the court—namely, cash down, etc.—either by exchange or the sale of securities.

"After the banks were closed on Saturday, the Crown Prosecutor informed my representative that he did not propose to adhere to the arrangement made regarding the 100,000 marks, which had in fact been deposited that forenoon; but required the full amount of half-a-million by 10 a.m. on Sunday morning. My representative, completely taken aback, pointed out to him that this course was in direct contradiction to the distinct agreement entered into by himself, and confirmed by the payment of the 100,000 marks; and that it rendered my situation hopeless, all the great banks being closed. The Crown Prosecutor merely replied that 'he was an official of State, and made his decisions accordingly.'

"There could be no further doubt that I was to be arrested, and I tried to reconcile myself to this despotic proceeding, against which I was entirely helpless. Of course I was aware that after the sudden interruption of the cure and the great agitations of the last few days, this arrest—as a prologue to the re-opening of the case, which was to take place early in July—must seriously injure my health; as no doubt it was intended to do.

"My family were indignant beyond measure; for, as I have said, the required securities were forthcoming, yet could not be drawn upon in consequence of the banks being closed. A final attempt was made by my eldest son. On the evening of Saturday, June 12, there was a large meeting in the Busch Hippodrome, summoned by the business community to protest against the Conservative tariff proposals. The Director of the Deutsche Bank, Mankiewicz, had been among the thousands present, but my son was told that he had just gone home to prepare for a journey. However, my son was fortunate enough to catch him at his house; and he showed himself to be a man of truly noble feeling, for on my son's appealing to him, he put off his journey and despite the Bank's being closed, completed the transaction—saying that it was 'a mere obligation of decency.' About 10 p.m., my representative Wronker took to the Crown Prosecutor's house the Deutsche Bank's guarantee for the 300,000 marks still owing. Thus, before Saturday night was over, and after all the banks were closed, I was saved from arrest by the kindness of Herr Mankiewicz. According to an officially-inspired notice in the newspapers, 'all preparations for arrest had been made.'"

Next day, June 13, the Prince was able to return to Liebenberg. The first thing he had to do was to recover from the effects of the interrupted cure. As things had turned out, it had done him more harm than good. We get some idea of his feelings from a document which was found by chance among his letters, diaries, and other papers a year after his death.

"*Avowal*:
"*June* 16, 1909.
"It is impossible, or almost impossible, to attain any inward tranquillity when I contemplate the new situation. It needs superhuman

fortitude to re-enter the gates of hell. Only he who knows that hell can estimate what it means to display the sort of courage that nevertheless I do manage to display—what it means to take part gently, patiently, even cheerfully, in the daily interests of my family and those belonging to me. This courage is founded on two things: love and —despair. So long as I am spared to my dear ones they shall be shown that courage, as the best expression I can give to my love and gratitude. Not as a display of defiance, but as a sign of inward tranquillity, equilibrium, faith. They must not suspect that I am a prey to despair in the shape of despondency, failure of energy and vitality; that a terrible weariness, a sort of cheerless indifference about the horrible eventualities has taken possession of me, and terrifies me because it almost seems like a lapse of moral consciousness. It is the logical result of nearly four years of incessant mental tension in a battle against the superior forces of despotic, omnipotent, and utterly unscrupulous opponents who have made up their minds to brand me as a criminal—partly so as to throw a sop to that great mass of the public which always declares that it is unfairly treated, a sop in the shape of a 'Prince'—nay, of 'the Emperor's friend'! Fodder for the wild beast whose hunger they dread.

"The terrible facts that I must now look in the face—for in nearly three weeks the trial will be re-opened—are as follows. I have to anticipate:

"1. Collapse of my physical or mental energies in the course of the trial; and I fear that this may come to pass, because my constitution is much enfeebled by the exceeding mental distress and physical suffering I have gone through. That would mean a continuance of the present situation, which is untenable, unendurable. Outlawed, persecuted as a mortally wounded animal may be by the herd.

"2. A sentence of, say, one or two years in a penitentiary, or as an alternative to that degrading penalty, imprisonment. It is overwhelming to write those words—I tremble only to look at them. Then what would the reality be? To me, to mine! O God in Heaven, grant me mercy after all my terrible sufferings!! But I ought to, and I must, look these horrors in the face. What shall I do if this happens? Of what avail would be the indignation that all Germany, nay, all Europe, might possibly feel? Of what avail to me, to my poor, poor children, to my Augusta? What would my life be worth if I survived the shame put upon me, the contempt for me and mine, though I be a hundred times innocent? Suppose they do sentence me? O God, have pity on me!

"Or else I have to anticipate:

"3. Acquittal. Well, suppose acquittal. What then? Am I not filthy in the eyes of all the world? *Would acquittal save me? No.* Not any pronouncement of the court, not a whole succession of duels—nothing, nothing will cleanse me of the filth so criminally cast upon me. Acquittal would be—a pebble in the ocean. Less than that. For the fury of my enemies will pursue me—pursue me to my last breath, that in their envy and hate they thirst for.

"Or there remains to me:

"4. That flight to the Infinite which men call suicide. No! and again No! Why should I, an innocent man, bring down upon myself suspicion of guilt? That would be madness. Who would believe that I, having come to the end of my endurance, merely wanted to escape from the terrible, the unbearable conditions of my life? Nobody! 'Guilty, guilty'—they would say. And dare I inflict such a thing on my dear ones? Force them to behold the body blown to atoms by my own hand? Give them, as the climax to my awful doom, the hideous spectacle of self-destruction? ... No, and for ever No. I have always disagreed with the conventional view that suicide is cowardly, for I had looked upon the resolve and the execution as a courageous deed, when it was not the outcome of sheer madness. But in this case I think otherwise. In this, it *would* be cowardice. For to escape from my doom, forgetting the incalculable debt of gratitude which I owe to my dear ones and my faithful friends, and which bids me spare them the horror of my suicide, would be rank cowardice. Nothing else. But it would be courageous to bear this frightful existence for their sake, to take up my cross, though a hundred times I sink beneath it.

"Our Saviour, too, bore His Cross; He, so pure, so innocent, so great, so holy—and I am only a man, an erring man as others are, dragging a mortal body and mind with all their weaknesses through the gloomy valleys of this mortal life. What is my innocence beside the innocence of the Saviour? Why should I complain of this terrible doom, when such is daily, hourly appointed to mortals? With what right do I claim to be an exception? I have to bear my cross with no hope of rescue, liberation, redemption—until death by God's will comes to my pillow as the great and glorious liberator. This is my duty—a sacred, a terrible duty. In another life I shall see and understand why it was appointed to me to suffer beyond all measure—so far beyond it that with my mortal mind I can but say: ' I know of no crime so horrible as to merit such suffering as I have borne for nearly four years now.' For even the death-sentence would be like redemption when compared to the torments I have borne, and bear. Woe, woe to those who are responsible for my agony! For there *is* a Divine Justice, though with my earthly understanding I can see no reason for my doom."

The case was to be re-opened on July 7. But was the Prince fit to stand his trial—was he any more so than he had been the year before? His physician, Dr. Genrich, and the police-surgeon, Dr. Stoermer, expressed the keenest apprehensions. The Crown Prosecutor (not now Isenbiel who, himself a broken man, was nearing his end; but Dr. Preuss, with whose later achievements we are acquainted), was determined not to be taken in. He set the " Deputation of Scientists " to work. This " most distinguished group of State authorities," consisting of an anatomical pathologist, a surgeon, and a children's doctor, made a cursory examination and delivered a verdict which forcibly recalls that famous one of King Solomon's. They described the Prince as being " probably—though, in view of his neurotic temperament, not certainly—capable of undergoing many hours, extending if necessary over many weeks, of daily attendance in court as a prisoner on trial." Whether his force of will would suffice to overcome occasional lapses of mental power and memory—whether after weeks of trial his psychical organism would be capable of functioning, " is a question which we do not consider it possible to answer with any confidence." In other words—the gentlemen were in favour of renewing the process of slow torture, and demanded of the accused that he should do his best not to deprive them of that enjoyment. They could not, however, guarantee success.

Any impartial reader of these contorted phrases must come to the conclusion that the proceedings could not be begun, since it was uncertain how long the accused would be able to follow them. The exalted legal mind of Dr. Preuss informed him, on the contrary, that the " probability " of an attempted flight would be considerably strengthened directly the accused was " informed of the diagnosis " : *i.e.*, he was not only fit to be tried, but fit to be arrested. Thereupon it was decided to re-open the proceedings. The two doctors succeeded at any rate in preventing arrest. The Prince was required to be at his destination in Berlin a week before the trial by jury began, there to be under observation by three police-surgeons. The President of the Court, Herr Kanzow, gave as his reason for this that " in the interests both of the administration of justice and the accused himself, adjournment of the proceedings, once they have begun, must in any circumstances be avoided."

Must in any circumstances be avoided. . . .

On July 7 the trial was re-opened ; and in barely an hour, before the formalities were over, it had to be stopped and indefinitely adjourned. For the accused, as a result of violent cardiac spasms, had fainted dead away and was only with difficulty restored to consciousness. In vain had his doctor advised that the early forenoon should be avoided, the invalid being specially subject to such attacks at that time of day. They had stubbornly insisted on beginning at 10 a.m.; and what the doctor had foretold came to pass.

The ghastly scene was at the time (for the public was not at that stage excluded) quite truthfully reported in the newspapers. The Prince who, from the moment he appeared, was visibly suffering and could speak only slowly and with difficulty, had nevertheless to submit to being harshly accused by the judge of making-believe to be ill. " You really cannot expect us to sit here every morning and wait to see whether and when you are capable of following the proceedings." " It looks to us as though you were turning your illness to good account." When this pattern of a fair-minded judge actually insinuated that the Prince had " got up " a heart-attack during the examination, his victim did for a moment lose control of himself. He smote the table with his clenched fist, and cried : " That is not true ! " Meanwhile the Crown Prosecutor had not been idle : he had applied for an immediate arrest on the ground of simulated illness and intention of flight.

Intention of flight, in an accused man who had voluntarily returned in all haste from abroad to appear before the court ! There was a general sensation, two sets of doctors nearly came to blows ; and Dr. Genrich, never given to mincing his words, very freely expressed himself to the judge on the subject of the famous " Deputation of Scientists." The court then decided that more light must be thrown on the matter, and arranged for the Prince to be examined by the medical authorities present (there were six doctors in court). It was at this moment that the Prince lost consciousness. The court was immediately cleared. When after some time the proceedings were resumed, the Prince was still motionless and much confused in mind. One after the other the doctors gave their opinion, in which they were now entirely unanimous—the accused was not able to defend himself; in no circumstances could he be proceeded against. Even the Deputation of Scientists ate their words. The foreman of the jury rose, and declared in the name of all his colleagues that they could not exercise their functions in face of the invalid's condition. Then the lawyers had to own themselves ashamed, beginning with the Crown Prosecutor, who applied for adjournment with a cheap display of humanity and compassion. So with the presiding judge; the decision of the court, delivered by him, was: "It has been shown beyond all possibility of doubt that the accused is not at present fit to stand his trial. The proceedings are therefore adjourned *sine die.*"

To complete the picture, let us give the Princess's description of the scene:

"I do not know who was compassionate enough to send for me. A sympathetic official had, on his own responsibility, permitted me to wait in a room on the same floor, so that I might be within easy reach of my suffering husband. When I came breathlessly hurrying in, what I beheld was sufficiently disturbing, for my unconscious husband was surrounded by a group of hurriedly summoned doctors. Everyone was most sympathetic, pressing my hands and my son's, trying to reassure me. But their looks and the way they questioned one another was enough to give me the terrifying impression that they feared the worst. But, thank God, his devoted attendant Bartsch soon arrived, and restored respiration by the means my husband was accustomed to. The invalid chair in which he sat

—and on which the President had so unpleasantly commented, saying ' that an accused man was supposed to be in the dock and not in an arm-chair '—could fortunately be arranged for him to lie flat. Our old family-doctor gave him a camphor injection. The pulse, which had been registering 140, fell a little, and so the principal danger was over. Filled with inexpressible thankfulness, I spread my cloak over the dear invalid, who was breathing a little more peacefully. He was half-undressed, and there was nothing else at hand. When they again removed me from my husband's side, I made no resistance. They said that ' as I wished to give evidence, I must not be present at the close of the day's proceedings.'

" And so his wife had to leave him; this was no place for her, but only for the bench and bar, the jury, and—fortunately this time—the Press of all shades of opinion. The moment had not yet come for excluding the public. There must have been some hundred listeners—in this instance, spectators rather. They had at all events seen what in a court of justice was an unusual spectacle.

" When the second adjournment was announced and the Crown Prosecutor had withdrawn his application for arrest, the court was instantly cleared. So that, coming back, I encountered many sympathetic faces, especially among the jurymen, and at the conclusion I actually heard *one* kindly speech from the President, insisting on quiet ' out of consideration for the invalid.' The same invalid who an hour before had been supposed to be ' making-believe ! ' One of the humane police-surgeons was left alone with us. Stretchers were brought from the nearest ambulance, and in a couple of hours my husband, escorted by all the sympathetic servants of the court and the police, was carried down the steps and brought back to our abode."

V
THE EBBING TIDE

THE second adjournment meant the end of the proceedings. As was to be foreseen, the Prince was never again well enough to appear before the court, unless at the risk of a repetition of the painful scene of July 7. His ailment—rheumatoid arthritis—was of the kind that might grow worse, but could never grow better. Still, when the terrible experiences of the last five years had been lived down, he might have hoped for brighter days. But the police-surgeons, whose duty it was to examine him every six months, were never able to vary their report—" Prince Eulenburg is not fit to stand his trial." So it went on, even when the Prussian monarchy had fallen and the Revolutionary authorities occasionally thought of re-opening the case. The doctors then sent to Liebenberg could give no different verdict. Finally these examinations were done away with, and the case declared to have been closed. The Prince never had justice done him in this life. All that was granted him was the peace of gradual oblivion. When, twelve years after the trial, the news of his death appeared in the papers, it is probable that many were amazed to learn that he had lived so long.

The most devoted care had succeeded in prolonging his days, but it was the existence of a hopeless invalid, hourly menaced by death, and a prisoner into the bargain. He left his beloved Liebenberg only once, for a few hours, when a medical consultation in Berlin became necessary. He suffered sorely from this captivity, and never ceased to long for the hills of South Germany, of which he had been so fond. But travelling was not to be thought of, even when the authorities ceased to make difficulties. No doctor would have undertaken the responsibility of sanctioning it.

Even in the most terrible days he had never quite lost his tranquillity of soul. Now he regained it completely. He had not failed to make arrangements for clearing his reputation, and for the sake of his descendants had seen to it that one day the world should know what had been inflicted on him, and who were the guilty persons. But having done that, he closed the account. To those around him he appeared calm, composed, even-tempered, in his best moments actually cheerful. Few suspected how difficult it was for him so to appear. He used to say that it was his aim, while he was forced to go on living, never to be a grief to his belongings by letting them see how intensely he suffered. The love they showed him he hoped to repay by giving them a picture of one at peace with his conscience, and humbly submissive to the Will of God. How well he succeeded in this, how much he still had to offer his family and friends, all those who had the privilege of seeing him can testify. He seemed sincerely to have forgiven his enemies. From his lips there never came a bitter word, scarcely even a complaint, about his terrible doom; and the complaint was less for himself than for those who had suffered through his misfortune—the Fatherland above all, which (as he did not fear to say) had been sorely injured by it. If one ventured to express astonishment at the fortitude displayed in such patient endurance, he would put the subject aside, saying it was a grace from above. "The capacity to bear the burden laid upon me is the outcome of a profound, ineradicable faith in God and the Divine Justice." This man, whose doom seemed unique in its refutation of the idea of a beneficent Providence, found his solace in faith in the Divine Justice. And his whole existence was a sermon on the truth that suffering nobly borne is the highest patent of nobility granted to mortals.

When he contemplated his Fatherland, fresh drops of wormwood seemed to be poured year by year into his daily cup of gall. Though shunned and outlawed, he was not so entirely isolated as not to become acquainted with much that was going on behind the scenes, and his intimate knowledge of the persons concerned caused him to watch the tragedy of Germany with eyes that saw differently from those of others, and could earlier than they discern the terrible climax. And when his painful anxiety about the future awakened memories of other years, he would take up his pen and seek, by profound and earnest reflection, to combine past and present in such a way that the question "*Quo vadis?*" might receive an answer, mournfully resigned though that answer could not but be. Thus many a prophetic saying is to be found in these writings; the trained observer of men and events had perceived the advent of much at which others shrank in horror and amazement when it came to pass. He had not lost the clairvoyance that had distinguished him in the past—indeed, it seemed intensified now that he no longer stood in the midst, and that his voice could be heard only within four walls.

Year by year he saw fulfilled the gloomy forebodings which so long had haunted him. When the Government went through the serious crisis of

November, 1908, it was manifest that he had been right when in the 'nineties he had frustrated Holstein's design of relegating the Emperor as a controlling factor in the conduct of affairs. The opportunity presented itself in 1908. An end could then have been put to personal rule; but the Reichstag showed itself incapable of seizing the moment. The political representatives of the nation failed in their task, the people were not ripe for self-government—exactly as Eulenburg had long ago foretold.

With 1909 came the fall of Bülow. Could anyone have blamed Eulenburg if he had felt something resembling malicious pleasure in that event? Bülow, the only man who could have saved him, had left him in the lurch—the old friend to whom in his youth he had written: " I shall never forget what you have done for us ! " To remain in office had been his motive; and the sacrifice of his friend had availed him nothing—for when the Eulenburg case was compulsorily adjourned for the second time, Bülow was no longer Chancellor. Who would not have known a kind of satisfaction in this retributive justice? But the Prince was far from doing so. He had indeed felt keenly the failure of his friend to stand by him in the hour of trial; yet he had forgiven and excused him. For in fact Eulenburg thought he knew that Bülow had long been in thraldom, unable to act freely. And on various occasions he did confess that this Imperial Chancellor, who in fact owed his position to him and for whom he therefore felt in some degree responsible, had not fulfilled his expectations. " I had," he said, " the highest opinion of Bülow's talents, his intellect, his erudition; and in those respects he never disappointed me. But I did overestimate his character. As a character Bülow has

BERNARD VON BÜLOW

failed—I cannot deny it. But how could I have suspected, after all, that he would ever have got into such terrible thraldom to Holstein ? " About the self-satisfaction so freely displayed by Bülow in his *Deutsche Politik*—ostensibly a tribute to the Emperor —Eulenburg remarked sarcastically that the publication was, to put it mildly, an indiscretion, and all the more so because the author imagined that he was recommending himself as the successor of his successor ! There was a certain effrontery in Bülow's references to his own political consistency ; they could only be justified " if he had also told us how and when and why that consistency failed to impose itself—how and when he allowed himself to be turned aside. For in those frustrations consists the real history of Bülow's administration."

Nor did the Prince deny that Bülow had shown himself wanting in his attitude towards the military camarilla round the Emperor, as well as towards Harden's campaign of slander. But he looked at the position from every side. " As a result of the halter Holstein had fastened round his neck, Bülow was in a horrible dilemma with regard to me, and so I don't want to throw any big stones at him—only just a little one, perhaps ! To which I would add that famous statesmen have rarely, very rarely, had blameless characters. . . . When he was selected for Secretary of State, from which the Chancellorship developed, the principal thing I thought of was intellect. If a man so intimately connected with the Emperor in the conduct of home and foreign policy did not possess a commanding intellect, both were lost, their days were numbered. Odd enough, when one thinks how little the Emperor cared about intellect in his military environment ! "

In this connection the Prince took the trouble to

state exhaustively in writing why he had thought it his duty to nominate Bülow. Of the 17 heads of foreign Embassies who might at that time have been candidates for the posts of Secretary of State and Imperial Chancellor, only five besides Bülow had been considered by him, namely :

"1. Count Hatzfeldt : quite in the first rank, but very frail in health, and hence not available.

"2. Prince Münster : very clever, too old, too much of an Englishman.

"3. von Radowitz : thoroughly suitable, but too much hated by Holstein to have any chance of surviving in Berlin.

"4. Baron von Marschall : thoroughly suitable, but hated by the Emperor, who is urged thereto by A.D.C. intrigues.

"5. von Kiderlen : well-adapted for State Secretary ; but hitherto hunted from Court by military intrigues. His way of life would preclude his ever becoming Chancellor.

"Who remained to us ? Only Bülow. In that ebb-tide I could perceive but one wave that exhilarated the spirit, salty, full-flowing—and breaking smoothly upon any and every shore ! No one who did not understand every turn in affairs could say why Bülow came to power. If in the end he was, like many others, ground in the mill by Holstein, that was merely the logic of grim facts."

Thus it was, perhaps, only a much qualified recognition of superiority which made Eulenburg then and afterwards declare that his friend Bülow was the only possible Imperial Chancellor. But he stuck to his guns ; and of Bülow's fall he said that it was nothing less than " a national calamity." When Bülow was succeeded by the entirely un-

The Ebbing Tide

sophisticated Bethmann-Hollweg, with no one better than Herr von Schön to support him as Minister of Foreign Affairs, Eulenburg observed with caustic wit: " I feel as though I were sailing in a ship where the captain is an actor, the first mate a professor, and the second an Alpine climber."

He was terribly perturbed by the notorious Zabern incident in December, 1913, when the great majority of German representatives thought the moment had come for fulminating against German militarism, though the sharpened bayonets of their neighbours were already pointed, East and West, at the breast and back of the Empire. The Prince had long had his very sceptical ideas about the Alsatian question. He thought that since in forty-two years Germany had not succeeded in really attaching the originally German Alsace to the German Empire, it was hopeless to think of achieving it, for the only safe and effectual method —namely " five-and-twenty years with no Prussian soldiers or Prussian officials "—was " for many reasons impracticable."

But the way in which the Reichstag handled the incident (in itself so unimportant), laying bare that weakest point in the Empire for all the world to see, made the Prince " buckle on his armour again," and during a sleepless night he confided his indignant reflections to paper.

" Small blame to the Reichstag " (so he wrote), " for its vote of want of confidence in the Chancellor, though in general it is wiser, if one has no gun, not to talk about shooting people—but only an utter lack of political common-sense could have afforded *urbi et orbi* such a spectacle in connection with such an incident. Not another nation in the world would have made such a show of itself. That serious politicians should have babbled, for Europe at large to hear, about Zabern and the military and civil antagonisms there—so great a lack of political sagacity I should not have thought possible, despite my low estimation of our political abilities. I was absolutely beside myself. There are plenty of committees and other secret conferences in which an incapable Chancellor can be got rid of by hook or by crook. But alas! there was another reason for my being over-wrought during that restless night after the debate in the Reichstag. I could so plainly see in imagination all the figures at Donaueschingen,[1] whom I know to the marrow of all their bones—laughing, mimicking the Alsatian dialect, making fun of the Chancellor who, though he 'hadn't tried to slither out of the mess,' *had* 'faced the music' too late, 'when the fat was in the fire' and couldn't be got out of it between the final 'spicy bit out of *Ulk*' and the cranking-up of his car for the drive back.[2] I could hear the other remarks about 'that aggressive blackguard,' Lieutenant Forstner, 'for ever grousing about what isn't in the least his business'; and 'the impudence of those Alsatians that some day we'll properly hamstring by snipping off their precious "constitution," if this sort of thing goes on.' Yes—I could hear everything that was said at Donaueschingen and in the Reichstag, and went through an entirely superfluous night of pain and sleeplessness, in the course of which I wrote down these reflections. My only consolation was the thought that lying in bed with gout and heart-failure is less of a hell than having to take part in that piece of tomfoolery which calls itself the German Government."

[1] The Emperor was just then at Donaueschingen with all his suite, on a visit to the Prince zu Fürstenberg.

[2] The Emperor's suite had contrived that the sovereign should have "no time" to hear the Chancellor's detailed report.

The Ebbing Tide

With growing anxiety the Prince, throughout all these years, followed the movement of the thunder-clouds that drew nearer and nearer, and finally seemed to darken the German sky from end to end. It was the period of the grand Fleet-building. In a comprehensive memorandum of 1912 the Prince, moved doubtless by the negotiations then in prospect with England for mutual limitation of shipbuilding, set himself to analyse the problem. He had never been able to believe that Germany's future lay on the water; a battle-fleet on the English pattern seemed to him a contradiction of nature, since Germany " is neither an island like England nor a boot pushing out into the sea like Italy ; but a splendid green pasture on terra-firma, where the sheep are full-fed and guarded by the military sheep-dogs, and the cattle chew the cud of politics." And when the fleet-building went on and on and on, the Prince regarded it as a challenge to England which would inevitably lead to war— a war which in Germany (as he had every reason to know) neither Emperor nor people desired. He was not among the convinced Anglophiles, being rather inclined to regard England as the steadfast foe to German development, and he looked sceptically on her friendly advances. But he thought there was another and less perilous way of opposing English hostility : " Quiet and consistent execution of the programme once representative of the broad lines of our policy—namely, the attainment of a coalition between the Continental Powers of Europe." These possibilities were in his view frittered away when in 1905 (owing to pressure from Holstein) the understanding with France— which Eulenburg thought was then, if rightly handled, in a better way than ever before—was for all time ruptured by the aggressive treatment of the Morocco question, while simultaneously the Russian alliance had been stifled at birth by the Emperor's blundering rashness at Björkö. Whereon the Prince commented sardonically : " One should never forget that a discussion between two monarchs is propitious only when it confines itself to the weather."

When the battle-fleet was nevertheless proceeded with and made still more powerful, though it was wholly unprotected, without Continental backing of any kind, the Prince beheld what he considered a challenge to fate. There was now only one prospect—war. " If successful—*tant mieux!* Then we could honestly and undisguisedly pose for good and all as a militarist state ! I almost believe that although we should be feared, we should be more respected, less hated, if we appeared in our naked Prussian aggressiveness.· But what would be our lot if, isolated by political blunders, we fell as a prey to united Europe, with our dreadnoughts, Zeppelins, and big guns ? Would not a latter-day 1813 succeed to a latter-day 1806 ? "

Two years after those words were written the war broke out—the war which was to lead to the latter-day 1806. The Prince was among those most sorely afflicted by it. His second son, Count Siegwart, who inherited his great musical gifts, and whose very promising compositions had even then (to the pride and joy of his father) attracted notice, died severely wounded in the lazaretto at Jaslo in Galicia on June 2, 1915. Two sons of his servants, whom he had seen grow up and cared for as if they had been his own children, never returned. And with these most intimate and irretrievable losses was mingled the searing agony of his country's downfall.

From the outset of the war the Prince had had his

very considered doubts of the issue, for he knew too well the personal inadequacy of German political leadership, in its whole disastrous extent. The terrible mistakes committed by the Government immediately before the war broke out were to him, as an expert of many years' experience, from the first apparent. In his opinion Germany's only chance of averting war was by way of a European conference—it might mean losses for her, might even mean grave developments in internal politics; but it would not be a complete collapse. In his view it was regrettable that the proposal for a conference should have come from England instead of Germany, and that Germany's answer was not conciliatory made matters worse than ever. The subsequent revelations on the Austrian and German sides confirmed him in this opinion. " I am not sorry," he wrote at this time, " that my official activities came to an end quite twelve years before the outbreak of war. But one feeling does perpetually torment me—that if I had still been at Tschirschky's side as Ambassador in Vienna, this terrible war might possibly have been prevented."

That it did come to war, and come in the way it did, he—doubtless quite correctly—attributed to the fact that the whole political situation was misjudged by those in authority, because all the prominent representatives abroad were at that time hopelessly inefficient. This again seemed to him a result of " the Old-Prussian stinginess which, despite the enormously increased national resources," kept the Ambassadors and Ministers on such low salaries " that we were not able to select the best brains from the cultured and—so far as good breeding goes—most representative circles, but had to content ourselves with those men whose private means sufficed to supplement the inadequate provision for expenses of State. Thus it was more or less a lucky chance when we had a really brilliant man in a foreign post." To this was added false economy with respect to the foreign Press and the intelligence-service. "If a Government sets up moral scruples about espionage and bribery abroad or seeks to economise on that service, it comes to grief by its own stupidity; and I am afraid that the renowned German common-sense has long, in that respect, been wearing the cap and bells of folly. If I had been called to a leading position in the Foreign Office, I should have taken a very firm stand against this cardinal error." Another unfortunate factor was the constantly predominating influence of the military elements in the Emperor's environment. Foreign policy became more and more "the battlefield of an embittered conflict between the Office on the one side" and the highly-placed military authorities on the other. "And again, between those antagonisms stood the Emperor, conducting a policy of his own as between sovereign and sovereign. Inevitably this made the Prussian Army a political factor. But, as a result of inadequate training for the political sphere, it followed that the best army produced the worst politicians."

And yet, as the war went on, even the Prince came to wish that the Army Chiefs had the last word in policy. When Germany was reduced from Bethmann to Michaelis and Hertling; when the Reichstag and the parties insisted on their say, until the world at large looked on with derision at the farce of Brest-Litowsk—then the one-time diplomat and statesman, who had fought a life-long battle against the political influence of the officers, would fain have let the Generals take the reins. "How horrible it is," he exclaimed, "to

have lions at the front, and asses in power at home !
May God grant us enlightenment in these fateful
days, that we may call the lions to the rescue ! "

After all he had seen and known, and interpreted
with unerring insight, the ultimate catastrophe
could not surprise him. It distressed him none the
less for that. Far from " feeling the sort of satisfaction a fortune-telling gipsy might at the fulfilment
of her prophecy," to him the fulfilment of the German doom was likewise the seal set upon his own
ruined life, the " deadly outcome " of his agony.
He was for ever trying to form some clear conception of the how and why of that dread issue. In
solitary reflection—" scared by the flames of the
World War, stewing in the juice of the brainlessness
of a genuine German revolution, when the modest
practical aim was strangled by the sentimental unpractical "—he would muse on the past, going
back to the days when Bismarck was fighting the
Crown Princess and teaching her son, the future
William II, to hate England ; when Emperor
Frederick died, and his death cut short the normal
evolution towards different forms of government,
which under Bismarck's personal leadership would
have resulted beneficially. The seed that was then
sown, he now saw ripen. Even the connection
between his own doom and that of the nation
became terribly clear to him. The events from
1907 to 1909, his victimisation, the November
crisis of 1908, the fall of Bülow, had been the
earliest heralds of what came to pass ten years
later—the first unmistakable signs of the universal
futility and mediocrity, the first utter breakdown
of all the political factors. What had then been no
more than a disturbing symptom now proclaimed
itself beyond all doubt. " Behind the mask of
power and wisdom was suddenly visible the feeble

countenance that bespoke an immature political body, which was smitten to the earth by the stupendous bludgeon of world-history, and has become the football of unbridled popular passions—for the masses are as one ravenous wild beast escaped from the cage. Where is their tamer? I cannot perceive him. For we are confronted with the spectacle of a whole nation unripe for policy, a nation without brain or brawn, a nation that resembles a neurotic, hysterical woman."

Events never ceased to confirm that judgment.

"It will always be a puzzle to me," wrote the Prince on May 6, 1920, "how Germany could come to such utter grief as she did in the sphere of statecraft and diplomacy. No better than Hohenlohe at Prenzlau in 1806—after Jena. We farmers now and again find that a pedigree bull, which has cost his owner an enormous sum of money, is utterly useless for breeding. Once upon a time we had statesmen like Stein, Hardenberg, Bismarck. And to-day? The Guards and Borussa systems really seem to have destroyed the attributes necessary to keep the stock in good case for breeding. The Guards and Borussa were sterile bulls. . . . The powerful Prussian nobility has been enfeebled instead of strengthened by its submergence in the purely military ideal, in the military service of the State. Even its finest flower, Bismarck, destroyed what he sincerely wished to foster by the fact that he always, at home and abroad, appeared in uniform."

Just as in this instance he unerringly laid his finger on the sore spot—the defective training given to the sons of the governing classes—so did he seek and find the ultimate causes of Germany's collapse in the same quarter which had occupied his thoughts when in 1903 he wrote his prophetic essay on Old

Prussianism. He traced these causes to the want of any real connection between the twin poles of German life—the Prussian army on the one side with its markedly material outlook, its prejudices and foibles; and German science on the other, with its pedantry, its conception of "science" in the broadest sense as a term not only for the claims to respect rightly put forth by the savants, but for the entire educational system. He recalled the frequent pronouncements of both Hohenlohe and Bülow that "in Germany the professor rules"; though at the same time the military, that opposite pole, seemed to have forcibly acquired equal authority over the "nation in arms." A state in which theory and practice, mind and matter, had so simultaneously and uniformly developed, might well have presented the ideal, had not the connection between the twin poles been lacking. "The bridge was not there." The bridge between the German professor and the German subaltern was no less absent than that between the civilian and the soldier. "It was natural that in the critical hour of 1914 both poles should be fused in the blaze of enthusiasm. The bridge seemed to emerge —but it was constructed of flame, not of stone and iron. And the flames parted company when it was a question of uniting in the time of trial which tests a nation to the utmost, and forces it to discriminate between the genuine and the spurious. Therefore we went under. I see the cause of that going under in the want of a *juste milieu*, in the non-existent bridge."

But however gloomy the present might be, the Prince refused to despair, though his hopes were modest. "The great question is—are we going through a fermentation from which some profitable ingredients may be isolated, or a process of disintegration which will leave only ashes behind it? These two possibilities torment a thinking man as he gazes timidly upward to the sword of justice, hovering above in the clouds, and beside it the spirits of our fallen heroes, who have laid down their lives for *this* Fatherland! I, who despite my country's doom still carry about a tabloid of optimism in a little pill-box, incline to the former possibility. I leave the other to my pessimistic friends."

For nearly three whole years the Prince had to look on at the grisly spectacle presented by the German State since November 9, 1918. Perhaps he was able to endure it only because in spirit he already belonged to another world. His wiry constitution resisted these fresh blows, despite the many assaults it had already suffered. " I am a dog on Fate's vivisection table," he wrote in February, 1921. " It is really miraculous how long some kinds of dog can resist the poison injected into their veins. No one is more astonished at this than I am. It is now nearly twenty years since I had my first dose, and I am still alive, though of course in reality done for." It even seemed as if his energies were reviving. The beautiful summer of 1921 afforded him days more endurable than he had known for many a year.

Then on September 12 he had a slight sore throat, which at first seemed nothing. Gradually it grew more alarming, and the doctor was summoned. But before the remedies instantly applied could take effect, his heart failed, and finally ceased to beat—the heart which had borne and suffered so much. In the Princess's arms, with the Pater Noster on his lips, the Prince passed away peacefully and painlessly on September 17, 1921, at three o'clock in the afternoon.

Five days later he was borne to his last rest in the mausoleum on the estate. The entire population of Liebenberg and the neighbourhood, without distinction of class or party, and numerous friends from a distance followed the body to the grave. May the time be at hand when the rest of the world shall recognise his achievements, do honour to his name—and know him for what he was : a pattern of Prussian conscientiousness, a victim to his German conception of fidelity to friends, a truly noble, truly good man.

APPENDICES

I

The Real Privy Councillor Fritz von Holstein

IN September, 1919, a friend of the Prince's, who had been permitted to look through his private correspondence, put the following questions in a letter to him :

" If your correspondence is at any time to be published, the world will probably raise the question of why the Emperor's most intimate friend set himself in opposition to Holstein's views, when the latter—so early as 1895—resolved to make personal government impossible for the Emperor. The letters give no answer to this, or at any rate not an explicit one. Nor is that to be expected. For it is easy to conceive that even to Holstein himself it could not have been fully explained. I have long considered the point, and was at one time inclined to regret that Holstein's intentions were not carried out. But afterwards, as a result of further reflection, it became clear to me that this was a mistake. Suppose things had gone as Holstein wished, and the Emperor been obliged to give up personally interfering with affairs of State—what would have been the consequences ? William II would never have genuinely acquiesced in that relinquishment ; he would have taken every opportunity to shake off his ' trammels.' Such an opportunity he would have found, unless he had been confronted by a steadfast and united authority, capable of taking and keeping the lead. Where was that to come from ? Officialdom *qua* officialdom—never ; even if it had been at one with itself, instead of being divided by a hundred antagonisms both personal and practical, and internally at war. The logical consequence would have been that the decision would have lain with the national representatives. That would have meant that the catastrophe would have come from the other end, or rather that it would have been accelerated. With such a Reichstag as we had had since 1890 (and more and more so as time went on), the Empire would have rushed to its destruction ten years earlier. It seems to me that these recent years have put the question to the proof. What Holstein wanted in 1895 came to pass in 1908 (possibly he himself brought it about). What good did it do us ? By 1909 it was a thing of the past, and the only thing that could then befall was—the rule of the Centre Party ! In 1895 exactly the same would have resulted. It would certainly have saved us from the errors of 'world-policy' and fleet-building, but would have left us poorer by the loss of a great memory ; and memories are now our only capital.

" Am I right in these reflections, and have I come near to divining the motives which urged you, Excellency, to protect the Emperor's person against the assaults of Holstein and Co. ? It would be of great value to me—and in future to all who may read the letters in question—to have a word of explanation."

To this the Prince replied on September 28, 1919 :

" You ask me why I set myself in opposition to

Holstein's views when he resolved to make the Emperor's personal government impossible.

"The reasons you suggest for my attitude, in putting me that question—one which will undoubtedly be raised by many readers of my correspondence—broadly correspond with the reasons I would now myself advance. But I shall be obliged to be somewhat exhaustive, if I am to give my reasons the necessary 'backbone.'

"In this matter the first step is to give you a veracious picture of *Holstein's personality*, and then to depict the effect of such a personality as framed in its office of State.

"The personality of that singularly complex man is plainly revealed to us in the countless letters forming my correspondence. Together with the shrewdness of his practical ideas, the intensity of his desires and anxieties, there emerges a certain excess of feeling—which I might go so far as to call effeminate. Take it for all in all, undeniably a most interesting psychological type.

"But one does not really learn to know a man from his letters alone. The real self will be obscure for anyone who has not seen the mind and body of him, in light and shade, in passion and repose, palpably and visibly expressed in daily intercourse.

"Throughout years of intercourse I came to know the man better than perhaps I knew any others. The mortal enmity which separated us and led to the tragic conclusion of my public and social life is an essential feature in his portrait—the portrait of a man whose genius was obscured by the pathological trait which was his (and, being his, became my own) disaster.

"If you, dear friend, had known Holstein

personally, and known him so intimately as I did, you would have shared Bismarck's opinion—that he was gifted, but must always be held in check, because he was crazy. As a matter of fact Holstein cannot be rightly judged unless one includes the pathological element.

" 1. He suffered from political delusions, with regard to which I estimate that out of ten political opinions of his, between six and seven were useful and often very subtle; while on the contrary the rest consisted of absolutely unreasonable conceptions—or more justly, hallucinations—which he nevertheless held to be genuine grounds on which to construct combinations and schemes —these being, as I have said, absolutely without foundation. Many of them were such transparent nonsense that I never would be persuaded even to discuss the question.

" 2. Another and even more exceedingly dangerous pathological trait was a kind of thirst for slaughter. Bülow and I used to call him the ' weasel,' for that animal never stops until it has slaughtered the whole henhouse. In this was revealed Holstein's *impulsive sort of smothered inward fury*. An attribute with which I made personal acquaintance in his great prototype, Bismarck. But with Bismarck it was unconcealed. With Holstein there would be the most sudden outbursts; often merely, for instance, if some one had not bowed to him—from across the street, and even though the offender might be short-sighted ! And so this somebody, who for one reason or another had not answered Holstein's salutation—no : ' The fellow didn't bow to me yesterday.' That was enough to start a persecution of the ' enemy ' which never came to an end. Or a word that somebody might somewhere have let fall—and not even directly against him, but one that might 'have reference' to some opinion that he, Holstein, had expressed—this sufficed to establish a lasting enmity.

"The amount of time and trouble it cost me, during our long intercourse, to talk him out of such nonsense, is beyond calculation. In that respect he undoubtedly betrayed persecution-mania.

"3. And not less, indeed, in his singular horror of encountering strangers or people with whose characters he did not believe himself to be thoroughly acquainted. He would hide himself; he never left his address (except with those whom he thought he could absolutely trust) when he went away; and it was perfectly futile to look him up—he was never at home.

"4. He could look no one in the face, avoided every eye. But in the brief seconds when one did contrive to meet his eye, the glance combined a painful unsteadiness with a kind of melancholy which always stirred me to pity.

"5. He regularly frequented the shooting-gallery, and talked of it even oftener. It was such a favourite subject that one could not help involuntarily asking one's-self 'Why?' It would take me too far if I were to enumerate all the idiosyncrasies of Holstein which must at least be described as 'eccentric.' For the reflective observer the general impression was, and remained —a big interrogation mark.

"When it became clear that we should have to part company, I often found myself thinking of his perpetual allusions to the shooting-gallery and his own pistols. For I had had an opportunity of assuring myself that Holstein's pistols were not to be taken too seriously.

"This No. 5 of my experiences undoubtedly strengthens the impression of persecution-mania. However, I am not enough of a psychologist to be able to give an expert opinion.

"6. His quite extraordinary cunning, secretiveness, and unconcealed preference for going the roundabout way when there was not the slightest reason for dealing with the matter anything but frankly, likewise belong (so far as I understand the subject) to the protean obscurity of the pathological domain, to which genius is beyond doubt more or less closely related.

"Holstein's genius was entirely concentrated on politics, one might even say on intrigue. To be sure, intrigue is always at the bottom of politics.

"My friendship for this Holstein had two foundations. The highest admiration—not so much for his infinite craftiness as for his subtle intelligence, his eminent political and literary learning, his undeniable gift of divination ; but more than this, the deepest compassion for that self-tormenting, evasive, even craven nature, subjected to the psychical sway of neurotic tendencies that were not to be denied by any observer.

"And then I was touched by his kindlier moods. There were moments in which I felt that he was really fond of me ; and besides, he was friendly with his underlings at the Chancery —friendly as a dog-lover is with a dog. For those poor tormented creatures, and the secretaries and councillors no less, had all suffered from Bismarck's outbursts of fury and Herbert's bullying—both of which were traditions even when the Bismarck era was a thing of the past, and from which the liverish, hæmorrhoidal, and susceptible Secretaries of Legation had never really recovered.

"Holstein, who was very well off, never had a private man-servant. A horrible old woman, whom I once saw, made me think that he must be of opinion that a man-servant would take bribes, thieve, or murder his master.

"Everything in, and concerned with, Holstein had something mysterious, something oddly disturbing about it. Even his friendship with the Jewish Frau von Lebbin, born Brandt (her father had been ennobled, and was of Jewish extraction), who was an inquisitive, clever woman with a racy Semitic tongue.[1] He went to tea with old ladies only—never with anyone else. For a long time it had been Frau von Kleist-Retzow, wife of the renowned Conservative leader. But Frau von Lebbin's Semitic intelligence won the day.

"Another thing that stirred me to pity was the loneliness of this remarkable man's existence, despite all the people he had to see on Foreign Office and political business. For I am one of the sociable characters who cannot exist without friendship.

[1] When I was Secretary of Legation in 1887, I was asked at a dinner-party at War Minister's von Kaneke, a friend of my parents, to take in Frau Geheimrat von Lebbin. She snubbed me and answered only with Yes and No, for what was I but an attaché. Towards the end of dinner her other neighbour whispered to her that I was Prince William's friend. "You are Prince William's friend!" she exclaimed, and her long nose and beady brown eyes gleamed with curiosity and delight. "Why didn't you tell me that?" Then she abounded in politeness—but it was my turn to answer with Yes and No. That was my only meeting with Frau von Lebbin.
[The lady died in 1919. Holstein's posthumous writings, which were in her possession, were said to have been left to her nephew, and he was said to have disposed of them. To whom? Probably to someone who had an interest in suppressing certain matters.]

"When in 1886, struck by my official reports and private political letters from Munich, Holstein first approached me, I felt much flattered. Then I became personally fond of him, because I felt sorry for him. That was the grand trick played upon me by good-nature—my pleasant but perilous inheritance from my parents and grandparents; perilous when one has to be a sort of tight-rope walker on the slippery parquet floors of Court and politics, and carry day and night the pole that keeps one in equilibrium between the too-much and the too-little —and a very precarious sort of balancing it is!

"But by means of my friendship with Holstein I at any rate discovered that the only soil in which that plant can never thrive is politics. The chemical ingredients are literally poisonous. They irremediably ruin foliage, flower, and fruit. Hence politics is the ground on which the old saying is most frequently proved true—that friendship can generate the profoundest hatred.

"And in that soil my friendship with Holstein went to rack and ruin—in the form of a 'hate' which made use of the most utterly unscrupulous methods. Still, even there I would call him 'pathological.' It was an instance of his hallucinations, which could construct a veritable crime on no basis whatever.

"Now, my friend, I think I have given you Holstein's personality in its broad outlines, like a painter who depicts his model in *négligé*. I am indeed among the few men who are in a position so to depict Holstein! Now that time and age have cooled me down, I have taken some trouble to paint my picture veraciously and fairly. I could not now depict him as so horrible and cruel as at the time when all my wounds were bleeding. I have tried to use the balancing-pole on the tight-rope of this description, to say neither too much nor too little; and in doing so have realised that age is the best of all balancing-poles.

"And now, to complete my portrait, a word about Holstein's methods at the Foreign Office.

"Holstein's work in the vast domain of foreign policy can only be justly estimated by the light of the existing official documents. The memoranda drafted and revised by him, which it was the Imperial Chancellor's business to forward to German representatives abroad; the expositions of important political matters which he wrote for the Chancellor or in certain cases merely for the archivists; special reports, made by him at the Emperor's command or, in consequence of Imperial marginalia, drawn up in the Chancellor's name for the Emperor's information on questions of foreign policy—all this most interesting and abundant material, preserved in the Foreign Office archives, can alone give any adequate idea of Holstein's powers in his official capacity. And undoubtedly it is a shining testimony to his great ability. His verbal pronouncements, deeply impressive though they were, will soon fade from memory.

"How the historian will estimate the importance—that is to say, the success—of the course he took in policy is quite another question. The work as such, and the subtlety of his arguments, will in any event be admired.

"Holstein's political judgment was, after Prince Bismarck's retirement in 1890 until his own in 1906, the preponderating one in *all* important questions of German foreign policy. Neither Caprivi nor Hohenlohe nor Bülow ever promulgated an edict on even the most insignificant political matter without Holstein's putting in his oar ; in some instances he drew up the document with his own hand. All these edicts, however, though they are testimony to the degree of Holstein's industry, were modified by reason of *the Emperor's very frequent interference* in foreign policy. And this because of His Majesty's direct telegraphic communication in cipher with his Royal colleagues, or the despatch of A.D.C.s with private letters to a sovereign, or brusque marginalia and commands on the reports from the German Ambassadors and Ministers, etc. This caused perpetual changes in the political temper of the Foreign Office.

" In such circumstances there could be no such thing as independent action on the part of Holstein, or the Imperial Chancellor, or the Secretary of State—or even the Emperor himself. For the Imperial interventions would soon be made to chime in with the policy of the Office—that is to say, would be re-modelled, brought into conformity so far as might be, and would then receive official countenance—meaning Holstein's countenance as we were accustomed to see it ; and *that* means a melancholy one !

" But there is no doubt that Holstein's policy would have been paramount, if the Emperor's interference had not so frequently given State affairs a turn which did not represent Holstein's views. I want also to make it clear that in every instance of the Chancellor's or the Foreign Minister's asserting himself on a serious matter of foreign policy, Holstein was always the *spiritus rector*. On the other hand, whenever Imperial commands and desires had to be given some expression, Holstein was reduced to the position of an editor—unless, in his bitter resentment, he refused to take any part whatever in the transaction.

"Another question is how far the temperament, the *idiosyncrasy* of Holstein was able to subordinate itself to the aims of foreign policy. This was often a danger, and errors no less often resulted from it. For the Chancellor in office was not seldom obliged to ask himself which would be the greater mistake—to give Holstein his head, even in apparently dangerous transactions, or to accept his resignation? They always chose the former! And the fourteen farewell letters—which all met with the Chancellor's refusal to accept, until at last State Secretary von Tschirschky (when Bülow was ill, but not entirely without his knowledge) laid the 15th before the Emperor—are sufficient evidence for Holstein's method of imposing his will. On each of these occasions he had begun packing up in his room, so as to show he was in earnest.

"It is manifest that with this system of giving in to Holstein, his monomaniacal tendencies were sure to impose *their* will; and in that way an aberration—let us say—of Holstein's could always be attributed to the existing Government.

"When one studies the Holstein era, one finds that during Bülow's Chancellorship *he*—Bülow—was the moving spirit, in so far as the Emperor's interventions did not take him by surprise. But Bülow had always come to a complete understanding with Holstein before he acted. As to Caprivi's and Hohenlohe's foreign policy, in neither case did any such thing exist—they were purely 'Holsteinish.' Bülow did discuss matters with Holstein, and on occasions asserted himself. But he always told me it was hell—and hell it was in the end, for him,

"You once wrote to me, dear friend, saying that ' Emperor William II had become the football of others.' One cannot exactly say that. It was not always so in questions of foreign policy. True, I must admit that the military Cabinet and his suite acquired more and more influence as time went on. These men, with their everlasting Berlin ribaldry, systematically derided the Foreign Office. "The King of Prussia must show these pen-pushers their place—phrasemongers who have forgotten what a Royal Command means. Muddlers who turn the simplest things into a problem are only fit to be commanded from the saddle. A curt military command, a clear uncompromising order, can bring so-called diplomatic obstacles into line as easily as it can a squadron on the Bornstadt field at Potsdam.'

"To write those words is to record the tone and substance of utterances that I have heard over and over again from the Emperor's lips, as the faithful echo of his military suite's ideas, when (I could not tell you how often !) I undertook the task of explaining the point of view in important political affairs of Chancellor, State Secretary, and Foreign Office, and winning him over to their side. As I myself had been a Guardsman and was therefore able to adopt the Berlin tone, I usually ' delivered the goods,' and laughed off the snub that loomed in the offing. It was merely a question of manipulation and independence of character. Anyone without such assets was lost with our Emperor. But one cannot be funny all the time, nor can one hope always to bring things off by cutting jokes, though there never was a Court in the universe where the tone was so slangy as at Berlin.

"But I should be unfair if I gave the impression that it was only this sort of thing which succeeded with the Emperor. That was not so. On dark days I talked like Ristori (whom I very much admired) and had a similar success. These are mere matters of instinct, and of really understanding one's friend. But I, the friend, was not always on the spot—and if I had been, my counsels would have lost their potency. For nowhere are men so quickly wearied-of as at Court. Nobody's mind is inexhaustible, and the pursuit of novelty is the ruling passion of every ruler, especially when he is an ebullient, impulsive William II.

"The Emperor often messed up our difficult foreign relations by his interference. In that respect I grant he *was* a football—but the football of his own character, his sudden 'inspirations,' his conviction that he must instantly realise some 'brilliant idea, before it loses all its grit in that confounded Foreign Office melting-pot.' That the unfortunate Foreign Office had to toil for months at mending his broken crockery was what never occurred to him.

"If you add to this Holstein's ungovernable fits of temper, which emphasised the Imperial blunders or impetuosities by all sorts of characteristic outbursts indicative beyond all doubt of his neurotic condition, you will have some idea of Bülow's hell—and mine too.

"I was often—very often—called to the rescue. For the Foreign Office, from the Chancellor to the most subordinate of the archivists, laboured under the strange delusion that I had unlimited influence upon the Emperor. Because I had occasionally succeeded in convincing my temperamental Imperial friend that 'it really *was* the Foreign Office's business to get over a difficult piece of ground, and that he ought not to expose his Imperial person in thorny political situations '—they thought I was always to be relied on to do it. For it was long reported of the Emperor that he could be influenced by no one. But only so long as A.D.C. politics were without *their* crude and positively devastating influence. Doubtless I often was of use in steering the Imperial desires, views, and even aberrations into the navigable waters of the Foreign Office channel ; and as I had never done anyone any harm with the Emperor, they trusted me in that respect also. There would have been a certain sense of impotence but for my part of mediator between a hyper-temperamental Emperor who would fall like lightning from heaven upon the assembly at the Foreign Office, and a brilliant, domineering Privy Councillor of marked pathological tendencies, to say nothing of an Imperial Chancellor who, always very sensitive about his dignity, regarded the said part as a necessary evil and, despite all his mumbled expressions of gratitude, never could really like me.

" Your survey, dear friend, is particularly concerned with the period 1894 to 1895 ; that is to say, the end of the Caprivi and the beginning of the Hohenlohe eras. Indescribable was the game of cross-purposes played at the seat of government—that is to say, the Foreign Office in the Wilhelmstrasse, which is at once the headquarters, the dwelling-place, and the workroom of the Imperial Chancellor, and to which the workroom of the political conspirator Holstein stood in the closest proximity. A slight clearance of the permanently thunderous atmosphere did take place in 1897 with Bülow's appointment to

APPENDIX I

be Secretary of State, but only to assume before long such forms as led with ever-increasing velocity to the great catastrophe of 1908 to 1909.

"In the transition period between Caprivi and Hohenlohe, the extremely gifted Finance Minister Miquel played a very prominent part. I have seldom met a man whose intellect, knowledge, and brilliant conversation fascinated me so much. But he was undeniably a mischief-maker, of the slaughtering type to which Holstein, that badger in his hole, was irresistibly attracted. The only thing to be said about *them* is 'Birds of a feather...!' But the methods of these two conspirators were so different that even there quarrels and the resulting enmity soon sprang up.

"At that time I often asked myself of what nature could be that modification in the parliamentary system which alone presented any hope of getting the Emperor to abstain from his sudden interventions. Old Hohenlohe had always been a Liberal at heart, and bore the stamp of a statesman who, though somewhat used-up, was all the more experienced for that. Miquel would have been the 'Speaker'—and Holstein the chucker-out!

"What would have been the result? Precisely what you now write, as the outcome of your survey of my attitude at that time. It would not have come to an end without conflicts and a terrible cleavage between the very powerful East Prussia, and Western and Southern Germany. The Emperor, after the first flames of enthusiasm in the telling part of 'national benefactor' had died down, and with his A.D.C.s gathered in close formation around him, would not only have fulminated against Hohenlohe, Miquel and Co. as 'traitors to their country,' but would *now* have for the first time done *regular, secret, and direct* political business (and that without ever telling the outlawed Wilhelmstrasse a word about it) with his 'colleagues,' as he always called the other monarchs. Wholly untenable positions, together with great encroachments in home affairs and the resulting conflicts, would very soon have been the outcome of any such modification—conflicts which must quite inevitably have ensued on the upheavals (of the most distressing nature conceivable) caused by the flagrantly autocratic and prejudiced foreign policy, strongly smacking of intrigue, which would have been pursued by the Emperor. For, as I have said, these meddlings of the Emperor's *could not have been prevented.*

" 'An end with a fright, or a fright without an end '—so he had said. But what was to have been the end with a fright at that time? Merely, perhaps, that our Emperor was to be relegated. But in what way? Revolution? That would have meant civil war in the German Empire, and most likely interference from outside—hence, war. Poison perhaps? You already know (if not through me, I imagine through the other side) that Holstein seriously suggested to Prince Bismarck that the Crown Prince Frederick should be poisoned. If you were not acquainted with this fact, I am prepared to name the authentic sources.[1]

---

[1] He did so later on. The Prince named Prince Henckel, who had it from Bismarck himself; and Herbert Bismarck, who laughingly told Eulenburg of it, as " characteristic of Holstein's lunacy." The Prince added : " There is no doubt whatever that the elder Bismarck told the story to some of his circle, as for example Busch and perhaps Rottenburg. . . . And I explain Holstein's terrible hatred for Bismarck by its having come to his ears that the Chancellor had betrayed this criminal proposal."

"The end with a fright promised quite as great a fright in every respect as the fright without an end, the duration of which after all depended, so far as human eye could see, upon the accidents that lie in God's hand to dispense.

"Though I was perfectly clear in my own mind about the great dangers of the existing situation, I was upheld by the consciousness that the unique sense of duty native to Prussian officialdom would, by its steadfast loyalty, probably steer the old kingdom aright through the mountainous billows of the storm-tossed waters. In the same way as that very officialdom had, all by itself, contrived to withstand without a quiver the battle between the greatest official that Prussia ever possessed and the Emperor—from 1890 to 1898.

"Reichstag rule, then! How could that have been possible with our Emperor, who nevertheless could not be poisoned? You say very justly: 'Our fate would have been the rule of the Centre Party, *sans phrase*.' But at the same time, the undermining by the Vatican of the Protestant Imperial House would have assumed such forms as would finally have led to the disruption of the Empire, and delivered us up to our enemies.

"Such were, in general, my reflections; and so there was nothing for it but to consider whether we *could* go on 'ringing the changes'; that is to say, go on balancing the one personality against the other—Holstein's and the Emperor's. For with the Emperor and his surprise-packets, there was—God help us!—no use whatever in thinking of another form of government. The only saviour I could see was Bernard Bülow. I knew that he, with his brilliant intellect, his many-sided erudition, his charming manners, and his tact was perhaps the only person who could, on the one hand, restrain the Emperor politically, put on the curb, so to speak; and on the other contrive to get on with Holstein, whom he more or less, like everyone else, regarded as indispensable.

"Thus Bülow, in those years of my heaviest toil, represented for me the only chance of a possible improvement in our manner of 'ringing the changes.' But I was still young enough not to think the Emperor quite hopeless as a ruler. He had undeniably some of a ruler's virtues, which manifested themselves in an honest, eager endeavour to make the German nation great and powerful; and he was eloquent enough to give striking expression to his ideas. Besides, he was a loyal friend, which tells strongly in favour of a character. But his temperament was the trouble. His utter lack of equilibrium was what utterly upset his apparatus of government. If we could have established at least a certain degree of harmony between *some* of the men at the wheel of the ship of State, we should have had one slight stand-by in the chaos of transactions and opinions.

"Bülow's resistance to being merely a cog in the governmental machine is comprehensible enough to me. For he, too, saw that existence with Holstein was simply torture. But I am inclined to think that it was much less Holstein's unscrupulousness that he feared—for in life that takes men farthest, though it certainly won't in Heaven; it was more the feeling that Holstein might soon drive him out, and for ever destroy the career to which he clung with every fibre of his being.

"As a 'weasel' Holstein certainly was insatiable and absolutely unscrupulous. A weasel is not afraid to attack bigger beasts than himself. In that way Holstein had slaughtered Bismarck. It was a logical consequence of his psychical make-up that he should want to slaughter the Emperor too, once His Majesty tried to break his magic circle. I had to see that, in the end—and he conspired to do it with Harden, whom till then he had hated like poison. From the fact that I, neither as friend nor as decent man, could or would consent to be Holstein's henchman in the slaughtering—that is to say, the putting in cold storage!—of the Emperor, arose the antagonism which finally parted us. My reason for *not choosing* to be that henchman was—quite apart from my friendship and loyalty—that I saw the *terrible danger* of Holstein's having unlimited authority as leader of the Government, unless there was some sort of control by the Throne. For every Imperial Chancellor, be he who he might, who had been in a position to command without any interference from the Emperor, would have 'ruled' only so long as he blindly followed Holstein's lead; and Holstein was, as Bismarck said with some exaggeration, but rightly enough—*crazy*.

"Bismarck was the only man who ever kept Holstein under his thumb. I, on my side, lasted as long as I did with Holstein—or perhaps I ought to say *under* him—because, as I have already mentioned, he imagined that everything the Emperor did aright in his, Holstein's, opinion, was my doing.

"But that the Emperor's reign would end in disaster of some kind I saw as clearly as Holstein did; and this from the time when my serious illness began gradually to release me from the service and from my perpetual attendance on the

Emperor. But I still hoped on for a while. After the critical years of 1908 to 1909, not any more. For as we had not succeeded in arranging a new alliance with Russia, but instead were building a battle-fleet which must turn England into a mortal enemy, everything—Emperor and Empire—seemed to me irretrievably endangered by the Emperor's interferences and aberrations.

" I frankly own that I could often have caused Holstein to be dismissed, for the fury of the A.D.C.s against the man in whom they—not without reason—saw him who had brought about Bismarck's retirement, knew no bounds. But I had no doubt whatever that Holstein, despite his pathological and other traits, was *indispensable*. No Chancellor would or could have done without him ; [1] it was clear to every one of them that in view of the stupendous difficulties caused by the Emperor's meddlings and private policies, which were incessantly putting the Foreign Office into the tightest sort of holes, Holstein *alone* possessed the qualities to steer the ship of State *tant bien que mal* out of the Imperial whirlpool, without veering from Scylla to Charybdis.

" With Bülow's appointment to be Chancellor (1900),[2] there came a period of blessed relaxation for me. (I had been closely intimate with him from our youthful days, and had smoothed over his differences of opinion with Holstein, who by reason of Bülow's erudition and skill barred him out from the Foreign Office.) For the Emperor,

[1] " Even Bülow could not let him down—to be sure, there were particular reasons for that ; because the noose Holstein had put round his neck was not to be got rid of with the best will in the world. . . ."
—P. E.

[2] He must have meant Bülow's appointment to be Secretary of State.

to whom I had constantly pointed out Bülow's great abilities, soon got up a flaming enthusiasm for him, and joyfully exclaimed, ' He shall be my Bismarck ! '

" That was unfortunately *not* the case. Bülow, at first in the Emperor's full confidence, did for a time contrive to prevent the Imperial meddling. On a basis of Holstein-Bülowish understanding the Imperial chariot ran quite smoothly along the road of foreign policy. Even the A.D.C.s kept as quiet as they were ever known to do, and were actually solicitous to feed Bülow up with ' the most important news ' from the Palace. *Tout allait au mieux dans le meilleur des mondes*—such was then the general impression. But doubts soon arose in my breast as to whether our vessel had really landed us on the Fortunate Isle. For the big war-boats, Weltpolitik, Kiao-Chao, etc., were being trumpeted over the universe. True, Bülow *plus* Holstein still stood at the wheel, and the two were mutually amicable ; but before long some political traits of a lethal nature—which were known only to me—began to reveal themselves in the new ' Bismarck.' The Foreign Office poison, with its mingling of A.D.C. and Big Fleet policy, was suffusing the goblet that stood on Bülow's writing-table. To myself the old friend of my youth grew gradually, gradually colder ; and Friend Holstein found that I supported his ' enemy,' Count Goluchowski. This I did with a good conscience, and it was shown to be the right course by Goluchowski's attitude at the Algeciras Conference, which gained him the all-too notorious telegram from Emperor William : ' You have drummed us out to a jolly good tune, like a loyal comrade-in-arms.'

"Holstein began to nag at me. Did he think he could manage with Bülow alone? Had I become too powerful for him? Who shall divine his reasons?

"For me, in the last issue, it was not an end with a fright, but a fright without an end; and into the gulf dug in the Hohenzollern universe by Holstein's alliance with Harden after Tschirschky *plus* Bülow had dared to remove him from office, Bülow too plunged headlong.

"But the Reichstag's collapse! I shall never quite understand how that came about, when in consequence of the 'revelations' about political indiscretions so carefully staged by the Holstein-Harden conspiracy, the Reichstag had been put in a position to take a real stand against the Emperor!

"That was a manifestation less—much less—of loyalty on the part of the national representatives than of *immaturity*, of *indecision*. I saw at once that the Reichstag was *not* the factor, *not* the 'backbone,' which might protect us against the Imperial aberrations. And this came to seem a proof that I was right in my feeling that it would be a disastrous experiment to vote for converting our Emperor into a parliamentary ruler. Only *without* him could that form of government have been feasible.

"But I have already said that it was my lively conviction that the Empire, apart from such experiments, was heading for catastrophe. I felt this directly the idea of building a big battle-fleet took tangible form—that is, during the Caprivi-Hohenlohe era, when those exalted beings had very little conception of what was going on in the heads of the Emperor and his Admirals.

Appendix I

"Disaster, doom, wherever I looked! Many a man comes to grief by trusting to luck. But what else had I to trust to?

"When my active official life had long been a thing of the past, Holstein nevertheless still saw the Emperor at my side as a *friend*. So I might still, he thought, frustrate his schemes. I must be *got rid of*, in that case; and he set about accomplishing this with the tenacity of purpose, the vehemence which were his when he was fighting an 'enemy.' For I had become his 'enemy' from the moment I refused to fight his enemy Goluchowski, who thirty years (!) before had dared—in Paris, when Holstein at the German Embassy was occupied in causing the downfall of his Chief, Arnim,[1] and the fashionable heart-breaker Goluchowski was Secretary at the Austrian Embassy—had actually dared to treat the *loup-garou* Holstein *de haut en bas*!

"In another place I have exhaustively depicted the course of Holstein's destructive campaign against myself. Here I need only mention that this undermining was manifested beyond all doubt when in 1906 Holstein—after his dismissal from the Office—made peace with Harden, and together with that most unscrupulous of all poisoners of public opinion persuaded the world in 1907 that 'the Emperor's most intimate friend' (as I was always called!) was a disreputable person. What good were my pistols and my sworn declaration of innocence against that? The unfortunate Emperor failed in the part of friend, under pressure from his military suite, who out of their venomous envy joined in the hue-and-cry against me and, blinded

[1] Holstein spied on Arnim's correspondence, and betrayed him to Bismarck.

by hatred, committed the stupendous blunder of endangering the Emperor's own reputation by that campaign against his intimate friend.

"April, 1908, saw the undeniable success of this conspiracy. The second act followed in November of the same year, with the dragging-in of certain political utterances of the Emperor's—which, crying indiscretions as they were, led (as a result of the campaign in Harden's press) to those well-known interpellations in the Reichstag which so very gravely compromised the Emperor's political prestige.

"I have already alluded to the collapse of the Reichstag in connection with that Holstein-Harden proceeding—to which, as a 'stunt,' I will not refuse my admiration, though it is with loathing that I survey such an abyss of depravity as is represented by the methods of both conspirators.

"Still, regarded in a purely objective light, the collapse in the Reichstag was no more than a disastrous incident in the history of Germany; though at the same time a nemesis for Holstein, who to revenge himself for his dismissal staged the collapse of the Government in which and for which he had worked in a prominent position at the Foreign Office—and who, after that collapse, went disappointed, embittered, and exhausted to his lonely death.

"I would say of Bülow too, though with reservations, that nemesis awaited him. His double-dealing with Holstein and the Emperor broke his nerve, and the ambiguous attitude he took in the great Reichstag drama of 1908 caused his own downfall. The soldiers and courtiers round the Emperor, who a few years earlier were all for Bülow, thenceforth called

Appendix I

him nothing but 'a traitor to the realm'—*and so did the Emperor.* Holstein died in May, 1909, and probably the veritable cause of his death was the moral shock of having had his resignation accepted in that April of 1906. The poor fellow was often seen at night, all alone, in the Wilhelmstrasse, gazing up at the windows of the Foreign Office. A moving story, which shows how completely that then well-nigh living ghost had identified himself with the rooms that in his great days he had occupied."

II

THE PRINCESS ZU EULENBURG'S RECOLLECTIONS OF
HER HUSBAND'S TRIAL IN 1908

Written, 1909.

ON May 8, 1908, my husband was taken, from the bed he had not left for weeks, to the Charité. Throughout the hot summer months he lay in the little low, airless room, fighting against the most distressing heart-trouble and fainting fits. For years, when he was suffering in this way, nothing but fresh air had done him any good. Here the two windows, both on the sunny side, had to be shaded all day long by thick hangings. The poor invalid was obliged to lie in darkness if he were not to be suffocated by the heat. Often there was a blessed shower of rain—and then, down with the curtains, up with the window, and a breath or two of real fresh air ! But, poor fellow, he could not long stand the noise, for the railway station was close by, with trains perpetually puffing in and out. He did so crave for peace and quiet—the window had to be shut, and the air in the little low room got stuffy again, and the continual opening and shutting of the ambulance-station gate was even worse than the noise of the train. At night the watchman and porters kept talking and laughing so as to pass the time—their work was so distressing and the night-watches were so long that they had to do something to enliven themselves. Those were the nights he had, to refresh him after the day of torment ! Think of lying like that for weeks and months, and at the same time preparing for such an ordeal as the trial. . . .

At first the excitement sustained him, and so he could concentrate. But there were many terrible attacks after he had been very much wrought-up—nervous break-downs as, for example, when, dozing towards morning after one of the sleepless nights, he was roughly awakened by two policemen asking for the keys of his writing-table. They had been ordered to go to Liebenberg, there—for the third time!—to make a thorough search.[1] Or else the prosecution would suddenly, as often happened, bring some of Harden's witnesses to be confronted with him. He had to let himself be stupidly gaped at by low, degraded creatures like that—once it was actually a handcuffed criminal. Not one of these men confirmed Harden's suspicions. He had, with Bernstein's help, collected about 150 such incriminations. The poor invalid became more and more incapable of attending to business, as the preliminary investigation drew to an end. This made things very difficult for his defending counsel. How often had Wronker to go away, shaking his head, because his client was too ill to follow his review of the evidence!

The noble, humane doctor of the Charité, the kind matron—these best knew how ill he was, and how much worse he grew with every day. Never shall we forget the comfort their visits were to us, though their skill could avail him little in conditions so unfavourable to a patient suffering as he was from arterial trouble, deprived of fresh air, of any possibility of movement, and never free from

[1] The Prince was convinced that the sole aim of these repeated domiciliary searches was to get hold of his private political correspondence. He had good reason to think they were instigated by Holstein, who hoped by this means to be able to destroy his own correspondence with the Prince.

noise by day or night. I have not a word to say against the Royal Charité on this account. These were the only quarters that offered any privacy, for they could be shut off from the main building, and there was a room for the policeman on guard and a little ante-room for my husband's devoted valet and nurse, Emanuel Bartsch. The only favour accorded to us was that Bartsch was not separated from my husband, and from my heart I am grateful for it. For on account of the alarming heart-attacks the Prince could not be left alone for a moment. This faithful man knew better than anyone else what to do for him. And his presence was absolutely necessary throughout the night, so that his bed had to be placed in the sickroom, though this made the atmosphere even closer. The whole arrangement was provisional—only for a few days, as they thought at the hospital. Nobody could have supposed that a man so ill would have been refused bail. Even the prosecuting counsel, who had solemnly assured me to the contrary, could not quite conceal his amazement at that unexpected order of the court.

At any rate, I and the children were allowed to visit him daily on production of a pass. I was thankful for that, though I often trembled at the thought that this alleviation of our misery might not long be afforded us. For there were many indications that the authorities were only waiting for the doctor in attendance to sanction a transfer to Moabit prison.

To pass the time I used to read to my dear sufferer, sitting beside a chink in the curtains, which were always drawn on account of the unendurable glare. Simple little stories translated from the English.

How sweet and reposeful were our quiet times

together at the end of the day—but how sad it was for me to take my lonely way at night to the little temporary abode which for all its modesty seemed to me like a palace after *his*. My way always took me through the Tiergarten and past the war-memorials, in one of the groups on which our ancestor Wend zu Ileburg stood in the place of honour beside his feudal chief, whom he faithfully served until the enemies of his lord flung him into his own dungeon, and there let him starve to death.

At last the longed-for jury trial drew near. The joyful hope of speedy vindication and acquittal had an inspiring and cheering effect on the martyr in body and spirit. Even the thought of again being able to breathe fresh air on the drive to court made him forget the distress connected with such a transit. A motor ambulance was ordered, so that he could lie on a stretcher going and coming. As the drive took only a few minutes, the defending counsel later requested the President of the court that the car might go a little way round through the Tiergarten, and the request was granted. These were the " daily drives " which the Press represented as a " peculiar favour."

It was indeed a *little* favour; one which would not have been granted to any other invalid inmate of the Charité—but for the simple reason that a less remarkable personage than Prince Eulenburg would not, in such a state of health, have been subjected to trial at all. I know this quite positively, from an authoritative medical source.

The miraculous force of a clear conscience upheld my husband during the first week of the trial. The doctors were astonished, shook their heads, and said : " How long can such superhuman energy last in a man so ill as he is ? " The defending

APPENDIX II

counsel wondered and rejoiced—they had never seen their client like this! For the first few days he seemed to be master of the situation. His accurate memory and power of concentration came back again. But alas! that tremendous effort was all in vain. The proceedings were so drawn-out, ranged so far and wide, and entailed so many repetitions that when after a fortnight his powers visibly failed, and alarming symptoms and fever made their appearance, and finally the adjournment took place, only the least important of the incriminating witnesses had been heard.

Among the many who had so long vainly exerted their influence in the Prince's favour was the venerable and honoured hero of 1870, with the Order *pour la mérite*, General von Leszczynski, to whom the Fatherland owed so much when he was Chief of Staff to General Werder. He could have revealed many things about the political side of these machinations. But since in this most political of all political trials, politics might not even once be mentioned, the two miserable incriminating witnesses, Ernst and Riedl, were repeatedly put in the box, and the Munich judges and sheriffs examined as to the credibility of these creatures. When my husband utterly collapsed, after sixteen days of trial, the entire Munich Commission was summoned by telegraph, as though the Berlin judge and jury had to apply to the Munich court for their verdict! The notorious witness, Ernst, had shortly before returned from a recuperative visit to his home, which he had been permitted by the court to make; and he was greeted by the President—before all the witnesses—with marked cordiality, and enquiries after his own and his children's welfare. Not once was any sympathetic enquiry made about the suffering

APPENDIX II

Prince, who daily grew iller and iller. That again might have looked like " favouritism."

During the last few days of the trial he was no longer able to sit upright on the stretcher. This was very disadvantageous to the defence, for it was difficult for counsel to consult with their prostrate client. When the feverish condition grew more marked, the doctors urgently applied for an adjournment. The Charité doctor and the police-surgeon were entirely unanimous in their opinion. For two days I was able, like other—oh, how enviable!—wives, to nurse my beloved husband without any kind of annoyance from either side. The fever ran high, and all the symptoms were very grave. I had forgotten the trial and the whole outer world. On the third day there was no change for the better.

But now the court began to worry us again, for naturally enough they wanted to get in one more day, if only *pro forma*, in order to prevent the actual adjournment. So little did the authorities know about the accommodation in the room where their victim was lying prostrate that they actually suggested holding a sitting of the court in the sickroom! To be sure, the three judges could have sat upon the servant's bed, and the defending counsel on the little table; then there would have been two chairs for the twelve jurors, but not another inch even of standing-room.

When from the little window on the ground-floor I watched the court with its servants and documents coming over to the Charité to assemble in the Committee-room opposite, I was seized with deadly panic at the thought of my poor patient's having to undergo the transit. I placed myself at the door of the sickroom, fully determined to resist the authorities and let no one in, not even the defending counsel. But then one of the kind police-surgeons came with Professor Kraus, and they calmed me by promising not on any account to allow the patient, suffering as he was from dangerous thrombosis, even to stir, let alone be carried down steep stairs. These men, whose right to speak could not be contested, even arranged that they should, in presence of the constables who acted as warders, photograph the invalid's legs, so as to give documentary evidence of the alarming swelling of the right one; and thus the High Court had to submit to a higher authority.

The night was again a bad one. Towards morning the fever somewhat abated, and immediately the invalid's energy was restored. The one thing he begged for was " no adjournment ! " And indeed it was even more vital for him than for the court that the trial should proceed to its end. When I arrived in the morning, I found the little room empty. He had wrung permission from the doctors to be carried, on his own responsibility, down and up the steep stairs into the Committee-room opposite. On account of the swollen leg, which might not be touched, he could not be dressed; but was merely wrapped in sheets, like a dead body, carried in on the stretcher and at once, behind a screen, transferred to a bed. Thus I found him, still feverish enough, but resolute to fight on. I could only submit.

The doctors had begged that he might be spared to the utmost. My son, who was anxious to give an account of a chance meeting with Ernst and of the man's despair immediately after the Munich trial, as well as I myself, were on that account withheld from giving evidence. I waited in the ante-room for two or three hours, getting more and more uneasy. They would examine no one but the patient, who needed so urgently to be spared ! I will assume that this neglect of the medical men's warnings occurred because now, for the first time, a conscientious and unprejudiced prosecutor had been admitted to the case, and so a sort of recapitulation of the prisoner's evidence was considered necessary. I do not now want to think, as I did then in my despair, that they wanted to lay snares for him, and take advantage of his illness and feebleness to make him contradict himself.

At the end of three hours he was utterly exhausted, and the proceedings had to be stopped. Wronker came to me overjoyed, and said : " We've got a good deal further to-day, and to-morrow will certainly see you clear of it."

It took a long time to empty the Committee-room. Then arrived the kindly Professor Steyrer, who knows so well how to cheer his patients. He had the bed removed from the dark corner into which it had been pushed at the close of the proceedings, and placed beside the window. There lay the beloved invalid at the open window, looking for the first time in two and a half months at the wide blue sky, enjoying a fine sunset, and collecting his energies for the exertions that were to come. We were both so thankful, so hopeful. We could not but think it a visible sign of the Almighty's protection that he had borne the transport so well, with that dangerous thrombosis against him. God would not refuse us further aid ! We separated that evening, in that firm conviction. The fever had been slight ; the big airy room, the window open on the peaceful broad courtyard, where there were even some trees and flowerbeds—all this had had a beneficial and soothing effect.

So it was all the more terrible for me when,

Y

completely unprepared, I heard the news next day. The trial indefinitely adjourned, the Prince still under arrest ! For the first time I completely broke down, lost all control of myself. How could my poor husband survive this blow ? When he had fought so heroically against the adjournment, now after the endless discussion to find that it was decided on and announced! After that last supreme effort he fell back on his couch, unable to listen any further. He was unconscious ; and when with glances of sympathy the last jurors had left the room, and the old servants of the court, with tears that they no longer sought to conceal, had collected their piles of papers, the faithful Bartsch and I had to call on the nurses to help us in holding the delirious patient down in bed.

This violent fever lasted through the night and for some days afterwards, leaving behind it such utter exhaustion as seemed to threaten his life. The trial had completely vanished from his memory ; it never made part of his delirium. His whole nervous system had undergone such a frightful shock that he could no longer think coherently.

When after some days he was brought back to the familiar little room, this delirium gradually ceased. With returning consciousness came great apathy and indifference. Those were grievous, melancholy, hopeless weeks. Everybody was away on holiday—not only judges, jurors, and defending counsel, but also the professors and head-doctors, finally even the dear matron. Even the two policemen, to whom we had gradually got used and who gave such willing help during the worst attacks, were on leave. Everybody could get away ; my poor sufferer alone had to go on suffocating in the heat.

I was filled with the profoundest bitterness.

I felt as though I were forsaken by God and men. Then I understood the desperate deeds of the persecuted and oppressed. I even understood how people who have seen their dearest persecuted and martyred, and who have not the inward support of religion, can be driven to take their own lives, when they have lost all hope of justice. The continued arrest was an unparalleled atrocity, for it prevented any possibility of re-opening the trial.

The junior doctors in our division of the Charité were as conscientious and sympathetic as their chiefs had been. But they doubted their ability to overcome the severe illness, in the circumstances now prevailing. The frequent relapses had affected the patient's lungs, fever and a racking cough persisted for several weeks, and the alarming heart-attacks, alternating with congestion, were more frequent. Cerebral anæmia, too, often caused hallucinations.

No one ever heard a complaint, not for a moment did he show any impatience under this martyrdom. He thought only of others—that I should have some fresh air daily, and the faithful Bartsch as well ; that the children should not come in too frequently to the hot city ; that the Liebenberg servants should be made comfortable, and so on. Once or twice, by his express desire, I had to leave him for several hours and go myself to Liebenberg, so as to look after some of our people who were unwell. We ought not to envy others, and yet how I envied our own servants and wage-earners their care-free lives ! Even when I drove past the poor little tea-gardens I wished God had given us the humble lot of the working-man, who enjoys his evening leisure after a hard day of toil. All I could bring my poor dear from Liebenberg was a few photographs of the beloved home, which he kept beside him in bed—and there, in real life, at Liebenberg, everything was flowering and sparkling and smelling so sweet, and it was no good to him!

At last, after nearly two months, came the end of the vacation; by the middle of September they were all back from their holidays, refreshed and invigorated. That of course meant: "Now we can start again!" A fortnight before, one of the police-surgeons had been ordered to examine the patient, which he did on many occasions at different times of day. Professor Kraus and the doctors of the Charité were naturally offended by the doubts thus cast on their conscientious reports—why should a police-surgeon be sent to confirm them! However, he too was obliged to state that my husband's condition was so little improved since the adjournment that there could be no thought of pronouncing him fit to stand his trial. "But he *is* fit to be arrested," was the reply. "Surely he must be well enough by this time to be transferred to Moabit from the Charité, where a room cannot easily be spared for so long. That short transit could not hurt him." That was the way the doctors were urged to sanction it. But the police-surgeon could not honestly say that he *was* fit to be arrested, even though the move itself might not be injurious. He could only confirm what Professor Kraus and the Charité doctors had said—that long-continued confinement, even at the Charité, might endanger his life.

The Crown Prosecutor, on receiving *this* diagnosis, applied for my husband's transference to Moabit! The defence applied for release from arrest.

Meanwhile preparations were being made at Moabit, in the infirmary of the prison. How fond we got of the little sickroom at the Charité, during

Appendix II

that horrible period of uncertainty! Even that room might soon be taken from us. Every morning, when I came to the Hospital, I was afraid I should find it empty. Once I really did, and the woman who was brushing it out was in tears. My blood seemed to freeze in my veins. But it was a false alarm, and the good woman was crying because this had been her first sight of the poor sufferer for a long time. What had really happened was that the doctors had had him taken to the X-ray room; they wanted to examine his heart, for there had been alarming symptoms which made any great excitement extremely dangerous, and in that phase of his illness it was rather good for him than otherwise to undergo some physical exertion.

After long, anxious days of uncertainty the 25th of September came at last—the day of decision. Throughout the endless hours from the early morning, when the court was to open, until late in the afternoon, my beloved husband thought only of me and how to distract my mind. But how could that have been possible? Our children all came in from the country . . . the awful suspense! It was like waiting for an execution. At last Wronker came panting to tell us that the arrest had been raised. Next day, before the relapse feared by the doctors could follow on the great agitation of mind, my husband was brought in the motor-ambulance so familiar since the beginning of the trial, to Liebenberg, where our children and the servants had prepared a moving reception for him. He was carried upstairs and put to bed at once—the bed from which he had been dragged nearly five months ago.

Those are my recollections of the terrible trial. I will now add what I had intended to say in the witness-box. Had I been called, as I daily expected to be, I should have spoken as follows:

I have myself requested to be called to give evidence, and I am glad that the moment has at last arrived when before God and the whole world I can testify and swear to my husband's absolute innocence. I am proud to be able to contend against falsehood for the best and noblest of husbands. I am prouder still to be at his side in bad fortune as in good—the good fortune for which we have been so envied.

It is seldom enough that happy marriages are brought before a court of justice, where usually divorce or separation is dealt with. Despite my grey hairs, it is not easy for me to speak of the most intimate matters relating to our happy married life. They are sacred; one does not care to make a public show of them. But I will answer all questions calmly and reasonably. I will try to overcome my indignation and pain at the base falsehoods which I am here to contradict, so far as to answer calmly.

First of all I declare on my honour as a wife and mother that the accusations here put forward are from A to Z lies invented by envious enemies and false friends; and that in the long period of thirty-four years comprising our married life, I have never perceived the smallest sign of anything but a perfectly normal emotional life or even manner of life. Nor can I understand how any reasonable person can venture to speak of abnormality in face of the fact that in the first ten years of our marriage (1876 to 1886) eight healthy children were born to us. But in Germany people have sunk so low that even the most normal and the happiest of marriages are not safe from such "modern" suspicions, or even the accusation of notorious "relations" of the kind.

My husband was always the best and most faithful of husbands, as he was the best of sons to his noble mother. That such infamies should be attributed to him is as monstrous as though I, the Princess Eulenburg, should be accused of poisoning, or one of our daughters of high treason. It is a terrible thing for so idealistic and strictly moral a man as my husband to be exposed to just such miserable and degrading calumnies as these. However, it is a convenient way of ridding one's-self of a man of honour whom it is desired to ruin, and who cannot be attacked in any less indecent fashion.

Everyone who ever knew us at all intimately, as well as our own servants, can testify with me to our happy family-life. Among thousands of marriages it would not be easy to find one like ours, in which there was such perfect confidence and such a community of intellectual work and interests. Therefore I can declare without hesitation that no one knows Prince Eulenburg so well as I do, who am fortunate enough to be his wife.

A life of the most loyal obedience to duty lies behind him. At the sacrifice of energy, time, and money he has never done anything but good to his fellow-creatures; and it is that kindness of heart, that wide philanthropy, which is now made a reproach to him; his enemies are making use of those virtues to cast suspicion on him. The many benefits and services done by him to his fellow-men are now tracked down by these despicable hounds, for the purpose of collecting their "great, overwhelming mass of incriminating evidence."

But no matter how craftily they may have done it, not a single person who knows Prince Eulenburg could believe these calumnies. Everyone who really knows him cannot but know, too, that any impurity, any deception, is absolutely incompatible with his nature. But the big public which does not know him, all those people who have never had anything to do with us—how should *they* be able to divine that all these accusations are empty air, that there is not one iota of truth in them—nothing but sheer envy and political intrigue?

There is scarcely a man in the whole world who is so misjudged and misunderstood by the great public as my husband is. The Press has invented an Eulenburg with whom he has nothing in common but the name.

" Phili, the Emperor's friend ! " Alas, yes—the Emperor's friend for more than twenty years ; and so he had to be stamped as a careerist and intriguer, and as that was not enough to bring down a faithful official who had served the Fatherland loyally for something like forty years, his morals and his honour had to be attacked. That is your latter-day way of sapping and mining.

There was a good deal of cunning—or there might have been—in referring these base suspicions to so remote a period, when he was between twenty-five and thirty. But they forgot me, his wife, and the counter-evidence *I* could give. And they forgot our faithful servants too, who were with us then and can support my testimony.

When my husband was overwhelmed with work in Munich, being much occupied with literary and artistic matters as well as his official responsibilities, he handed over to me—so early as the beginning of the 'eighties !—the entire management of our income. All payments, even of his personal expenses, were made by me. He took only a little pocket-money for daily purchases. So that I knew all about his outlay, all about every journey, however short. He was never away for half a day without leaving me his precise address. Being a fond and anxious father, he always wanted to be easily reached, in case any of the children were at all ailing. And whenever he was absent I was entrusted with the opening of his private letters, in case they should need to be answered or forwarded.

His literary works belong to those happy youthful years in Bavaria, which have since been the subject of these calumnies. The published writings are but a small part of what he did at that time. In everything he wrote, prose or poetry, his pure noble nature was mirrored—his devoted love for his saintly mother, his love and subtle understanding of children, joined to a true Christian piety and enthusiasm for all that is sublime, unsullied, good, and beautiful.

Those very years from 1881 to 1888 in Munich and Starnberg were the happiest of all, the tenderest of all, in our whole married life. In earlier years we had lost our two eldest children. This great grief had, if possible, drawn us more fervently, more closely, together. And then came the lovely happy time in Bavaria, especially the summers at dear Starnberg.

Surely it must be evident to any reasonable person that if there had been the slightest stain on his reputation at that time, a clever man like Prince Eulenburg would not, after a year's absence, have returned to Starnberg and bought a house there! For it was not until 1889 that our little abode was purchased for the family to inhabit during the yearly cure at Gastein, and as a special provision for our daughters in days to come.

It was then, too, that the notorious Jacob Ernst was installed as house-steward. The Prince could not have done that, either, if he had had any reason to fear common talk. That "common talk," if there really was any such thing during the latter part of our stay at Starnberg, could only have been started by my husband's present enemies. The other fishermen in Starnberg may often have felt jealous of our always taking the Ernst family's boat when we went to the lake. But it was only natural that we should turn, on our first arrival and settling down in Starnberg, to our nearest neighbours. These were the Ernsts. The nearest way to the lake from the villa we then had led through their garden; and as there was only a terrace in front of our house, the children and their nurses were fond of going there, and thus made acquaintance with the good old mother. She was called "the poor fishermam," for she had had much grief with her children—one after the other her eldest son and a pretty grown-up daughter had died of consumption. Fortunately she did not live to see her youngest and only surviving son turn slanderer and perjurer.

He was then a good-natured youth, and we thought he was grateful for all the kindness shown him. At first we interested ourselves in him out of pity for his parents. Once my husband took him to Meran when he went to his mother there, because the poor boy had been coughing so incessantly. How often, when he was rowing us, we would say: " Not too fast, Jacob—don't strain yourself! " In a few years his lungs got better. He and his old uncle were our oarsmen for years. Almost daily we went on the lake with our children and my parents, and naturally we became more intimate than ever with the two Ernsts. In Bavaria, as in all mountain-districts, the people of the place are much more informal and (as they say themselves) more easy-going with visitors than they are with us in North Germany. My husband especially had always liked talking with such simple, unsophisticated folk on his trips and climbing tours. It is the same kind of change, the same kind of relaxation, as being with children when one is over-tired and run-down by intercourse with the great world and the intelligentsia. Jacob Ernst, besides, had another good quality— he could hold his tongue so well when one was not inclined to talk.

When we saw him again, after some years and particularly after his wife's death, he was evidently going downhill. I was then in Munich with my daughters—it was the winter of 1905 to 1906; and I went to Starnberg expressly to see after him and his motherless children. I found him very much changed. I thought he might have taken to drink. He said himself: " Since the wife's death I never sleep; it can't go on like this. There'll soon be an end to it." His only consolation was " his beer," to which he had always been addicted more even than is usual in Bavaria. Even as a young man he used to tell us that he never took any breakfast—only " his beer," before the midday meal. Every year he seemed to grow slower-witted and deafer.

And this is the man to whose oath more

credence is given than to that of Prince Eulenburg—a Bavarian peasant, once a worthy man, but now retrograde and afflicted with deafness! But as until now he was of good repute, it was quite a clever stroke to get hold of him and use his evidence to confirm the bought false witness of the infamous Riedl.

The friendly letters written by Prince Eulenburg to this Ernst, and of course carefully preserved by him, are now turned into "highly suspicious documents." Why should not the Prince have written to him in a friendly sort of way? He does, to everyone; it might even be said that he thinks too little of class distinctions, takes too familiar a tone. But that is his way. His writings are enough to show his freedom from any such prejudices.

But the world knows very little about such wide humanity, and a perfectly selfless nature will always be a puzzle to it. Most men confine themselves to "getting something out of" that unselfish sort of kindness. That was why from near and far they all, high and low, importuned him; and he, with his unique kindliness and conscientiousness, insisted on answering every application, on helping everyone everywhere, until his energies and nerves were broken down. What thanks does he get for it now? But at least a few faithful hearts have the courage of their convictions, and have not forsaken the friend and benefactor in his hour of need. Men and women both. Of his *women* friends I have not yet spoken.

It is a matter of course that the Prince's enemies, who have set themselves to track down everyone with whom he ever came in contact, should intentionally and completely ignore the female sex. Women would not have been of any service in *that* game—the young and the old to whom he gave a helping hand in need ; the beautiful and gifted who admired and still admire him so fervently, and of whom many are to this day his warm devoted friends. I am sorry that the officials who at the behest of their superiors repeatedly examined my husband's private correspondence at Liebenberg—letters which I had spent months in putting into chronological order—that those officials did not also take away with them some of these most interesting correspondences with distinguished and highly-placed women, all of them so cordially inclined to him. That would have given some real idea of his universal popularity, as remarkable with women as with men.

I was not jealous. For I knew that I possessed my husband's full confidence, and that he, though as a man among men and an artist he could not be entirely indifferent to such tributes, *had* preferred me to all others when he chose me for his lifelong companion ; and I knew, too, that he would be faithful to me.

My husband's habit of keeping all his letters made my work of arranging them very arduous. Along with the intellectual correspondences carried on with the most distinguished men and women of our time, he carefully preserved letters from people in the most modest positions —from his many protégés, the sons and daughters of former official subordinates, godchildren, wards of both sexes who had never forgotten him. For example, I had put Jacob Ernst's letters in the same packet with some from the little son of his one-time keeper, now his nurse, Emanuel Bartsch. Directly the news of that horrible Munich lawsuit, the Städele trial (our enemies' first deadly attack), came on us, totally unprepared as we were, I collected Ernst's letters, so as to have them at hand in case of any investigation. My husband himself never thought of them, never asked for them even when the persecution began. How could he possibly imagine that out of deeds of kindness anyone could construct so abominably artful a snare!

A man with a clear conscience, a man who never in his life has had anything to conceal, is besides incapable of imagining the labyrinths of cunning in which tortuous natures are quite at home. If my husband had had anything to conceal, he would have been more circumspect, and would certainly not have written Jacob Ernst a friendly letter even after the persecution had begun. Surely it is manifest that a clever man who has for years held an important diplomatic post, and is himself a lawyer, will not voluntarily put himself in such a position as his present one, unless he has a perfectly clear conscience, unless he can say to himself: "It is my duty to my family to prove and swear to my perfect innocence." When he was seriously ill he dragged himself, against his doctor's wishes, to the Bülow-Brandt and Moltke-Harden trials, to give evidence for his friends. He came back, composed and satisfied. Is it conceivable that so religious and conscientious a man as he is could be composed and satisfied if he had sworn to anything which departed from the absolute truth, even though it might be no more than a failure of memory? No—and again no!

But afterwards, when Harden was sentenced to a term of imprisonment and we were all rejoicing, my husband said with unerring fore-

Appendix II

sight: " That is the signal for fresh and terrible fights! Harden will not submit to imprisonment without having beforehand moved heaven and earth to do the Fatherland still greater and more irretrievable injury!" And he was only too right.

When at the end of April one horrible sensation succeeded another, he had been for two months laid up with acute rheumatism in his knee. The long incarceration in the little hot, airless room at the Charité had so aggravated his sufferings that he was never equal to preparing himself adequately for the trial, to the despair of his defending counsel. Yet he never for a moment lost his peace of mind; and in that time of sorrow I learnt from him to place my trust in God alone, and have no fear though all the powers of hell should conspire against us. He cannot and he shall not be the victim of base envy! Even in the scales of human justice my testimony must surely weigh heavier than the lies and inventions of his adversaries! The testimony of a wife who for 33 years has been devoted to her husband with boundless love and reverence, who has always possessed his full confidence, and in all those long years has never for a second doubted him in any respect.

III

THE DIARY OF PRINCE EULENBURG FROM APRIL 21 TO JUNE 24, 1908

April 21, 1908. Trial at Munich. Harden v. Städele, the editor. The witnesses Riedl and Ernst tell most horrible lies about me. The whole case looks like a public indictment of me. I am completely in the dark.

April 22. I read the report in the newspaper and went off in a faint, from which, alas! I recovered. Geritz and Emanuel Bartsch looked after me. Frightfully upset. Endless telephoning from and to Liebenberg. A terrible night. I feel that after two years of incessant battle I shall be laid low. Jews and their money, Court, Government—all against one man who never showed them anything but kindness. But the " Emperor's friend " is the real quarry. *Nil novi.*

April 23. Return of my dear wife from Brixen. She knows nothing yet.

April 24. I had to tell her that things are worse than ever. She was splendid. My faithful servants are all beyond compare in kindness and attachment.

April 25 to May 6. Awful days and nights of torment. Two surprise-visits from the investigating magistrate, accompanied by a police-surgeon and constables. Immediately after the terrible evidence at Munich, I had myself asked for an investigation. Now I am supposed to be guilty of perjury ! ! These surprise-visits are unspeakably distressing. For I am in bed with neuritis, together with heart-failure and nervous exhaustion.

May 7. The witnesses Ernst and Riedl were confronted with me, in my bed at Liebenberg. They stuck to their infamous evidence, which was only to be expected, for if they didn't they would go to gaol. The investigating magistrate declared me to be under arrest. Doctors Hoffmann and Genrich stated that I was fit (!) to be transported to Berlin, for incarceration in the Hospital. During the night two constables kept guard in the two rooms opening off my bedroom (lest I should make my escape ! !)

We tried to obtain immediate bail in half a million marks. Endless telephoning. A terrible sleepless night. My poor son Fritz Wend came back from Austria in the afternoon.

May 8. At 3 o'clock we left Liebenberg ; difficult business, getting me into the carriage. The Commissioner of Police on the box. In the carriage Augusta, myself, the doctor, and Emanuel. Agonising departure from my home, branded as a criminal. God is trying me harder than I could ever have imagined ! . . . On the way great pain and faintness. We often had to stop. Arrival at the Charité in Berlin at 6. I lost consciousness when being lifted out and carried in on the stretcher, but the quarters are tolerable, and our reception was kind. I was very tired, but managed to sleep with the help of powders. Emanuel sleeps in my room. Next door is the nurse ; a room close by for Emanuel to sit in during the daytime ; and there is a room for two quite friendly constables who are my warders. Augusta is staying in our rooms at 42, Königin-Augusta Strasse.

May 9. After all it is better to be here than at Liebenberg, guarded by police in my own house! Augusta came in the morning. I slept a little. Visit in the afternoon from my dear children Siegwart and Tora. The former, though he is still very ill, had come from Munich to see me. Fritz Wend came a little later. The 500,000 mark bail refused. I am to be a prisoner. This is to give the Press its sensation. I am the sop that the Government and all the authorities are throwing to the Cerberus of the " people " (the Press)—and I shall be gobbled up. My only chance would have been to be plain Mr. Schulz. Visit from the doctors, Professor Kraus and Dr. Steyrer. Both from Steiermark—full of kindness, sympathy, understanding. Also a visit from my lawyer, Wronker; these discussions are frightfully tiring—and what will they all amount to? Nothing! I must suffer—I am *intended* to suffer; but my innocence gives me inward strength. Visit from the investigating magistrate, who is kindly inclined and procured me these quite private quarters, which are not at all so bad. Later, Augusta came again. I was worn-out with pain. That enabled me to sleep.

Sunday, May 10. Bad heart-attack and fainting-fit in the morning. . . . Felt a little better in the afternoon, but not till then. Dr. Steyrer sent me some branches of budding larch from Steiermark, and I was deeply touched by his kindness—and skill.

May 11. A troublesome morning after a bad

night. A long time before I could pull myself together, and I stayed in bed. At ten the two doctors, Kraus and Steyrer. Very upsetting sort of interview. I told them all about the pains in my head that I have suffered from for years, and that I ought not to confess to now, lest it may give the impression that I want to be considered a mental case. Kraus suggested that I should see a psychiatrist. I refused. . . . More and more sympathy for me in many quarters. What good will that do? " Hosanna," and then " Crucify him ! " I know my doom . . . I was very much upset, worrying myself about the visit from County-Court Judge Schmidt, for I am not equal to these discussions, either physically or mentally. Towards evening came Dr. Steyrer, for whom I feel a great liking. He is a real comfort to me. . . .

May 12. My own dear Augusta's birthday—a terribly sad one ; she is like an angel, soothing my pain. I awoke after a good night, but felt very tired. I sent Emanuel with flowers and a little present to Augusta. Then arrived Kraus and Steyrer. A long talk, which upset me. I stayed in bed nearly all day. The air in this little room is not good ! I can take about eight paces in it—like a caged hyena. God knows how long this will last ! Soon after 12 came my darling Augusta. At one o'clock the dear children—the three boys and dear sweet little Tora. God bless her ! And so we kept the birthday here—united in such love. In the afternoon I tried to sleep. At 5 came Wronker. Things look bad for me. The preliminary inquiry will last some time longer. Harden daily sends bundles of denunciations

—about 140 (! !) witnesses are to be heard. What will be the end of it?

May 13. Bad night. I took no sleeping-powders, and had to pay for it. Great weakness. A short sleep in the afternoon. Visit from kind Dr. Genrich, who is still frightfully indignant. Otherwise nothing new. Things are in the same state. Hopelessly against me. God alone is my refuge.

May 14. I slept with the aid of veronal powders. At 7 a.m. appeared a police-sergeant, wanting the keys of my writing-table at Liebenberg ! ! I was startled out of sleep, and fainted. Emanuel called Dr. Steyrer, and I did not recognise even him—not for two hours. Then I did, and Kraus too. My condition very trying and alarming—heart-attacks and dizziness. Visit from Wronker, who told me that bail has again been refused (which I expected). I shall probably be here for weeks and weeks ! In the afternoon I at last felt better. Visit from Steyrer, whose sympathy profoundly touched me. Fritz Wend tells me that four police-sergeants spent four hours looking through my letters, and took several away with them. I must indeed pray God for patience —it is all I can do.

May 15. A tolerable night. At 5 came the investigating magistrate. Two men were brought to my bedside, with whom, according to Harden and Co., I had had sexual relations (! ! !). I had never laid eyes on them ! Thank God, both declared on oath that they had never seen me before. I can't bear this any longer. What will happen if such men swear they *do* know me? I am in the power of terrible forces. God's visitation is harder

Appendix III

than I have strength for. Oh, if it would but come to an end ! I feel that the terrible pains in my head, which are getting worse and worse, will incapacitate me mentally. Besides the fight for my existence, my family, I have to contend with these inner foes that seem likely to deprive me of my reason. The effort to retain facts is sometimes superhuman, unbearable, beyond mortal power. Terrible weakness results from it, exhaustion and a passionate craving for death. And God will not have it so ! . . . I can't bear all these strangers, these questions, the ghastly politeness which is so well-meant, yet masks such infinite cruelty. What can be God's purpose in this? Certainly I have merited punishment for many things, but not really more than plenty of other people. And yet I have to bear the stigma of abominations that I never committed. I suppose I shall understand it some day, but not here, for I am a broken man. Oh, if God would but grant me release —but not in the most terrible way of all, by losing my reason ! . . . Laemmel arrived. I was terribly upset at seeing him again, and at our conversation. Everything seems confused. I have only the dimmest recollection of what happened yesterday. I must have been very ill.

May 16. Passed the night in a kind of stupor. A bad morning ; my head in a whirl, and great oppression on the heart. Emanuel's care quite affecting. He is like a good spirit by my bed. I cannot write ; the words get all mixed-up. Dr. Steyrer has become a friend. He soothes me, and I know he believes in me and understands how wretched I am. But he will not be able to save my brain. I know there has been a change since yesterday, and that no doctor can do anything. Oh, if I can only keep my sense of all the love that people show me!

Sunday, May 17. A tolerable night, but I am very weak in the mornings. I can scarcely talk or do anything to pass the time. Still in bed. I am frightfully nervous and restless.

May 18. Weaker than ever after a passable night. Visit from the doctors. They want to call in a psychiatrist. The beginning of the end! A short visit from Wronker, which of course upset me. I feel that these things are bringing me lower and lower. Augusta—and I too—received many tokens of deep sympathy. Afternoon visit from my dear Dr. Steyrer, who gave me a beautiful photograph—his own work. In the evening I was most horribly weak.

May 19. Very weak this morning. But I had the joy of a glorious vision, which fortified and consoled me. Fritz Wend and Tora told me a lot about Liebenberg. Oh, how I long to see the spring! Last year I was very ill in bed—now I am in prison! Shall I ever see the spring again? . . . I was so weak that I stayed in bed all day; got up for a little while in the evening. In the afternoon a short visit from Wronker and a long one from my dear Steyrer. —— sent me a splendid bunch of carnations. So there are still some people who believe in me. And how will it end? Persecution, hatred, lying—more and more of it all!

May 20. Very bad day. In a sort of dream all the morning. Geritz came from Liebenberg. I can't remember what he talked about. In

Appendix III

the afternoon came the psychiatrist of the Charité, a specialist, Professor Ziehen. It was a terrible effort to tell him about all the confusion and pain and torment I have had for so long in my poor head—to recall so many things of which I had only the dimmest recollection, and which were connected with awful mental tortures. God alone knows whether it was wise to take this step. I cannot even say that it has relieved me. I had a whole series of fainting-fits—until 9.30 p.m. This increasing weakness is not unpleasant, except for the difficulty in breathing. But that does not last long, as a rule.

May 21. No sleeping-draught last night. More stupor than sleep. At eleven Fritz Wend came unexpectedly from Liebenberg, for Marie and Adine were arriving from Austria. Both came to me straight from the railway station. I took great pains to seem composed, so as not to distress the poor things. Professor Ziehen in the afternoon. Stirred up most painful recollections of my mental state. Most distressing to me. My good Dr. Steyrer came and cheered me by his affection and sympathy. A letter from Field-Marshal Hahnke, Chancellor of the Black Eagle Order, was brought to me—it had been opened by the magistrate. The Emperor, as Grand Master, has ordained that " since in my present state I can neither wear the Order, nor keep it in safety, I should send it to the Chancery *ad depositum* " [that is, till the decision is made]. What a ridiculous fuss about a bauble ! What did I ever care for Orders ! And now, when all this slander, envy, hatred, is heaped upon me—when they accuse me of perjury—me, a man who before

God can say with a clear conscience that he never felt anything but love for his fellow-creatures, and always did what lay in his power for them ! How absurd these things are, how unimportant !

May 22. Bad night. It is beginning to get very hot in my little room. Morning not too bad, and the doctors came. Kraus and Steyrer had a friendly talk with me about the situation, and implored me for God's sake to reject any idea of suicide. It would be the greatest of mistakes —and do the greatest harm to my dear ones. (And yet three of my best friends advise it !) What terrible questions and discussions. In my awful situation the wisdom of man is of no avail—God shall be my guide and I will bear the cross that He lays upon me, and that others have borne before me. And in days like these, to have to write a letter about an Order ! How it revolts me ! But I will bear this cross too. I will set down for those who shall one day read these lines what monarchs are, who say to their " best friend " that " until their last breath they will never forget what he did for them."

" *To His Excellency the Chancellor*
" *of the Black Eagle Order :*
 " *General Field-Marshal von Hahnke,*
  " *Berlin. Kurfürstendamm* 252.
       " Berlin, Charité.
       " *May* 23, 1908.

" In reply to Your Excellency's letter of the 20th, I have the honour to inform you that as a result of my application to the Crown Prosecutor—of which I had the honour of informing Your Excellency in my last communication—the preliminary investigations concerning me have been begun. The result of these investigations, which have not yet been concluded, will furnish the material for a decision for or against an indictment. Since the witnesses Riedl and Ernst have, as was to be anticipated, held to their evidence (fearing punishment if they should take the contrary course), the investigating magistrate has placed me under provisional arrest, and despite my feeble state of health I have been transported from Liebenberg to Berlin. Both my condition, and the impossibility of corresponding privately with Your Excellency—I am guarded in the Charité by two constables, whose duty it is to take every letter written by me to be opened by the magistrate and at his discretion forwarded—preclude me from giving Your Excellency any further information; for I should not wish such painful communications as those relating to my present circumstances to pass through the hands of a stranger. The letter written to me by Your Excellency was taken to the court of inquiry, there opened, read, and (as the enclosed envelope will show) forwarded open to me through a messenger of the court, that is to say, a policeman. In these circumstances I am in the distressing position of being obliged to send this strictly confidential document unfastened to Your Excellency.

"I shall not, however, be able to give Your Excellency any further information as to the course of events. My health is so enfeebled that I am no longer equal to writing. Doubtless Your Excellency will be informed from other quarters of the progress of these proceedings. However they may end—a Prussian officer and functionary who has spent more than forty years in honourable service to his king and country, a Philip Eulenburg is incapable of taking a false oath—no matter what the other oaths opposed to his.

"As regards the delivery of the Orders *ad depositum*—which shall be done this day from Liebenberg—it is entirely in accordance with my wishes. I shall have the honour of adding to the specified decoration all those other Orders and decorations conferred upon me by His Majesty; such as :

"1. The Hohenzollern Order with Star.
"2. The Red Eagle Order with Crown.
"3. Their Majesties' Silver Wedding Commemoration Order.
"4. The medal struck to commemorate Emperor William I's Centenary—for I do not consider that any discrimination should be made between distinctions of this kind.

"But I have another reason for saying that it accords with my wishes to hand over all the Orders and marks of distinction conferred upon me by His Majesty. Throughout the whole course of my life I have felt a certain repugnance to the conferring of Orders as a reward for the fulfilment of duty, however conscientious that fulfilment may have been. And I have had no opportunity to do more than my loyal duty. But because of the peculiar favour with which His Majesty has distinguished me for more than twenty years—and which to the end of my life will be remembered with profound gratitude !—I have set an entirely personal value on the conferring of these several Orders and decorations.

"Hence these objects became wholly valueless to me in the moment when His Majesty, urged

Appendix III

thereto by public and private opinion, suddenly deprived me of his countenance and support.

"I am aware that Your Excellency will probably feel these expressions to be somewhat irrevelant to my official reply. But since, as I have said, this will be my last communication with Your Excellency, I expressly request of your kindness that you will permit the contents of my letter to be conveyed, without any abridgment, to His Majesty the Emperor and King.

"I have the honour to subscribe myself Your Excellency's most respectful and humble servant,
"Eulenburg—H."

May 23. A tolerable night with veronal ; very low throughout the day. Couldn't brace myself to get out of bed—except for half-an-hour in the morning. Wronker came at noon for a quarter-of-an-hour. Up to the present the Munich inquiries have yielded no results. Professor Ziehen with me for half-an-hour. In afternoon Dr. Steyrer, bringing the news that the High Court has decided to revise the Moltke-Harden case ! How horrible ! If the Crown lawyers had a spark of feeling for the Fatherland's well-being they would have left that shameful case, that crying scandal, alone. But the letter of the law, with those who should uphold the right, has always been more honoured than good sense and enlightened counsels.[1] "A fight without an end "—a fight to make one despair ! But God shall still be my shield in all these utterly incomprehensible doings.

[1] The reason was that a witness who had previously been dismissed from the case, and whose evidence was anyhow irrelevant, had been re-examined without being expressly reminded of the oath he had taken in the earlier trial.

Sunday, May 24. A bad night in spite of aspirin. I was very much upset. The interview with the doctors taxed my energies. At 11 came Fritz Wend from Liebenberg, and refreshed me with his dear presence and his talk of home doings. How God has blessed me in him—and what pain it gives me to cause him such misery as one cannot see an end to. He had called on Varnbüler, whose inexpressibly loyal friendship deeply moved him. Augusta had a visit from August Eulenburg, whose loyalty and sympathy for me were infinitely touching to her. Laemmel from Ruppin came to see me. He was a little more hopeful. Why? It is true he does not know of all the forces that are bent on my destruction. Where is hope to be found? Not here on earth! But I know where salvation awaits me. God will give it me, and " there remaineth a rest."

May 25. A goodish night with sleeping draught. The whole forenoon very bad. Great weakness and dizziness. At 6 Wronker, with news from Munich—not so bad ; examination of witnesses proceeding. What good is it? What good, though public opinion seems to be turning in my favour? I am not even physically capable of fighting it out. One against a hundred—the odds are unfair! I feel as though a mountain had fallen on me—yet I go on living. But the few hands that are trying to extricate me are as the digging of tiny insects.

May 26. Night not so bad. Augusta came with the dear children Adine and Tora. How glad I was to see their darling little angel faces! I made them tell me about Liebenberg, now sparkling in all its beauty. The poor little

APPENDIX III

things imagine that I am longing for all the loveliness that my ancestors and I have fashioned. But they are wrong. My life has grown too grievous for me even to think of the possibility of such delight. When I hear of it, it is as though they were reading to me from some beautiful refreshing book—a novel in which one loses one's-self, in which one knows and loves the characters and their surroundings; but quite impersonally. And that is just why it does one good. I felt scarcely equal to seeing Schmidt, who told me that all the Munich depositions have brought nothing but *on dits* to light. He said, too, that the whole Press in Berlin and Germany is furiously attacking Harden. A complete *volte-face*. What does that signify—one thing to-day, another to-morrow. Finally Schmidt produced yet another abject wretch, whom Harden had described as one of my intimate acquaintances. The abominable creature came right up to my bed—but afterwards swore he had never seen me before. My God, what torments! Suppose he had been bribed, and had sworn he did know me? I don't know how I manage to endure it all! What a terrible power of resistance is mine against this misery. " Be still and clear and strong, unhappy fool. Thy misery is now thy strength." I heard that in Liebenberg on the night of April 23, 1908. And Romans 8, 18, says : " For I reckon that the sufferings of this present time are not worthy to be compared with the glory that shall be revealed in us." So I must go on suffering and enduring, and think I am passing through a dreamland of terror where, though my hands cannot touch them, my eyes can see in the distance quiet, peaceful, overarching glades.

May 27. A tolerable night; but a very bad morning. Attacks of breathlessness, and my head unutterably confused. Steyrer came early. Afterwards again with Professor Kraus. Towards noon a slight improvement.

Ascension Day, May 28. Now Nature is in all her glory, and I can see nothing of it but the flowers that kind people bring—as to a corpse. The night bearable, but again very weak. Nearly all day I had to read the evidence taken from Munich and Starnberg witnesses. A frightful ordeal, to which I am hardly equal. Even though these things are only rumours, idle gossip, nothing directly incriminating, I cannot get rid of the feeling that all the filth in all Germany is smothering me. How am I ever to get away from this cesspool? How stand up to these adversaries?

May 29. Night not so bad. Fainting fit in morning. The doctor sent for. Better by noon. An indescribably painful day. The investigating magistrate began going over all the incriminating material with me—such a pile ! From 3 to 7.30. The necessity of keeping my attention fixed, the frightful revelations of calumnies, suspicions from all my friends, officials, servants—lie upon lie ; I was well-nigh suffocated. What earthly good is it for me to declare again and again : " Lies ! I never did any of these things, I don't know any of these people, etc. ! " Will they—*do they want to*—believe me ? I feel that only God can be my judge. Men will condemn me. May God grant me strength—for life is becoming a hell. Can I go on bearing it ? I am physically and mentally weaker, my nerves are beginning to go. My angel Augusta consoles me. The good Emanuel's care is touching.

May 30. The night not a good one. The day was trying. Yesterday's effort has done me harm of some kind. And I am suffering badly in the moral sense, because I cannot get over the impression of all that pile of incriminating material. I have been flung into a sea of infamy, and when I try to swim to shore, criminals and murderers beat me back. How is the poor wretch to land? Only God can help me—and He has veiled His face. Jacob Ernst's evidence is an enigma to me. What *can* be making him accuse me? Am I really to be condemned and end my life in shame, and are my poor children to have *their* lives made hideous by this discord that no harmony can prevail against? I pray to God so often, so fervently for them—for myself I have ceased to pray. —— sent me some splendid carnations and a profoundly moving letter. Her fidelity is a precious gift from God. If my King had only been a tenth part as loyal as she is, I should not have to endure the agonies that are overwhelming me, and that show me to myself as " guilty " indeed—but only as all erring, weak humanity is guilty. Even under the impression of that mass of accusations, I cannot regard these men as greatly guilty—merely as victims of error. But I will not acknowledge myself " Guilty " towards the Divine that is in me! I have done wrong—I *have* been guilty of many an error, many a sin, for I am a man faulty and weak as we all are. Yet I know that God is just, and never will I doubt His justice—though for a while He "hide His countenance from me." Nevertheless, my guiltiness towards God is no more than this—that wealth and rank impose on us the duty of giving, of helping. Under the pressure of daily cares and toil I have not done enough for my fellow-creatures in their hour of need. For to feel love is a long way from being active in love. And when I make even the briefest survey of my life and my deeds, I feel lost in a sort of fog of perpetual " putting-off." Yes —I, too, am a wrongdoer. And therefore I accept the heaviest trials as a punishment, an offset for what I have neglected, for what I have sinned in. It is for God to ordain the form. The kind of offset He has chosen seems difficult to me, the " why " still more difficult. But what are mortal destinies ? Nothing but offsets for much that we know of, and much that we do not—but shall, some day. Therefore :

> Nehmen sie den Leib,
> Gut, Ehre, Kind und Weib—
> Lass fahren dahin !
> Sie haben kein Gewinn !
> Das Reich Gottes muss uns bleiben.[1]

But for all that, suffering still means anguish, and the mortal body writhes beneath it as do the mind and soul. Yesterday's reading of the evidence gave me some kind of physical shock, and I know why it was—apart altogether from the spiritual pain of the afternoon. Quite unexpectedly Adine and Tora, my darling children, came with Augusta. I had to make

---

[1] Though they take your life,
Home and honour, wean and wife—
Let them go their way !
Not to them the day !
God's great realm for us abideth.

a supreme effort, or I should have burst into tears. I must not let the poor dear children see how I am suffering. They have enough to bear on my account. My composure must be a help to them; their young lives must not be darkened by the sight of human anguish. They are darkened enough, without that. But they came to-day like angels from Heaven, and their chatter made me feel as if we were at home, framed in the paradise of my Liebenberg. I breathed again, and was so thankful to be able to.

Sunday, May 31. Very hot weather. I still feel the physical change resulting from that awful evidence. Chiefly rushes of blood to the head, which are something quite new to me. The doctors think my condition very unsatisfactory. That attempt to " put through " the long study of the evidence has done me a lot of harm.

June 1. Very hot again. Night tolerable. My state of mind the same. Very weak. Geritz came at 10. The poor fellow beside himself about Harden's calumnies. How painful for me to see all my loyal officials publicly reviled, slandered, attacked, on my account! All, all have to suffer for me; and I want to show them nothing but affection, make their paths smooth for them.

1. I must keep it well in mind that I have put a great part—perhaps the greater—of my path of suffering behind me.

2. I ought not to forget that I have suffered so fearfully that even the disaster of being condemned has lost some of its terrors, and I am probably capable of bearing even those torments.

3. The consciousness of my being a victim

would mitigate the fact of being condemned. Not only in my own consciousness, but in that of many groups of people.

4. A very large group would, despite the sentence, believe in my innocence. Another group would consider me a homo-sexual, but would excuse the false oath :

(*a*) Because I would have wanted to save my reputation, and after all would have injured no one.

(*b*) Because I would have taken the oath to save the Emperor who, if I were condemned, would certainly be branded as a homo-sexual (and that is the terrible mistake the Government has made in letting things go so far)!

A third group would regard me purely and simply as the victim of a political conflict, in which homo-sexuality had played an extremely insignificant part—and only as a means to an end.

A fourth group would regard me as a " signal proof " that Article 175 is untenable, and that there must be a reform in the administration of the oath.

A fifth would forgive me everything out of sheer human sympathy for the vastness of my suffering—even if they considered me in some sort guilty.

Take it for all in all, the case has so many sides that a condemnation would not be judged by ordinary rules.

5. The preservation of my life and health is an essential factor if my sufferings are to be brought to any sort of an end—either by my being cleared, or finally sacrificed.

6. I must try without ceasing to rise above my sufferings and look to the end where, after

APPENDIX III 355

all, there is still the possibility of some sort of endurable existence.

7. Suicide would be simply a confession of guilt, and would mean a greater triumph for my enemies than condemnation would.

8. Death in the course of nature would be a relief for the Emperor, the Government, the justiciary, the authorities of the Crown; ultimately for my family, my true friends—and myself.

That lies in God's hand—and His justice is my solace, even if human justice, haloed as His representative, should condemn me.

Such was, in essentials, what I said to N. N., who was sent me by ——, so as to hear from the doctor how I am, and what is my spiritual state. N. N. is not only a man of powerful intellect, but a good man too. Full of understanding and a friend in need. I knew him already, though not as a consoler—as a man whose whole personality was inspiring in its strength. And so ——, the finest, bravest, truest of women-friends, has done me yet another kindness by sending N. N. But how I grieve to think of that noble woman's pain—she who, so exalted, can nevertheless see and feel for these things with such intense sympathy! I hear that the Emperor is distressed about me. I can well believe it. But his stupefying life leaves him no time for reflection, and he will never own to himself that he is in any way to blame for my misfortune. Perhaps he puts the responsibility on other people—but not on the right ones, so far as my knowledge of him goes. In the afternoon from 4 to 6.30 more reading of evidence. Frightful, appalling things. One lie after another. What good is my eternal " No " ? They will smother me, throttle me, drown me in this cesspool. God be merciful unto me—for in truth I see that my earthly weapons are of no avail.

June 2. Terribly hot. The night bad. The results of all that agitation yesterday plainly to be felt. At 11 a visit from Wronker, and we went over all yesterday's incidents. Then came the good Laemmel from Ruppin. It was an inexpressible torment to go over again with him the things that yesterday almost killed me. But what can I expect but these ordeals ?—I tried to sleep, so as to be equal for to-day's evidence. At 4 came the investigating magistrate. The doctors had most strictly forbidden me to give more than two hours to it. To-day we got over something like 150 points of the material. More horrors, alternating with idiocy, absurdity, and heartlessness. Always my " No "—and then fresh accusations. There really are only a few of my friends, officials, servants who are not suspected, involved in this filth !

June 3. The night terribly hot. The morning correspondingly bad. Emanuel had to open the windows during the night, and that meant no sleep, for the noise in the street is appalling. This day very trying. I felt so tired, and yet I had to keep on talking and discussing all day long. The doctors came at 11, Wronker from 11 to 12, then Laemmel, then Wronker again, then Dr. Genrich, then the investigating magistrate. So on until 6.30, in such heat, not a moment's rest, perpetually called upon to fix my attention ! I don't know how I manage to bear it. This time Schmidt brought me a gaol-bird under the care of two warders,

Appendix III

of whom Harden declares that I have had relations with him. Thank goodness the fellow owned that he had never seen me before. But it was an excruciating ordeal. The martyr's path is appointed for me. God knows His Divine purpose. But I often think: " It is enough." I daresay that is very weak of me.

June 4. The night terribly hot. I suffered badly because of it. In the morning so disturbed in mind that I could remember nothing. Staff-Surgeon von Saar (deputising for Steyrer) came. He is a nice, kind man, warmly sympathetic for me. Wronker came, and we had a painful talk, which showed me in good earnest how badly things are going. Am I equal to standing my trial in court? I feel more and more doubtful about it. I know my physical energies are sinking, and the confusion in my brain sometimes lasts so long (as for instance to-day from waking till the afternoon) that I begin to think I am not quite right in my head. And my memory fails me alarmingly. What is to be the end of all this? I once wrote a fairy-tale—or was it a poem, or a song? —at any rate I remember a verse from it, which goes something like this:

> Geduld im Hoffen, du Kind der Zeit!
> Im Zügel der regsame Wille!
> Es hat ein Ende all Lust und Leid,
> Es kommt der Tag der Stille![1]

Sometimes I fancy that God must have given me my imagination and my talents simply for

---

[1] Thou child of Time, hope on and wait,
And thy rebel will subdue!
There comes an end to every fate,
And the quiet day, and the new!

the purpose of making it easier to bear the crown of thorns He has appointed for me—and which, for reasons that are hidden from me, I must wear.

June 5. A very bad night; 21 degrees Réaumur in the room throughout. The morning as usual very confused. Wronker came at 11. He struck me as being very much perturbed; he asked me—having begged me yesterday to be frank about my mental state—whether I would have a report on it sent in. This showed me that he thought my position very terrible, and I was so overwhelmed that my mental agony almost killed me. Unhappy wretch that I am! Scarcely able to control my mind, and physically so weak that I dare not leave my bed—and yet I have to make decisions so momentous as this! But I am utterly unable to do any such thing, I am not entirely master of my thoughts. How shall I decide? Finally I told him that there were only three possibilities:

1. *Acquittal.* Then my enemies will go on with the fight, I shall be driven to further despair, and there will be more false witnesses —and then will begin another prosecution for perjury.

2. *Condemnation.* I discussed that frightful possibility with N. N. some days ago, and wrote down my ideas. In that case I may be regarded as a martyr; but I shall bear the prison-brand on my forehead, and it can never be effaced—not even the love of my dear ones could efface it; and they, for all their intense sympathy and faith in me, will nevertheless come in time to feel the burden a heavy one.

3. *Declared insane.* That would end the proceedings; I should be supposed to be a

free man. But my " martyrdom," as some would certainly consider it, would take a different form. What good would it do me to feel and know that by my unspeakable sufferings I had been robbed of my former mental capacities ? What would it avail me if every clear-sighted person should say : " No wonder such an existence drove him mad ! " (Dr. Genrich, my own family-doctor, said only yesterday : " I can hardly understand how you have kept your senses ! ") Such a confession of mental disturbance would merely mean a confession of guilt. I should not be " the victim " then—the victim of a political party and base envy—the victim of justice, which *can* go wrong. No ; I should be deprived of the sympathy which might be felt for me in many quarters, and which would be some slight solace to my poor family. For the verdict of narrow-minded, hostile, calumnious society will in any event, even that of acquittal, be censorious enough to destroy me, cruelly and relentlessly.

4. *Suicide.* Then everyone would pity me, and it would be a kind of relief for my family. But the effect would be almost the same as if I were declared insane. So that, too, would mean a confession of guilt, and a terrible shock to my family, and a bitterness of feeling that nothing, not even the many years of life that lie before my children, could ever extinguish in them. For they love me far too dearly. Some sense of forgiveness would gradually permeate through their pain, they being so young as they are, if they could see me, however branded, slowly beginning to feel once more a sort of pleasure in living ; if

by their love they could rejoice me, who would have renounced all else that life might still have to offer.

Thus tormented by having to concentrate on the objective " I," all I could do was to wait for the investigating magistrate, who wanted to " produce " another witness from Munich—one who had, to be sure, given the emptiest kind of evidence. In the afternoon I received the appalling indictment-sheet from the Crown Prosecutor : " Indicted for perjury and attempted incitement to perjury." To see it in black and white was a terrible shock. I am confronted with such enigmas ! How is it possible that that harmless letter to Ernst can be taken as an incitement to perjury ? If I were guilty of such a thing, if anything so horrible had ever entered my head, I should certainly not have sent the letter by post. I should have had a go-between, should have despatched it by some hand I could trust. I should never have been such a fool, such a lunatic, as to go about a crime like that in that way ! But why do I wonder, why do I feel any surprise at all ? They want my head—and they will get it. Oh, how fortunate were they who had their heads sliced off by the guillotine ! But in the German *Kulturstaat* the procedure is more thoroughgoing, and am I not a Prussian—a man who has *travaillé pour le roi de Prusse !*

All the afternoon I lay in a kind of mental torpor with alarming fits of breathlessness. My good Emanuel's care was touching, like that of one of the Sisters, who are so kind. Not until 8 in the evening was I at all clear in my mind ; but then I got very excited and tried to jot down these notes while I *was* lucid. Dear Augusta came to wish me good-night. Has she any idea of my sufferings, I wonder? I have tried so hard to give her the impression that they are merely physical, the result of this intolerable heat.

June 6. The veronal took good effect last night. My exhaustion after those revelations helped, I suppose. I awoke from a soothing vague sort of dream, and painful reality came rushing upon me once more, and I utterly collapsed. What infinite refreshment there is in God's gift of sleep! If only He would let one not awake! The doctor comes twice a day. He is quite a young man, this deputy for my kind Steyrer, Dr. von Saar; a good, dear fellow, whose kindness does me good, and makes me entirely forget the military " form " which I didn't altogether like at first. In the evening, Dr. von Saar told me that the magistrate had asked whether I could not be transferred to Moabit. He examined me again, and said I could *not*. Late at night I felt very ill again.

Whitsunday, June 7. A flood of happy memories of childhood came over me. I have never been among those who cling to the thought of past happiness. Rather, I make a point of taking without flinching the wounds that life deals out to us, because I am convinced of the *necessity* in our destinies—and besides people of strong imagination are always strong in hope too. Augusta came and read me the Gospel for Whitsunday. The weather has got very cool. Little Dr. von Saar told me lots of things. I went to bed at 9.30, very much fatigued by an hour of great pain, sitting up in the armchair.

Appendix III

Whitmonday, June 8. My good Emanuel went off to Liebenberg for two days. To-morrow is his birthday. I hope the change will do him good. I can never speak of him without emotion, for the kindness, the self-sacrifice, the steadiness and self-respect of that simple fellow upset all our theories about education, culture, pride of birth. "But God seeth the heart"—that is the crowning beauty of Christian doctrine, what makes it superior to all other systems. Later in the day Kammer came to see me.[1] It touches me to see his loyalty, his attachment to me. But his unshakable conviction that I shall be acquitted gives me great pain. He said, "So we all think in Liebenberg and the neighbourhood." I begged him to remember what danger I am in—danger meaning uncertainty about the verdict. I had to give the poor fellow some idea of how serious the situation is. I didn't like to say more, because my hopelessness might have grieved him.

June 9. A confession of faith. The Emperor Marcus Aurelius (reigned 161 to 180) says: "[Reason] is thy ruling part; and here consider: Thou art an old man; suffer not that excellent part to be brought in subjection; suffer it not to be drawn up and down with . . . lusts and motions. Neither to repine at anything now present, or to fear or fly anything to come." And again: "Remember this, that unto reasonable creatures only is it granted that they may willingly and freely submit unto Providence; but absolutely to submit is a necessity imposed upon all creatures equally."

"Be strong and of a good courage; be not afraid, neither be thou dismayed; for the

---

[1] He was the land-agent at Liebenberg and Häsen.

Lord thy God is with thee whithersoever thou goest." (Joshua 1, 9.)

Job 5, 17. " Despise not thou the chastening of the Almighty "—2 Cor. 12, 10. "Therefore I take pleasure in infirmities, in reproaches, in necessities, in persecutions, in distresses for Christ's sake ; for when I am weak, then am I strong."

Why should a man of my age, who has thought much, seen much, suffered much, think and act differently from the Christians and pagans to whom their experience of life dictated such verses ? I say that to rise above our fate gives us a strength of which the man who has not been tried in the crucible of suffering has no conception. I know very well that a kind of stoicism, and certain ideas about predestination may be read into that outlook—and it does seem to preclude the energy that is demanded of a man, and the tiresome conception of honour which holds a pistol over one's fellow-creature—but I am not capable of seeing things otherwise. And if people think to see a sort of dull passivity, a " moral defect" in the strange fact that I cannot be angry with my enemies—that I could even talk and discuss matters with a Harden, a Holstein, a Bernstein, quite calmly and without bitterness—well, I have been so from childhood. My often having been incensed by some unjust action doesn't alter that. Marcus Aurelius says : " Such and such things, from such and such causes, must of necessity proceed. He that would not have such things happen is as he that would have the fig-tree grow without any sap or moisture. In sum, remember this, that within a very little while both thou and he shall both be dead, and after a little while more, not so much as your names and memories shall be remaining."

But though I forgive, that does not entitle me to ignore the punishment which it is a duty to inflict so far as I have the power to do so. Since God punishes us, He gives us the right to punish justly, and to teach a lesson. Profoundly convinced as I am of the wisdom and justice of God's purposes, I am now submitting to the doom which is a lesson to me. But I can reconcile myself to the defence I am putting up against my enemies *only* because I consider that in this instance my enemies deserve to be punished. For, purged as I am of all hatred, my own most heartfelt wish would be not to have to act at all in the matter, to be able to leave the verdict to God alone, with no lawyers at my side, no speeches, no defence of their making. What I should like best would be silently to acquiesce in the will of God, to see and feel what others do with a tranquil mind that knows not hatred. "How much time and leisure doth he gain, who is not curious to know what his neighbour hath said or done or hath attempted, but only what he doth himself, that it may be just and holy. . . . Not to look about on the evil conditions of others, but to run on straight in the line, without any loose and extravagant agitation." (Marcus Aurelius.[1])

My fervent love for those nearest me, the duty of doing everything that is best for them, is as a goad in my side. In full consciousness of thereby making a necessary sacrifice of my

---

[1] The English translations of Marcus Aurelius are taken from Casaubon's version. (Translator's note.)

own will, I put my faith in God's approving care when I thus forsake the path of passive resistance which my temperament, nature, and way of thought commend to me.

The morning was again peculiarly trying. I miss my good Emanuel, who understands my ailments and always does the right thing for me. After the doctor's visit and a painful talk with Wronker, to which I was not equal, came the dear, good children to say good-bye. Augusta stayed with me till 2 o'clock. But even the rest after my meal did me no good. I was horribly nervous and worried, and it was no better when in the afternoon my dear Fritz Wend arrived. Emanuel came back and told me all about the picnic I had arranged as a birthday treat for him and his family. They all seemed to have enjoyed themselves—I am so glad.

June 10. After a tolerable night a most unpleasant morning with fainting-fits and so on. Thank goodness I have Emanuel with me again. Long visit from the doctor. Then came Augusta, bringing me most touching letters of true sympathy. After my meal another alarming attack. If only my body were stronger and more capable of resistance! I feel my powers falling from me like autumn leaves that flutter gradually, daily from the tree.

June 11. The night far from pleasant, but the morning somewhat better than of late. I am gradually losing my hold on life. The situation is too alarming for me to be able to reckon on acquittal with anything approaching confidence. I can't help feeling that such a thing is really not to be hoped for.

June 12. After a bad night, during which I wrote and read, a morning of great pain. If only one didn't wake up! Emanuel massaged and looked after me, and at last I got a little better. Doctors Kraus and Steyrer came together, for the first time since their holiday. Both impressed by the turn public opinion is taking in my favour. That may do good for a while. But my enemies will see to it that things are different when the trial comes on.

June 13. Bad night, morning still worse. I had to send for Dr. Steyrer at 7.30 ; he found me extremely low, the pulse very feeble. That is my usual state in the morning. Not until 11 was there a slight improvement.

Sunday, June 14. I had a good, quiet night, thanks to veronal powders ; and a beautiful waking, for my mind was so lethargic that the daytime terrors scarcely loomed on me at all. Kind Sister Bertha [4] paid me a long visit, and her gentleness, mature judgment, and steadfast religious faith were a refreshment to me. She told me, as a sign of the times, that it is immensely difficult to recruit the nursing staff ; and that most of them are unbelievers, incapable of giving a word of spiritual consolation to the poor invalids who are in danger of their lives. They are always talking of their rights ; of their duty they never speak. So even in that calling, pleasure-seeking and egotism are beginning to prevail. Dr. Steyrer, too, stayed some time with me, and told me interesting things. I am glad to hear that he has been made a " Professor." That makes the future brighter for the excellent man—oh, how much brighter than mine !

[1] Fräulein Bertha Nitschke, matron at the Charité.

June 15. The mornings are always bad. Too weak physically to be able to offer any resistance to the thoughts that assail me ; they do with me as they will. All the misery of my existence comes over me, and God's comfort seems to fail me. But the old faith still survives, though it be only in the innermost recesses of my soul, and I wait longingly for the wind that will kindle the sparks once more. Thank God, I always do feel them kindling in the course of the day—and by God's mercy they will never cease to warm me. Else, how should I survive ?—I always enjoy my good Steyrer's visits. In the afternoon a bad fainting-fit. Wronker did not come—a relief for me. How could I have followed his statements ? Oh, if it would but end ! Such days of weakness are more trying than people think.

June 16. Restless and low. The trial is getting nearer, and means such horrors as I have not physical strength to encounter. I am too enfeebled by all I have suffered. In the afternoon came the tidings that June 29 is the date fixed for the opening of the proceedings. Wronker came for a short time. He seems to have little hope—he brought up points which are apparently very injurious to me. My God, what an abyss between guise and guilt—and what another abyss yawns before one, if the judge should take the guise for the guilt !

June 17. The night very hot, and so I slept badly, even with veronal. Even in the early morning it was almost unbearable in this room ; the whole day it was 23 Réaumur. Towards evening came Laemmel from Ruppin. He was more hopeful to-day. So he and Wronker play at see-saw, as one might say. One day I am uplifted, the next cast down. I can't understand a word of the lawyers' jargon in the documents concerning the trial. But a client finds the endless circumlocutions most abominably confusing, and loses the thread, can't get any idea of his own case. Laemmel is a true steadfast friend to me ; to my last breath I shall remember his fidelity, kindness, eager self-sacrificing devotion. To-day Emanuel rolled me in my invalid-chair to a window in the warders' room. For the first time this year I saw green trees in full foliage, and pretty shrubs.

June 18. The night bad, but the morning tolerable. At 11 came my dear Fritz Wend from Liebenberg. We had a great deal to discuss. While I was still at Liebenberg I wrote a paper to be published in case I was condemned—it showed my opinion of the depravity prevailing in other circles besides the Harden-Bernstein one, and also the infamous means they employed to ruin me. Fritz Wend had taken it to a man who is a better judge than anyone of the effect certain kinds of news is likely to have on Press and public. He said : " It is sensationally horrible—but not sufficiently so. If the public is to gloat to its heart's content, if it is to be made to take the Prince's side, quite another kind of hard-hitting is what is wanted (against the Emperor, Bülow, etc.)." For that I am too " decent "—even if I have to bear the prison-brand on my forehead. And so I shall be slaughtered, and never say a word—and God will understand me, if no one else can. It is terribly hot.

Appendix III

June 19. The night good in spite of all the heat, but just as I woke in the morning I had a fainting-fit which must have made my good Emanuel very anxious. I feel a great desire to be alone—alone for one whole day. For in this little room, the almost incessant presence of my people, Emanuel, the doctors, the lawyers, the Sister, the officials is like an oppression on my brain that makes me ill.

To his dearly loved Mother, in Heaven.
For June 20, 1908.

Als Du uns Haupt und Herz noch warst in unserm Kreise,
Geliebteste, erschienen Ehre, Ruhm, und Glanz,
Die auf mir Armen lagen, Deiner milden Weise
Wie treuer Mutterliebe stolzer Ehrenkranz.

Doch jetzt erst dürfen stolz aus Deinem erdentrückten Kreise
Die blauen Augen leuchten in verklärtem Glanz :
Du siehst den Sohn auf banger, schwerer Pilgerreise
Geduldig tragen seiner Leiden Ehrenkranz.[1]

PHILIP ZU EULENBURG-H.

June 20. My dear, dear mother's birthday. How great was God's mercy in sparing her a long life (she would have been 84 to-day), in letting

[1] While head and heart thou wert of our fond earthly home,
O dearest! glory, honour, and renown
Weighing on me unglad, to thy sweet soul did come
But as the loving mother's birthday-crown.

And now, perchance, at gaze from Heaven's eternal home
Those blue eyes proudlier see thy son's renown—
Wayfarer on a pilgrimage of pain to roam,
And meekly wear his thorn-set birthday-crown.

her behold from above, in all the glory of His freedom, what would have been such agony unspeakable to her in this earthly sphere. Now she understands the inner workings of things, the "why." She knows how to estimate my sufferings and can even realise their value to me, while my poor family is consumed with misery about them. . . . In the morning after a very hot night, I felt such a wonderful sense of serene composure. Again, for a moment, I had a vision of Mama, and knew joy amid all the wretchedness of my life, and cannot be grateful enough to God for that moment. Then came my dear good Augusta with a splendid spray of roses for the dear Mama's picture, which I had decked, in the early morning, with two beautiful Liebenberg roses. The kind G.P. sent me some very fine stocks; the dear —— a gorgeous bunch of many-coloured carnations of rare beauty, with some sweet words besides. So my little room looked quite festive; and as there was no lawyer's visit to dread, with its reminders of horrible actuality, I was able to keep the train of quiet thought which on my thorny path I need so badly.

Unfortunately I had a bad nervous attack later on, as I always do after any sort of excitement. Emanuel's stroking of my head and arms gradually soothed me again.

Sunday, June 21. A painful awakening. Very slowly my mind cleared, but I am low-spirited and nervous.

June 22. The critical days are approaching, and I am preparing my mind for them. Shall I be able to get through this purgatory? My energies have diminished, and I feel no con-

Appendix III

fidence in myself. If God does not give me strength, I shall have a physical breakdown. I wish it were a real battle, with bullets raining round me! But before a hundred curious spectators to have all that filth flung at one, to fight for one's good name in face of hatred, contempt, humiliating pity, without the support of health—was there ever such torture! I am fully conscious of the terrible danger I am in. There are two sides to it—Jacob Ernst's inexplicable statements; and the temper of the jury, who know me only in the light of the calumnies that for the last two years have filled all the newspapers.

As to Jacob, I do not for a moment believe he could be bribed. But I think I have a very good idea of the psychological process which made the poor deaf man fall a victim to the crafty Bernstein. They told the unfortunate fellow (or did he misunderstand them, in his deafness?) that there had been an eye-witness of some moral delinquency between him and me, and that this eye-witness had sworn to it. Therefore he, Jacob, would be sent to gaol if he did not confess to that delinquency. And he, distraught with terror at the thought of his children, his situation, weighed the gratitude he owes me against that prospect—and branded as immoral the confidential relation, perfectly impeccable as it was, in which he and I so long stood to one another. And so doing, fell into the trap; for to retract would have meant imprisonment. Thus he twisted the rope round my neck. For all my friendly intercourse, my letters, my presents—everything, everything that in all innocence and kindness of heart I bestowed on him, is now the overwhelming mass of proof which will inevitably destroy me in the eyes of strangers—*i.e.*, the jury.

When at Liebenberg, after having been confronted with him, I appealed with all the urgency I could command to his conscience, he cried in desperation : " But I'll go to gaol if I take it back now ! " " You were telling the truth, were you not ? " interrupted the magistrate. " Oh aye," said the distracted Jacob, pulling himself together, " I was telling the truth, all right." But that moment was enough to reveal his despair at the position he was in.

That they did play the trick of an oath by an eye-witness on the poor fellow is proved beyond all doubt by the curious encounter between my son Siegwart (coming from Brixen) and Jacob at the Munich railway-station, immediately after the close of the Harden-Städele case. Siegwart knew nothing about it, and spoke cordially to Jacob, who looked utterly unlike himself and most miserable. In the course of their conversation Jacob said, after uttering terrible curses on Bernstein and Harden : " Why, they told me there was a fellow that took his Bible oath he had seen something."

So stands the case. That is the explanation. But it alters his oath in no wise ; and though all Harden's 150 incriminating statements, some of which are senseless and some clever or clumsy inventions, could not in themselves suffice to prove me guilty, nevertheless many of the details and asseverations (such as Riedl's) would be substantiated by the weight attaching to Jacob Ernst's sworn evidence, and

Appendix III

so could not be lightly dismissed. Thus far does the unfortunate Jacob's evidence affect the case—and thus far does it intensify the danger which will probably mean my ruin.

For, as I said above, I cannot even reckon on the impartiality of the jury. In their eyes I am the degenerate intriguer, who for nearly twenty years has inveigled the Emperor into doing all those things which the people resent, who encouraged his autocratic tendencies, who brought the Fatherland to the brink of war—who, in short, is a perverted abnormal person of the most pernicious kind ! That is what the entire Press of Germany, poisoned as it has been by Harden and Holstein, has made of me. And quite openly made of me for the last two years, with no sort of contradiction from the Government organs. How should the poor jurors be " unaffected ? " It is absolutely impossible. Which among them knows me ? Which knows anything about my real nature, my opinions, my character, my heart, my genuine Liberal feeling ? Not one of the men who will now be confronted with the Ernst evidence, and have to deliver a verdict !

Is there any chance that they will be influenced by the patriotic feeling that my condemnation would put the Emperor in a terrible position ? That the stigma cast upon me would inevitably react on him ? Assuredly not. For in the course of this case, which is a purely political one, any allusion to politics will be sedulously avoided—so as to spare the " hallowed " personality of the Emperor. And to no one will it occur that he can only be spared by stamping the case as a political one, which it in fact *is*, and protecting the Emperor, as a mere man, from *my* condemnation. But after all would the jury be at all concerned to spare the Emperor, when the case is conducted as it will be conducted ? By no means. The tendency to asperse the Emperor (for whom, as is the way in Germany, every one has a bad word) has long prevailed—though quite surreptitiously.

That is the real snare. As hopeless for me as can be conceived. To the clear-sighted, very evident. For the optimists there is only one attitude to take : " It is impossible Prince Eulenburg should be condemned."

But the terrible misfeasance of the Government consists in *their* not having said to themselves while yet there was time : " It is impossible to condemn Prince Eulenburg, because we are a monarchical Government, because we are all bound to protect the Emperor's prestige."

Now it is too late. They will reap what they have sown. I am but a pawn on the chessboard—and the Government has lost the game, the Emperor's game.

It is human nature to feel anger against those who do us a bitter injury. The degree of that anger depends on the nature of him who is injured or accused. And so I did feel an ebullition of wrath against the unfortunate Jacob Ernst ; but soon it became more a sense of bitterness, for I was much wounded by his ingratitude—such ingratitude as could actually deliver me up to the law. But on calmer reflection I came to a different conclusion, and I think it is the right one. I now feel a deep pity for him ; and this leads me to

Appendix III

forgive him for the wrong he has done me, even though that has meant such martyrdom, appointed to me by God for my chastening. In the foregoing pages I have briefly sketched the process which deprived the poor fellow of his wits and self-respect. For I know the simple, unassuming, honest creature, his good heart, his tender love for his children ; and so I can perfectly understand the inner workings of his nature. He heard, or in his deafness he thought to hear (and was scared out of his wits by hearing), that a man had sworn to being an eye-witness of moral delinquencies between him and me. Simultaneously he was subjected to pressure of a really devilish description by Bernstein, defending Harden, and told he would be taken straight to gaol if he did not confess what the witness had sworn to. The County-Court judge pressed him in the same way. He was a prey to sheer panic. If that eye-witness had sworn to it—what use for him to tell the truth? He would be lost —he would go straight to gaol ! How was he ever to get out again ? His motherless children, his house and possessions, with no one at their head—they would come to utter grief . . . what could he do but confess to anything Bernstein and the judge might want? He could not set his gratitude to me higher than his duty towards his little children—but he completely collapsed when the consequences of his evidence were made clear to him. He knew that after giving evidence on oath he really would be sent to gaol if he retracted that evidence. He was under compulsion. In the further hearings he will have to make his evidence more circumstantial. This will necessarily bring in the various occasions on which he travelled with me in the capacity of valet. The unfortunate man feels the trap closing on him—and the anguish he suffers from the memory of me grows keener every day.

How can I be anything but profoundly compassionate? And who is the real wrongdoer? The real wrongdoers are they who extorted the so-called "confession" from the poor fellow; who, morally speaking, inflicted worse torture on him than did the inquisitors of the Middle Ages on their victims.

I feel that, before all else, I must try to be just, that in this devil-dance of fraud, calumnies, malice, envy, and stupidity I must strive to see clear, and stand erect. It is only by trying to realise the motives which govern the acts of one's opponents, and to master one's own human passions, that one can hope to attain that end.

June 23. A tolerable night with aspirin, but in the morning low and tired. It is only with the greatest effort that I can bring myself to react against it all. When one is physically and mentally exhausted, the imagination alone can restore one. Just as my meal was brought in, Laemmel appeared. For the first time he suggested my giving a political aspect to the case—if not explicitly, anyhow by implication. Thereby he simply acknowledges that I am right in thinking the case ought to be given the political stamp that really belongs to it. Oh, if God will but extract the sting of bitterness from the hearts of my darling children, so deeply implanted by the horrors of recent years! Only He, who is Love, can do it. They do not even understand me when I assure them that I, the source of all their anguish, am wholly free from any bitterness of feeling.

June 24. To-day I close these pages, which I could not possibly go on with up to the beginning of the High Court proceedings against me on June 29. These few days will be entirely taken up with painful consultations between the lawyers and myself. In the intervals I shall require complete mental rest, so as to keep what physical energy I have left for the battle. God has granted me a tranquil and resigned composure in all the battles of my soul. May all my dear ones, faithful ones, remember these battles—and that patience, if life should give *them* a " doom " to endure. It is more self-respecting, more salutary, to prepare one's-self for the inevitable patiently and without rebellion against the Will of God. For it alleviates the pain of those who love us if we try to be as little sensible as may be of our own suffering, if we try to curb the expression of it.

" Therefore despise not thou the chastening of the Almighty." (Job 5, 17.)

" For I reckon that the sufferings of this present time are not worthy to be compared with the glory that shall be revealed in us." (Rom. 8, 18.)

(Signed)
PHILIP ZU EULENBURG-HERTEFELD.

IV

A Witness for Prince Eulenburg

IN the year 1908 I made the acquaintance of Prince Philip Eulenburg during his stay in the Charité. He was entrusted to my personal care, so that I was almost daily in his company. It was with some comprehensible reluctance that I undertook this duty, which in the event became dearer and dearer to me. For in the Prince I came to recognise a high-minded man, a man of the greatest kindliness and the sincerest piety, joined to brilliant intellectual talents and wonderful versatility.

His unassumingness and gratitude were touching. He thought himself under an obligation when in reality he was always the gracious giver. What consideration he showed to those around him, despite all his own pain! It is with a sense of deep gratitude that I recall him and the many beautiful traits of his character, which drew me nearer to the human being in him, and have been an example to me that all my life I shall try, in fond remembrance, to emulate.

The idea that the Prince imagined or exaggerated his illness is one that I am in the best possible position to contradict. For I was the almost daily witness of his undeniably severe physical suffering, which was sensibly aggravated by conditions so unfavourable to the invalid.

His certainty of being some day vindicated sustained him through the worst period and fortified his spirit, though his physical strength ebbed away. That certainty rested on God; hence he could submissively and patiently bear his heavy cross with never a word of repining.

His thoughts were often with his late mother, in deep, grateful, childlike love. He was never tired of talking to me of her, as also of the sacred thoughts that ruled his mind, and gave him strength.

As in that distressing period, so in after years—the Prince was always the same; a true man, with the kindliest of hearts. I have the most profound belief in his absolute truthfulness.

At his death I lost—in this life—a warm, true friend. But the remembrance of that rare personality which God permitted me to know and appreciate lives on in me—unsullied, blessed, and vindicated.

Charité, Berlin. *August* 13, 1922.

(Signed) BERTHA NITSCHKE, Matron.

INDEX

Adolf of Bückberg, Prince, I. 70.
Aerenthal, Count, I. o.
Agliardi, Cardinal, I. 105, 136, 153, 228.
Albert, Archduke, I. 227.
Albert of Prussia, I. 70.
Alexander III, Czar, I. 132, 133, 139, 141, 143, 145.
Alexander of Battenburg, Prince, I. 105.
Arnim, Count, II. 311.
August Wilhelm, Prince, I. 42.
Augusta, Empress (Wife of Wilhelm I), 54.
Augusta, Empress (Wife of Wilhelm II), I. 42, 259 ; II. 22, 92-3, 221, 245, 281.

Bach, Frau, I. 48.
Baden, Grand Duke of, I. 83, 95, 253 *et seq.* ; II. 14.
Badeni, Count, I. 238 ; II. 76.
Banffy (Hungarian Prime Minister), II. 19.
Barrère (Ambassador), I. 107-8, 109.
Bartsch (Valet), II. 266, 316, 323, 333, 336, 339 *et seq.*, 361.
Beck, Baron, I. 238, 273.
Bernstein (Crown Solicitor), xxix ; II. 209 *et seq.*, 375.
Berchem, Count, I. 57, 59.
Bethmann-Hollweg, Count von, II. 275.
Bismarck, Count Herbert, I. 9, 24, 29, 31, 37, 39, 53, 55, 60 *et seq.*, 72, 73, 82, 92, 158, 265, 285 ; II. 6, 59.
Bismarck, Prince, I. 21, 33, 55, 57, 59, 60, 84 *et seq.*, 148, 155 *et seq.*, 233-4, 272, 292-3, 296 *et seq.*, 310, 314, 319, 323, 329, 344 ; II. 43, 63, 282, 292, 297, 304, 307.
Bismarck, fall of, I. 84.
Bismarck, Princess, I. 9, 92.
Bitzthem (Saxon Military Plenipotentiary), II. 54.
Bollhardt (cuirassier), II. 210, 220, 234.
Borries, Police President, II. 194 (note).
Botticher, Minister, I. 273, 313-4, 359 ; II. 16, 20, 22.

Brand (journalist), 213-4.
Brest-Litowsk, Treaty of, II. 280.
Bronsart, von, I. 301, 344, 348, 351, 353.
Brunswick, Regent of, I. 70.
Bülow, Alfred von, II. 25, 29, 181-2.
Bülow, Bernard von, I. 21, 22, 24, 36, 148 *et seq.*, 71, 83, 87, 88, 118, 119-21, 141, 158, 135-6, 194, 196-7, 221 *et seq.*, 240, 251, 263 *et seq.*, 280, 305, 307 *et seq.*, 311-2, 320 *et seq.*, 345 *et seq.*, 369, 383, 388 ; II. 3-41 *passim*, 43, 56-7, 66, 69, 70, 84, 88, 98, 100, 108, 109, 112-19, 125-30, 132, 135, 155, 158, 160 *et seq.*, 173 (*and note*), 174, 178, 179 *et seq.*, 181 *et seq.*, 192, 195, 196, 204, 213, 231, 272-4, 292, 297, 306 *et seq.*
Bülow, Carl von, II. 117, 118.

Cambon, Ambassador, I. 107, 108.
Caprivi, I. 80 (*note*), 95 *et seq.*, 111 *et seq.*, 119, 122, 129, 148 *et Chapter II passim*, 220, 247 *et seq.*, 341 ; II. 184, 297.
Caprivi, fall of, I. 247 *et seq.*
Carnot, President, I. 234, 252.
Chamberlayne, Houston Stewart, II. 79.
Chelius, Lieut. von, I. 82.
Chinese Expedition, II. 66, 269.
Chodziesner, Dr., II. 247 (*note*).
Crailsham, Minister, I. 58, 60, 47-8, 103-4, 119, 282-3.
Cretan Question, I. 374.

Dankelmann, Count, I. 82 ; II. 258.
Derenthall, II. 175.
Dietrichstein, Princess, 226.
Dohna, Count Eberhard, I. 75, 77, 136 ; II. 91, 249.
Dohna, Prince Richard, I. 82 ; II. 249 (*note*).
Dollinger, Dr., I. 106.
Donhoff, August, I. 298.
Donhoff, Countess (*afterwards Frau von Bulow*), II. 3, 6, 8.
Donnersmark, Prince von, II. 153.
Dresscher, I. 358.

Elbe, Frau von, II, 196, 214.
Engelbrecht, von, I. 141, 318 ; II. 9, 46, 48, 49, 50.
Ernest of Saxe-Coburg, Duke, I. 46.
Ernst, Jacob, II. 190, 217 *et seq.*, 231, 240 *et seq.*, 249, 311, 312, 314, 315, 320, 330-4, 337, 360.
Esebeck, W., I. 82.
Eulenburg, Countess Alexandrina, I. 3, 8-9.

INDEX 383

Eulenburg, Count August, I. 218, 290, 359 ; II. 22, 58, 180, 205, 211, 348.
Eulenburg, Princess Augusta, I. 22, 63, 64, 65 ; II. 90, 124, 156-7, 189-90, 245, 261, 266 *et seq.*, 285, 314-35 *passim*, 337 *et seq.*
Eulenburg, Count Botho, I. 84, 111, 176, 194, 247, 251, 252, 256 *et seq.*, 288, 298 *et seq.*, 322, 334, 370 *et seq.* ; II. 22, 36.
Eulenburg, Karl, I. 82.
Eulenburg, Count Siegwart, II. 221, 278, 338, 372.
Eulenburg, Count (father of Prince Philip), I. 3, 14, 71.

EULENBURG, PRINCE PHILIP :
Vol. I.—Early Years, 3-18 ; his emotional temperament, 4 ; aversion from speaking in public, 4 ; facility in making friends, 5-6 ; influence of his mother, 8-9 ; a clever musician, 10-11 ; and author, 12-13 ; joins the army, 15 ; enters diplomacy, 20 *et seq.* ; attaché at Paris Embassy, 22 ; marriage, 23 ; transferred to Munich, 24 *et seq.* ; suicide of King Ludwig of Bavaria, 27 ; meets Prince William (Wilhelm II), 31 ; correspondence with Holstein, 32 *et seq.* ; becomes close friend of Prince William, 38 *et seq.* ; his opinion of Bavarian catholics, 59 ; chargé d'affaires at Munich, 61 *et seq.* ; ambassador at Oldenburg, 65 *et seq.* ; correspondence with Herbert Bismarck, 30 *et seq.* ; corresponds with Wilhelm II, 74 ; intimate life with Emperor begins, 75 ; efforts to preserve understanding between Emperor and the Bismarcks, 84-5 ; final severance from the Bismarcks, 92 ; ambassador at Stuttgardt and Munich, 93-120 ; tete-a-tete conversation with the Emperor on Bavarian affairs, 114 *et seq.* ; established as Emperor's intimate friend and mediator between him and the Government, 121-214 *passim* ; Holstein's use of Eulenburg for his personal aims, 127 *et seq.* ; with the Emperor at Cowes in 1893, 142-6 ; advice to the Emperor on the Army bills, 150-6 ; correspondence with Waldersee on Bismarck question, 162-6 ; advice to Emperor on Triplice, 169-73 ; exempt from Emperor's practical jokes, 187 ; visit to Wusterhausen Palace, 189-193 ; stern remonstrance to Empe or, 208-9 ; and 211-13 ; ambassador at Vienna, 217-46 ; wanted as ambassador in London, 221 ; correspondence with Bülow, *ib.* ; his friendships at Vienna, 226 *et seq.* ; intercourse with Emperor Francis Joseph, 230-33 ;

Eulenburg, Prince Philip—*continued*:
relations with Russian ambassador at Vienna, 256 *et seq.* ; his dealings with the Emperor at times of crisis, 247-78 *passim* ; correspondence with Holstein at the time, *ib.* ; difficulties of appointment of new Chancellor, 270 *et seq.* ; his intercourse with Holstein, 279-343 *passim* ; emotional correspondence between the two, *ib.* ; he stands between Emperor and Holstein, *ib.* ; his frankness to Holstein, 304 *et seq.* ; writes to Bülow about Holstein, 309-10 ; *et seq.* ; writes to Emperor on Köller crisis, 331 ; acrimonious correspondence with Holstein, 336 *et seq.* ; struggle for Emperor's favour with Holstein, 344-88 *passim* ; writes to Bülow his alarm at Holstein's action, 345 *et seq.* ; Tausch's calumny, 357-61 ; seeks to get Bülow as successor to Hohenlohe, 387-8.

Vol. II (*including Appendices*).—His friendship for Bülow, 3 ; gets permission for Bülow to marry the divorced Countess Donhoff, 3 ; intimate correspondence with Bülow, 4-41 *passim* ; Bülow as a counterpoise to Holstein, 8-9 ; his advice and warnings to Bülow, *ib.* ; his reverence and love for the Emperor, 23, 36-7 ; preparing the way for Bülow, 30 *et seq.* ; comment on the "camarilla" of the military attachés, 43-51 ; dislike of von Engelbrecht, 46-7 ; writes to Emperor against Admiral von Senden, 52-4 ; influence with Emperor failing, 56-7 ; argument with Emperor on personal rule, 63 *et seq.* ; summing-up of Emperor's character, 73 ; loses interest in politics, 73-5 ; final years of diplomatic career, 76-141 *passim* ; sends New Year's wishes to Holstein, 81-2 ; end of friendship with Holstein, 83-6 ; raised to rank of Prince, 88 *et seq.* ; letter of thanks to Emperor 92-4 ; his affair with Pierson, 106-7 ; his action in the Wreschen affair, 107-9 ; thanked by Austrian Emperor for speech, 111-2 ; letter to Bülow on the political situation as regards the Triplice, 112-7 ; his health breaks down, 119 ; proposal to make him Minister of the Household, 125-7 ; health grows worse, 128-9 ; Emperor refuses his resignation, 129 ; resigns from ambassadorship, 135 ; farewell visit to Emperor Francis Joseph, 137-8 ; retires to Liebenburg, 145 ; story of the " Round Table " at Liebenburg, 148-9 ; his friendsnip with Lecomte, 150-1 ; awarded the Black Eagle, 153 ; remarks on the proposed big fleet and on the army, 162-6 ;

Eulenburg, Prince Philip—*continued*:
Holstein's revenge, 169-87 ; talks with Lecomte about danger of war with France, 171 ; disapproves of Holstein's policy, 173 ; his correspondence with Witte and friendship for Lecomte used against him, 173-4 ; challenges Holstein to a duel, 174-5 ; Holstein's apology, 175 ; Holstein-Harden attacks open, 278-9 ; Bülow's friendship cools, 181-2 ; the Press turns against him, 183 *et seq.* ; first charges of immorality and unnatural vice, 187 ; his friendship for the fisherman Ernst, 189-90 ; his name placed on the secret police register, 192 ; story of a blackmailer, 192-4 ; leaves Germany for a time, 197-8 ; enmity of the A.D.C.s and military circle of the Emperor, 200-3 ; takes legal action and definitely leaves the Service, 204-5 ; Harden's case, 207 *et seq.* ; seriously ill, 208-9 ; acquittal of Harden in Moltke case, 209 ; takes legal action against Harden and Bernstein, 211-2 ; his dramatic success in Harden case, 214 ; serious illness, 216 *et seq.* ; fear of coming witnesses, 217 ; case opens with evidence of Riedl and Ernst, 220-2 ; case decided against him, 224 ; Crown Prosecutor turns against him, 227 ; in bed is examined by a commission, 228 *et seq.* ; contemplates suicide or flight, 229 ; confronted with Riedl and Ernst, 231 ; arrested on charge of perjury, 232 ; imprisoned in the hospital of La Charité, 232 ; sympathy of the prison officials, 232-3 ; 145 accusers reduced to twelve, 234 ; proceedings at Moabit: evidence breaks down and is confined to Riedl and Ernst, 239 *et seq.* ; his collapse and adjournment of trial, 246-8 ; extracts from Diary, 248-50 ; farce of legal proceedings, 251-3 ; released from arrest on bail, 254 *et seq.* ; amount of bail increased, *ib.* ; returns to Liebenburg, 259 ; trial re-opened and again adjourned, 264-5 ; notes by Princess Eulenburg on the affair, 266-8 ; case declared closed, 269 ; 260 to end of Vol. II. ; survives the War three years, 284 ; death, *ib*. Notes on the real von Holstein, extracts from the private correspondence of Prince Eulenburg, 289-313 ; Recollections of the Princess zu Eulenburg of her husband's trial in 1908, 314-35 ; Diary of Prince Eulenburg from April 21 to June 24, 1908, 336-77 ; Sister Bertha's account of his life in hospital, 378-9.

Ferdinand of Bulgaria, I. 51, 64 ; II. 281.
Festetics, Count Tassilo, I. 227.

386 INDEX

Fischer, Dr., I. 125, 329, 358.
Fleet, Big, Proposal for, I. 146, 370 ; II. 9, 33, 51, 53-4, 56-7, 162-3, 309.
Forstner, Lieut., II. 276.
Francis Joseph, Emperor of Austria, I. 171, 175, 230, 232, 237, 241 *et seq.*, 364 ; II. 78, 95, 106, 110 *et seq.*, 137.
Frankenstein, I. 264.
Franz Ferdinand, Archduke, I. 234 ; II. 77, 92, 95.
Franz Salvator, Archduke, II. 116.
Frederick, Crown Prince of Russia, 30 *et seq.*, 63 (*note*). (*see also Frederick, Emperor of Germany*).
Frederick, Emperor of Germany, I. 51, 64 ; II. 281, 304.
Frederick, Empress, I. 175.
Frederick, William I., King of Prussia, I. 190.

Genrich, Dr., II. 208-9, 263, 265, 340.
Geritz (Valet), II. 336, 342, 353.
Giers (Ambassador), I. 127.
Goluchowski, Count (Ambassador), I. 237, 239, 240 *et seq.*, 375, 376, 380-1 ; II. 77 *et seq.*, 96 *et seq.*, 136, 309, 311.
Gorz, Count, I. 79 ; II. 65.
Gronsart, I. 301.
Guiche, Marquis de la, II. 95-6.

Hahnke, General von, I. 312, 351 ; II. 343 *et seq.*
Harden, Maximilian (Journalist), II. 178 *et seq.*, 187, 193 (*note*), 194 *et seq.*, 273, 307, 312, 315, 334, 335, 336, 340, 353, 372, 375.
Hartel, Professor, I. 227 ; II. 104.
Hatzfeld, Count, I. 143, 147, 221, 225, 235, 308, 309 ; II. 36, 274.
Hatzfeld, Elizabeth, II. 38.
Haussmann xxii ; I. 176 ; II. 252.
Hélene of Orleans, Princess, I. 23.
Helldorff-Bedra, Herr von, I. 257, 283.
Henckel, Prince, I. 285-6, 296, 306.
Henry of Prussia, Prince, I. 259.
Hertling, I. 280.
Hertzfeld, Karl von, I. 7.
Hertzfeld, Baron Samuel, I. 191.
Hess, Field-Marshal, I. 3, 231-9.
Hess-Diller, Fritz, I. 231.
Hesse, Grand Duke of, I. 321.
Hinzpeter (tutor), I. 75, 333, 335 ; II. 57, 58.
Hirschfeld, von, I. 160, 176 ; II. 214.

INDEX

Hochberg, Count, I. 82 ; II. 106.
Hoffmann, Privy Councillor, II. 246 (*note*), 247 (*note*).
Hohenau, General Count, II. 203.
Hohenberg, Princess, II. 95.
Hohenlohe, Count Alexander, I. 319, 347 ; II. 12, 20, 22, 23.
Hohenlohe, Cardinal, I. 106 ; II. 60-1.
Hohenlohe, Prince Constantine (Lord Chamberlain), I. 226, 244.
Hohenlohe-Langenburg, I. 259.
Hohenlohe-Schillingfurst, Prince (Chancellor), I. 259, 262, 269 *et seq.*, 277-8, 289 *et seq.*, 298-9 *et seq.* ; II. 10 *et seq.*, 49, 50, 123, 125, 192, 297, 302, 303.
Hollmann, Admiral, I. 370, 373 ; II. 181.
Holstein, Baron von, I. 13, 32 *et seq.*, 60, 61, 83, 95, 98, 99 *et seq.*, 102, 104, 107, 112, 123, 125 *et Chapter III passim*, 217, 220, 226, 235, 239 *et seq.*, 249, 255 *et seq.*, 276-7, 249 *to end of Vol. I passim* ; II. 8 *et seq.*, 35, 79 *et seq.*, 95 *et seq.*, 171-87 *passim*, 193 *et seq.*, 272, 273, 289-313 *passim*.
Huhn, von (Journalist), II. 176.
Hullessen, Inspector, II. 192.
Hulsa, Lieut. von, I. 79, 82 ; II. 47, 48, 202.
" Hun " Speech, The, II. 67-8.

Ilberg, Dr., II. 201, 246.
Imbriani, I. 128.
Isenbiel, Crown Solicitor, II. 216, 218, 225 (*note*), 226, 234-68 *passim*, 324, 360.

Jansen, Minister, I. 69.

Kaize, Minister, II. 77, 78.
Kalnein, Count, 82.
Kalnoky, Count, I. 167, 168, 171, 222, 223, 234, 235.
Kammer (land agent), II. 362.
Kanders, Dr., II. 128.
Kanzow, President, II. 235, 243, 264.
Karl XI of Sweden, I. 23.
Karl of Prussia, Princess, I. 233.
Kayser, Privy Councillor, I. 125, 256, 333.
Kessel, von (A.D.C.), I. 82 ; II. 148-9.
Keszcki, I. 82.
Ketteler, Baron von, II. 76 (*note*).

cc*

Kiderlen-Wachter, I. 79, 104-5, 116-7, 123-4, 132, 135, 140, 144, 149, 183, 195, 217, 247, 252, 259-60, 308 ; II. 22-3, 28, 35, 36, 56, 274.
King Edward VII, II. 72, 152.
King of Italy, I. 137, 193 ; II. 50.
King of Saxony, I. 155, 175, 191-2 ; II. 10.
King Oscar of Sweden I, II. 90.
Kistler, Secretary, II. 135.
Klee, von, I. 126.
Kleist-Retzow, Frau von, II. 295.
Koch, Professor, I. 130.
Kopp, Cardinal, I. 105.
Köller, Minister, 270 *et seq.*, 313, 315, 330, 342.
" Köller Crisis," 270 *et seq.*, 331.
Korber Minister, II. 110, 116.
Kramarz, II. 76, 108.
Krauss, Privy Councillor, II. 254, 324, 338 *et seq.*
" Kruger Telegram," I. 239, 240, 332, 367.
Krull, Dr., II. 147.

Laemmel, Privy Councillor, II. 206, 207, 208, 211, 215, 216, 224, 228, 348, 356, 367, 376.
Lebbin, Frau von, II. 295 (*and note*).
Lecomte, Raymond, II. 150, 151, 171, 172, 173.
Lenbach, Lena, I. 92.
Leopold of Bavaria (Prince Regent), I. 29, 30, 32, 44, 57, 58, 98, 102, 110, 175.
Lerchenfeld, Count, I. 57, 98, 129.
Lesczcynski, General von, II. 199, 201, 211, 318.
Leuthold, Dr. (Surgeon-General), I. 81 ; II. 57, 66, 67, 129.
Levi (conductor), I. 45.
Liebenau, Court-Marshal von, I. 64.
Liebenburg Castle, I. 8, 11, 65, 71, 81, 130, 178-80, 189, 193, 260 *et seq.* ; II. 33, 120, 121, 145-6.
Liebenburg " Round Table," II. 148, 151, 180.
Lindau, Rudolf, I. 82.
Lippe-Schaumberg, Prince of, I. 88.
Lobanov, Prince, I. 228, 315.
Loe, General von, 334, 335.
Lucanus (Chief of Cabinet), I. 188, 210, 338 ; II. 14, 17, 18-20.
Ludwig II of Bavaria, I. 27, 208 ; II. 189.
Ludwig Victor, Archduke, II. 193.
Lutz (Bavarian Minister), I. 53, 56, 57, 59, 97, 129.

INDEX 389

Lutzow, Police President, I. 351, 358, 364.
Lynar, Count zu, II. 203, 210.
Lyncker von, I. 81 ; II. 149.

Mackensen, General, II. 69.
Macmahon, Marshal, I. 107.
Marschall, Baron von, I. 83, 98, 102, 119, 122, 124, 132, 183, 201, 202, 203, 217, 235, 244, 251 *et seq.*, 271, 274, 288, 289, 313, 314, 322, 326, 344 *to end of Vol. I passim* ; II. 4 *et seq.*, 47, 274.
Mankiewicz (Banker), II. 259.
Mayer, Judge, xxx, II. 224.
Metternich, I. 144.
Metternich, Princess Pauline, I. 227.
Michaelis, Minister, II. 280.
Miljutin (Russian War Minister), 128.
Miquel (Finance Minister), I. 251, 266, 274, 322, 365 ; II. 33, 42 (*and note*), 303.
Mittnacht, von, Minister, I. 94.
Moltke, von, A.D.C., Count Kuno, I. 82, 182, 269, 273 ; II. 24, 149-50, 195-6, 201, 206, 207, 211 *et seq.*
Moltke, General Helmuth von, II. 171, 182, 183.
Monts, I. 338 ; II. 28.
Mottl, Felix (conductor), I. 44.
Müller, II. 181.
Münster, Prince, II. 274.
Murat, Princess, I. 246 ; II. 96.
Muraviev, Count, I. 127, 228, 367 (*and note*).

Nicholas II (Emperor of Russia), I. 140, 304, 321 ; II. 69.
Nigra, Count, I. 229 ; II. 100-1.
Nitschke, Sister Bertha, II. 233, 366, 378-9.

Object of Book, xi.
Oldenburg, Grand Duke of, I. 93, 94, 101.
Osten-Sacken, General von, 109, 228.
Otterer, Herr (Bavarian Deputy), I. 112, 117.

Papal Nuncie at Munich (*see Agliardi, Cardinal*).
Perlet (gamekeeper), I. 81
Pfuel, Herr von, I. 40.
Pientak (Polish Minister), II. 108.
" Pierson Affair," I. xxviii ; II. 106 *et seq.*, 129, 240.
Plessen, General von, II. 19, 49, 50.
Ponsonby, Sir Henry, I. 142, 144.

Pope Leo XIII, I. 43, 106, 107.
Pourtales, Minister, II. 35.
Preuss, Dr., II. 263, 264.
Prussian Civil Service, efficiency of, I. 122.

Radetzky, I. 231.
Radolin, I. 321, 326 ; II. 14.
Radowitz, von, II. 274.
Rainer, Archduke, I. 227.
Rantzau, Count, I. 57, 59, 60, 61, 89, 90, 96, 98, 102, 130, 282 ; II. 138.
Recke, von der, I. 275.
Recknitzer (Hungarian Jew), II. 97.
Reichach, Baron Hugo von, II. 175.
Renvers, Professor, II. 133.
Reuss, Prince, I. 175, 179, 220 *et seq.*
Richter, Eugene, I. 43 ; II. 15.
Riedl, II. 217 *et seq.*, 231, 240, 249, 250, 320, 337.
Rogati (police sergeant), II. 250.
Roosefelt, President, II. 152.
Rosebery, Earl of, I. 145, 237.
Resenfeld, Victor, II. 231.
Rothkirch, Alexandrina von (*see Eulenburg, Countess*).
Rothschild, Baron Nathaniel, I. 229 ; II. 238.
Rothschild, Baron Albert, II. 239.
Rotterburg, I. 89.

Saar, Staff-Surgeon von, II. 357, 361.
Salisbury, Lord, 237, 307, 315.
Sandels, Augusta von (*see Eulenburg, Princess Augusta*).
Schenk, Dr., II. 257.
Schlieffen, Count, II. 69, 71.
Scholl, II. 69.
Schon, Herr von, II. 275.
Schopf (Police Sergeant), II. 250.
Schratt, Frau, II. 79.
Schweininger, I. 176.
Schweinitz, General von, I. 139.
Sended, Admiral von, I. 370, 373, 378 ; II. 9, 10, 14, 49, 51 *et seq.*
Sauffert (Police Commissioner), II. 250.
Solms, Count, I. 141.
" Social Democrat " Party, I. 264-5.
" Spiritism " in Germany, I. 47 *et seq.*
Stadele (Editor), II. 219, 222-3.

INDEX 391

Stein (Journalist), II. 177.
Steyrer, Dr., II. 321, 338 *et seq.*
Stoermer, Dr. (Letter to Author), I. xviii-xxi ; II. 254, 263.
Suite of Emperor visiting Liebenburg, II. 148-9.
Swaine, Colonel (British Military Attaché), I. 315, 323, 325, 326.
Szell, Minister, II. 110, 117.
Szögyeny, Count, I. 242, 372 ; II. 97, 104.

Tausch, Commissioner von, I. 357 *et seq.* ; II. 11, 15, 19, 20.
Tepperlaski, I. 126.
Thun, Count, II. 76 *et seq.*, 104.
Tirpitz, Admiral von, II. 51, 57, 69, 181.
Treschkow, von, II. 216.
Trial of Eulenburg, 225-68 *passim* (*see also Appendix III*).
Tschirschky, Secretary, II. 172, 174, 175, 185, 299.
Tschischkin, I. 127.

" Urias " Letter, The, I. 175.

Valerie, Archduchess, II. 116.
Varnbuler, I. 82, 182 ; II. 150, 174, 175.
Victoria, Princess of Prussia, I. 55, 70.
Victoria, Queen of England, I. 225 ; II. 367.
Vladimir, Grand-Duke, 127, 128.
Voigt (Bandmaster), I. 41.

Wagner, Cosima, I. 44.
Waldersee, Field-Marshal Count, 18 (*note*), 46 (*note*), 73, 96, 129, 162, 197, 198, 257, 265, 272, 301, 306, 322 ; II. 43, 69.
Wales, Prince of (Edward VII), I. 142, 143 *et seq.*, 234.
Wedel, Count, I. 129 ; II. 46, 182.
Wend, Fritz, II. 337, 340 *et seq.*
Werder (Ambassador), I. 127, 139, 140, 318.
Werthem-Berchlingen, Count, I. 25, 28, 34, 52, 57, 58, 64, 77, 282.
William I, Emperor, death of, I. 51.
William, Prince (*see also William II, Emperor*), I. 38 *et seq.*, 56, 58, 60.
William, Crown Princess (*see Augusta, Empress*).

WILLIAM II, EMPEROR OF GERMANY :
    Vol. I (*as Prince William*).—Visits Bayreuth with

William II, Emperor of Germany—*continued*:
Eulenburg, 31 ; becomes cordial friend of Eulenburg, 38 *et seq.*; accepts songs and music from Eulenburg, 40-2 ; discusses politics with him, 43 *et seq.* ; a visionary and believer in " Spiritism," 46-7 ; conversation with Eulenburg in 1901 on " Spiritualism," 48-9 ; becomes Crown Prince, 51 ; constant correspondence with Eulenburg, 52 *et seq.*, his displeasure with Herbert Bismarck, 60-1.

(*As Emperor*).—His first visit to Munich, 63-5 ; first Norwegian cruise, 73-4 ; affectionate relations with Eulenburg, 74 *et seq.* ; visits Liebenburg as Eulenburg's guest, 77-82 ; speaks with gratitude of Eulenburg's help at the time of Bismarck's dismissal, 85-6 ; transfers Eulenburg to Munich, 101 ; conversation with Eulenburg during Norwegian cruise, 114-6 ; restless manner of life, 122 ; complete lack of statecraft and experience, 122 ; desires a nearer approach to France, 126 ; is dissuaded from meeting the Tsar at Dantzig, 133 ; meets Emperor Francis Joseph at Abbazia, 136 ; meets King of Italy at Venice, 137 ; at Cowes in 1893, 142 ; fear of France declaring war with England, 142-3 ; his obstinacy over the Army Bill, 148 *et seq.* ; advised by Eulenburg to be cautious in his New Year's Speech, 153-4 ; contemplates reconciliation with Bismarck, 158 *et seq.* ; his fondness for practical joking, 187 ; exaggerated notions of himself as Sovereign by the Grace of God, 197 ; his fondness for public speaking, 200-1 ; his mania for palace building, 208 ; drinks " brotherhood " with Eulenburg, 210 ; visits Rome, 211 ; divergent views from the Foreign Office, 244 ; at loggerheads with Caprivi, 247 *et seq.* ; effect on him of the assassination of Carnet, 232 ; unveiling memorials, 256-7 ; difficulties of choosing a new Chancellor, 262 *et seq.* ; the Konigsberg speech, 265 *et seq.* ; his action in the Köller crisis, 273 *et seq.* ; strongly asserts the " rights of the Crown," 276 ; his independent policy, 309 ; his personality a source of danger to the State, 310 ; visits Bismarck at Friedrichsruh, 314 ; devoid of all political tact, 315-6 ; persistent interference with the Foreign Office, 319-21 ; personal correspondence with the Tsar outside the Foreign Office, 321 ; his telegram to Kruger, 332 ; forces on the question of a big fleet, 334 ; his distaste for publicity and oral procedure in military affairs, 344 ; his unrelenting feelings against

INDEX

William II, Emperor of Germany—*continued*:
Marschall, 362, 366 ; continued antagonism to the Foreign Office, 380.
Vol. II.—In full accord with Bülow as Chancellor, 34 ; looks on Bülow as " his Bismarck," 41 ; his admiration for all Prussian officers, 44 ; influence of his A.D.C.s and Military Attachés on his conduct, 45 ; his obstinate confidence in Colonel Engelbrecht, 488-9 ; his excitement over the House of Correction (Non-Strikers) Bill, 57 ; his desire to be an absolute sovereign, 65 ; delivers the " Hun " speech at Bremerhaven, 67-8 ; regards the Boxer expedition as a purely military affair and not political, 71 ; disappoints all his real friends, 72 ; injudicious letter to the Emperor of Austria, 78 ; his refusal to countenance the reinstatement of an Austrian military attachéship at Paris, 98 *et seq.* ; refuses to accept resignation of Eulenburg, offers extended leave instead, 135 ; accept it at last, 136 ; visit to Liebenburg foundation for story of " Round Table," 150-1 ; meets Lecomte (French Attaché) at Liebenburg, 151 ; signs Holstein's letter of resignation, 176 ; less cordial to Eulenburg, 201 ; is informed of the accusations against Eulenburg, 203.
Appendix I.—289, 290, 297, 298, 299, 300 to end of Appendix I, *passim*.
Appendix III.—343, 346-7, 354, 355, 368, 373.

Wilczek, Count Hans, I. 227.
Windhorst, I. 43, 90.
Witte, Count, I. 187 ; II. 169-70.
Wolkenstein, Count, I. 238.
Wronker (lawyer), II. 255, 259, 325, 338 *et seq.*
Würtemberg, King Karl of, I. 94, 101.
Würtemberg, Queen Olga of, I. 94, 101.
Württemberg, King Wilhelm of, 101, 102.

Zanzibar, Treaty, I. 159.
Zedlitz, Count, I. 109, 110, 111, 322 ; II. 151 (*note*), 246 (*note*).
Ziehen, Dr., II. 343, 347.

Northern Michigan University

3 1854 000 785 223

EZNO v2
DD219 E8 H32 1971
Philip Eulenburg; the Kaiser's friend.

DATE DUE

GAYLORD — PRINTED IN U.S.A.